T0322951

NOBODY'S
KINGDOM

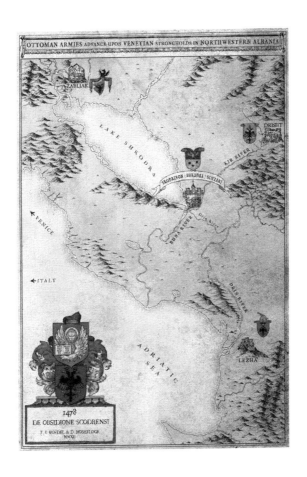

OTTOMAN ARMIES ADVANCE UPON VENETIAN STRONGHOLDS IN NORTHWESTERN ALBANIA

ZABLJAK

DRISHT

LAKE SHKODRA

KIR RIVER

SKODRINON | SHKODRA | SCUTARI

VENICE

ITALY

DRIN RIVER | DISAN

DRIN RIVER

LEZHA

ADRIATIC
SEA

1478
DE OBSIDIONE SCODRENSI
T. J. WINDER & D. HOSAFLOOK
MMXII

Also by T.J. Winnifrith

The Vlachs: The History of a Balkan People
Perspectives on Albania (ed.)
Shattered Eagles: Balkan Fragments
Badlands-Borderlands: A History of Southern Albania/
Northern Epirus

NOBODY'S KINGDOM

A HISTORY OF
NORTHERN ALBANIA

T.J. WINNIFRITH

Signal Books
Oxford

First published in 2020 by
Signal Books Limited
36 Minster Road
Oxford OX4 1LY
www.signalbooks.co.uk

© T.J. Winnifrith, 2020

The right of T.J. Winnifrith to be identified as the author of this work has been asserted by him in accordance with the Copyright, Design and Patents Act, 1988.

All rights reserved. The whole of this work, including all text and illustrations, is protected by copyright. No parts of this work may be loaded, stored, manipulated, reproduced or transmitted in any form or by any means, electronic or mechanical, including photocopying and recording, or by any information, storage and retrieval system without prior written permission from the publisher, on behalf of the copyright owner.

A catalogue record for this book is available from the British Library

ISBN 978-1-909930-91-9 Cloth

Cover Design: Tora Kelly
Typesetting: Tora Kelly
Cover Image: Edward Lear, *Ochride* (1848)
Printed in India by Imprint Press

CONTENTS

Foreword by James Pettifer vi

1. Divided Country: The North and its History 1

2. The Land 20

3. The Illyrians, 1200-230 BC 36

4. Rome, 230 BC-235 AD 57

5. Goths, Slavs and Byzantium, 235-1018 73

6. Albanians and Anarchy, 1018-1500 93

7. Ottoman Albania, 1501-1912 112

8. Independent Albania, 1912-1992 131

9. 1992 and the Future 152

Appendix I: Uscana 158

Appendix II: The Lissus-Naissus Route 161

Appendix III: Procopius' *Buildings* 166

Appendix IV: The Priest of Dioclea 171

Appendix V: The Albanian-Yugoslav Border 175

Notes 187

Select Bibliography 213

Index 229

FOREWORD

Tom Winnifrith was born in 1938 into an English professional family with a long tradition of public service and involvement in the main institutions of the state that were bequeathed by the Victorians to their twentieth-century successors. Close relatives served in the Anglican Church, Churchill's Cabinet Rooms in the Second World War and in education. As a child he grew up in Dulwich, in south-east London, and soon showed considerable academic promise as a boy. He attended Tonbridge School in Kent between 1951 and 1956, before gaining a place to read Classics, *Literae Humaniores*, at Christ Church Oxford, where he studied between 1956 and 1960. His family had a long connection with the College where he joined the Labour Club and excelled in the literature and ancient history parts of the syllabus.

Winnifrith's main intellectual influence and someone who was to play a key role in determining the direction of his later academic research and writing on the Vlachs in the Balkan mountains was Christ Church classics tutor and University Lecturer in Ancient History, Eric Gray. Gray was a Philhellene who spoke good modern Greek and who had during the Second World War been attached to the Greek ELAS *andartes* in the Arcadia region of the Peloponnese in mainland southern Greece. Gray's gripping descriptions of mountain warfare and the nature of Greek rural society before the Civil War inspired the young student to visit the region.

Nowadays Winnifrith would probably have stayed in Oxford to do post-graduate work but given his circumstances at the time an occupation beckoned, and after a period trying school teaching in London, from 1961 he was appointed to a post in Eton College to teach classics where he remained until 1967. This occurred in the last days of the traditional classical syllabus in major public schools, and when he was appointed, Eton had over thirty staff teaching classics and associated subjects. A major reform was instituted by the then headmaster Anthony Chenevix-Trench in the mid-1960s and Winnifrith, who had always been an avid reader of English literature, transferred to teaching a mixture of classics and English. School holidays, in the days when public school teaching had many fewer responsibilities than nowadays, took him to Italy and Greece, until the onset of the Greek Colonels' junta after the coup in 1967 reined in his travel and exploration. In 1966 he moved from Eton to a research post at Liverpool University where he stayed for three years, and as the William Noble Fellow in English also completed his PhD on the Bronte sisters as novelists. In 1970 he made a move to the newly developing Department of Comparative Literature at Warwick University, where he remained until he retired in 1998. In the earlier part of that period, he finished his first book *The Brontës and their Background*[1], and for a time became very active in the Brontë Society before becoming disillusioned by the intractable conflicts in that organisation.

When democracy returned to Greece after 1974 he concentrated his research in the northern mountains, encountering numerous Vlach pastoralists who then were still living according to ancient transhumance traditions. He became fascinated, as a serious Latinist, by the roots of their language, and began to teach himself Vlach, so following his nineteenth-century inspiration, Gustav Weigand.[2] It was many years since the Edwardian scholars Wace and Thompson had laid the foundations of Vlach scholarship in Britain,[3] and much had changed in the Vlach world in northern Greece and neighbouring countries since then but little had been published about it. His research during this period, before the end of the Cold War and almost exclusively in far northern Greece, was brought together in his first 'Balkan' book *The Vlachs: The History of a Balkan People*, a pithy and engaging study saturated with classical knowledge that cast light into an area of Greek life that up until then had only been the academic terrain of anthropologists like

---

1   Macmillan, London, 1976.
2   G. Weigand, *Vlacho-Meglen: eine ethnographisch-philologische Untersuchung*, J. Barth, Leipzig, 1892.
3   A.J.B. Wace and M.S. Thompson, *Nomads of the Balkans: An Account of the Life and Customs among the Vlachs of Northern Pindus*, Methuen, London, 1914.

John Campbell, who had little sustained interest in the Vlachs.[4] His sections on the Vlachs in late antiquity and their relationships to Byzantium were ground-breaking in their time.

The end of the Cold War in 1990 and the opening up of Albania and Yugoslav Macedonia to reasonably easy (if uncomfortable) travel and research led Winnifrith to explore the Vlach presence in first southern and then northern Albania, and in what was then south-west Yugoslavia. He brought together various experts on Albania in an edited book *Perspectives on Albania*,[5] and then published his own *Shattered Eagles: Balkan Fragments*,[6] with seminal papers focused on the region such as 'Minorities in the Prilep-Bitola Area' and 'Albania and the Ottoman Empire'. In the chaos of the time in both countries after the independence referendum in Skopje in September 1991, and with the ex-Yugoslav wars just beginning not far away to the north, Winnifrith was a resourceful and active traveller into old age, willing to rough it in order to speak to the people on the ground in often remote localities. He was a great admirer of Nicholas Hammond's scholarly researches that embodied practical fieldwork, particularly his pre-Second World War study of ancient and modern Epirus, with Frank Walbank, and both had common forebears in classical human geography in Strabo, Procopius (in his study of Justinian's buildings) and Pausanias.[7] He stood for the centrality of antiquarianism and the subjective factor in Balkan history research, and was often a critic of some academic historians of the modern Balkans.

The post-Cold War period and the subsequent Yugoslav conflicts also brought new research priorities. The explosive questions of Balkan minority rights and associated nationalism immediately came into focus, and Winnifrith spoke at a notable conference on the subject at St Antony's College, Oxford, in 1992, which was also where we first met. The political identity of the

---

4   Duckworth, London, 1987.
5   Macmillan, London, 1992.
6   Duckworth, London, 1995.
7   Nicholas Geoffrey Lemprière Hammond, *Epirus: the geography, the ancient remains, the history and topography of Epirus and adjacent areas*, Clarendon Press, Oxford, 1967.

Vlachs had long been uncertain and their loyalty divided largely between Greece and Romania. Mainstream Greek historiography, however, saw the Vlachs as Greeks, while Romanian historians viewed the Vlachs as Romanians, and it is this conflict that has defined the recent history of the Vlachs. Winnifrith became involved with a new movement among the Vlach diaspora in the United States that rejected this Manichean approach and asked why the Vlachs could not simply define themselves as Vlachs, regardless of the nation-state they happened to find themselves in, or pledge loyalty to. Tom was presented with a Mayoral Proclamation of 'Vlach Cultural Awareness Day' in New York City in honour of his visit and in the ensuing years contributed many articles to the *Newsletter of the Society Farsarotul*, a membership publication of the oldest and largest Vlach association in the US.[8]

A traditional classicist and Hellenist, Winnifrith was soon faced, as many other scholars were, with profound dilemmas about the emergence of a new Macedonian national entity in the region, and this is also reflected in his work at the time. As a moderate socialist veering towards liberalism in his personal outlook, he sympathised with many of the real achievements in the ex-Yugoslav republic in areas such as health, public transport, literacy and education compared to the absence of social facilities in pre-PASOK mountain Greece, and was concerned to see that as far as possible the peace in both Macedonias, Greek and Yugoslav, was kept and involvement with the conflicts to the north avoided. He became an active supporter of the Friends of Albania humanitarian relief organisation and its journal *Besa* under the leadership of Primrose Peacock, and an active member of the Anglo-Albanian Society.

In his next book, *Badlands-Borderlands: A History of Southern Albania/Northern Epirus*,[9] Winnifrith returned to familiar terrain. In preparation he spent a good deal of time in the library of the British School in Athens, drawing in particular on the papers of S.S. Clarke (1897-1924) whose fieldwork in the region preceded that of Hammond and Walbank in the early 1920s and who died

---

8   www.farsarotul.org
9   Duckworth, London, 2002.

an untimely death in a drowning accident at a young age after a brilliant military career in the First World War. Clarke - or at least his largely forgotten and unpublished materials - is in many ways the guiding star of this book, and it ends with Winnifrith's observation that in terms of field research on the Greek-Albanian border, 'a new Clarke is still needed for our age', although many of his friends and colleagues must feel that Tom was to fulfil that role very well himself in Vlach and associated scholarship. He is in some senses a writer in the tradition of the scholar gypsy of nineteenth-century literature, with profound curiosity for the textures and customs of life among a neglected minority living in the complex changing world of the modern Balkans.

Following its publication, his activity moved northwards and resulted in the manuscript for this book, *Nobody's Land: A History of Northern Albania*. It is a stimulating, complex text covering centuries and is Northern Albania seen through the eyes of a scholar very learned in the medieval and Byzantine worlds as well as the ancient classics. As a student of modern Balkan history and culture I have learned much from it and I am sure all readers will find the same, and it is best left to speak for itself.

Tom has fought a very brave battle against ill health in his final years after the loss of his much loved wife Helen and I have been fortunate to have been able to help finalise the text in some very minor dimensions and bring it to publication. I have also enjoyed many stimulating, witty and combative dialogues on a kaleidoscope of topics, from the future of classical studies, the House in the late 1950s, Brexit, the decline of British newspapers, some nightmarish and some wonderful pupils at Eton College - all a rich tapestry of memory and crisp anecdote. I am very grateful for the support of Tom's children, Tabitha, Tom and Naomi, his translator and sometimes travelling companion Lala Meredith-Vula for her photographs, and James Ferguson's expert work at Signal Books in Oxford.

James Pettifer
St Cross College
Oxford

July 2020

1. DIVIDED COUNTRY
The North and its History

Some years ago a now defunct company named Adelante Travel advertised a week's tour of Albania costing £1500. The company stressed Albania's rich cultural heritage as seen at sites like Durrës, Butrint and Apollonia, but then sought to justify its high prices by emphasising the rare and exotic nature of the country. This extraordinary quality was demonstrated, rather paradoxically in view of the expense, by the lack of creature comforts and modern amenities. In fact, it is possible to travel cheaply if not comfortably round Albania by public transport staying in simple hotels or even private houses, and comfortably if not cheaply by using taxis and staying in the rather grander if not luxurious hotels which can be found in most major towns. The North is less well furnished with tourist sites and hotels than the South, but there is adequate accommodation in Shkodër, Kukës, Peshkopi and Bajram Curri. Admirable guidebooks by Gillian Gloyer and James Pettifer show the way to a holiday including a cultural tour much cheaper than that advertised.

Pettifer in the various editions of the *Blue Guide* urges travellers to be cautious, pointing out a number of potential hazards particularly in the North. Yet events over the last twenty years have led to a large Western military presence in the neighbourhood and a fund of goodwill to Western travellers. Of course Albania has been difficult and dangerous in the past, and the title of this book and its predecessor *Badlands-Borderlands* play upon these dangers and difficulties in the same way as Adelante Travel once did.

But some prophets of gloom are too gloomy. The journalist A.A. Gill who declared that Albania was full of brigands and profiteers seems to be harking back to the past. Of course Albania was a closed book from 1945 to 1991 with only limited access to certain sites allowed to a few closely supervised parties, and progress since 1991 has not been entirely smooth with a terrifying outbreak of violence in 1997. It is unfortunate that two popular books about travel in Albania with particular emphasis on northern districts by Robert Carver and Dervla Murphy should have been published just after that year, giving an unfavourable impression of the country. My title may contribute to this impression, but this is a book about the past, not the present or future. Since I have met, especially in the North, with nothing but friendship and hospitality generously given it would be churlish to speak ill of a country just emerging from a long nightmare. It is because of this nightmare that few have been able to visit Albania or to view its history dispassionately, as the rest of this chapter will reveal. Moving rather oddly backwards through Albanian history I will aim to show the handicaps past historians of various nationalities have faced, aware that I too in my more regular forward narrative which forms the subject of subsequent chapters face the same handicaps since I am inevitably following in the footsteps of my predecessors.

Omne ignotum pro magnifico est, and ignorance and prejudice about Albania are sadly prevalent even among those who speak with authority about it. There have been some very good historians of Albania, but the area has attracted more than its fair share of amateurs, eccentrics and those whose work has been marred by political or nationalist bias. In 1997 the *Times* newspaper published a leader on Albania, blaming its troubles on · a fundamental division between the two main linguistic groups in the country, the Ghegs and the Tosks. This rather crude analysis was further marred by placing the Ghegs in the South and the Tosks in the North rather than vice versa. It is true that the struggle between supporters of the right-wing Democratic Party of Sali Berisha, mainly in the North, and supporters of the left wing Socialists of Fatos Nano, mainly in the South, might seem to reflect a Gheg-Tosk division. But a more important factor was the division in the Second World War when the communist partisans led by Enver Hoxha were strong in the South, and resistance to them and subsequent repression by them was marked in the North. Albania still divides politically along these lines, although there were communists in the North like Ramiz Alia, Hoxha's successor, and the pre-war left-wing leader Bajram Curri, who had a town renamed after him. But the wartime division does reflect a fundamental difference between the North and the South which I have followed in dividing my work on Albania into two volumes. The North has less to do with ancient Greece, medieval Byzantium, modern Greece or the Orthodox faith. It was more feudal, more tribal, more Catholic, more prone to Austrian and Italian influence. It has also a more savage climate and landscape and inhabitants endowed with little respect for law and authority, although paying great respect to a strange code of honour involving blood feuds and revenge.

In the Second World War British officers aided the Albanian resistance to the Germans and became involved in the struggle between the eventually victorious communists and forces hostile to communism, themselves divided between those loyal to King Zog and those opposed to him. British accounts of this period tend to reflect the views of the party to whom the authors were attached during the conflict. There used to be a similar division in accounts of Albania after the war with some idealists portraying Hoxha as building a Socialist Utopia, and others casting him as a brutish tyrant, but the former picture is clearly unfashionable, while the latter is hardly relevant. The American scholar Bernd J. Fischer using German sources has given a good account of Albania during the war and of the previous regime of King Zog, an ambiguous figure, although his name, comic to English ears, has contributed to the Adelante Travel approach to Balkan history. Other quaint but sympathetic views of the country are presented by Bernard Newman, Nigel Heseltine and above all the Gordons who travelled in difficult country in the North and provided amusing verbal and pictorial sketches. The great ancient historian of the Balkans, Nicholas Hammond, mainly confined his visits and his researches to Southern Albania. Margaret Hasluck published far less, and her work based on an extensive stay in the northern highlands has not received due recognition. Two other less scholarly but equally heroic figures, Edith Durham and Rose Lane Wilder, provide exciting accounts of life in high

Albania, although they were not historians and Wilder, with her schoolgirl crush on King Zog, writes too much about herself and not enough about the country she was visiting. Such travellers are now beginning to attract the interest of students of Albania, although their writing does draw attention to the fact that these women did not always agree or even get on with each other. The recent publications by Pearson of sources dealing with Albania in the first half of the twentieth century are admirably objective, although not all the sources are reliable.

Albania became independent in 1912, but the First World War almost immediately intervened to make the country divided and ruled by foreign powers as it had been so often in the past. There is no good overview of the First World War in this area, though there are some interesting studies of isolated episodes such as the heroic and tragic march of the Serbian Army across Northern Albania, not an episode conducive to friendly relations between Serbs and Albanians. For most of the First World War most of Albania was in the hands of the troops of the Austro-Hungarian Empire, and it is scholars from this empire who produce the best accounts of the North during the nineteenth century and the early years of the twentieth. Thus we find the eccentric Hungarian Baron Nopsca and the Croat Milan Šufflay, both of whom died tragically, and there is the great Czech historian of the Balkans, Konstantin Jiricek. Albanian archaeology was well served by Patsch, Hopf collected important literary documents and von Hahn did pioneer historical work

English interest belongs more to the first half of the century and was mainly confined to the South, when Ali Pasha was an obvious magnet for travellers from the West, whereas with the Austro-Hungarian domains reaching nearly as far as Shkodër the North was more attractive to Central Europeans. Much of Teutonic scholarship on Albania has been conveniently collected in this century by Stadtmuller who also published the accounts of Antonio Baldacciri in Italian. Baldacciri travelled as did Durham on foot and on horseback to areas which, the modern traveller, lazily dependent on the internal combustion engine, does not or cannot reach. Such a traveller anxious to explore the terrain of Albania in the hundred years before independence could do worse than consult the guidebooks of Baedeker and Murray which show routes not even marked as mountain tracks on modern maps.

The Ottoman Empire was not really accessible to Western travellers until the Napoleonic Wars which caused an interest in the Near East for strategic reasons and made France and Italy less attractive venues for the Grand Tour. Greece became the obvious place to visit after Byron, and there was a simultaneous revival in the study of ancient Greece. These factors as well as the presence of Ali Pasha caused Northern Albania to be neglected in favour of the South. Even the indefatigable Colonel William Martin Leake, still quoted as an authority on Albanian topography and a traveller to places virtually unknown by Western writers over the next two hundred years, does not have much to say about the North and tends to use Classical texts as his guidebooks, these texts also being almost silent about the lands north of the Shkumbin. Leake did after all call his great work *Travels in Northern Greece*. Pouqueville and Hobhouse, the friend of Byron, have the same bias, although they were less indefatigable travellers. Another contemporary Henry Holland, the physician of Ali Pasha, slightly confuses the issue because while admitting that the southern part of his employer's realm was largely inhabited by Greeks, he still calls the districts around Gjirokastër Northern Albania and never reached the area of our study over which Ali had no control. It is odd that two of Leake's family played a part in the history of modern Albania one fighting with the Partisans in the Second World War, one fighting against the Turks at the siege of Shkoder in the Balkan Wars. Records of and from this family might shed new light on post-Napoleonic Albania.

Before the Napoleonic Wars we are largely dependent upon Ottoman records for the whole period after 1500. There are modern Albanian collections of historical sources. Venetian documents mainly deal with the coast. Turkish *defters* (tax registers) provide an impartial record of the administration by Istanbul of its distant province, unfortunately divided and subdivided in ways that prevent us from seeing the Albanian nation, modern

Albania or even Northern Albania as a whole. The intricacies of Ottoman script are a further handicap, although the labours of the Turkish scholar Halil Inalcik have done something to reduce this difficulty. There is also the seventeenth-century account of the Turkish traveller Evlyia Celebi, well translated into English and German by Robert Elsie, who has also provided translations of Albanian folktales and a survey of literature in Albanian or on Albania. Celebi's enthusiastic account together with the fact that in the seventeenth century there was mass conversion to Islam should draw our attention to the popularity of Turkish rule in this part of the empire. In Northern Albania particularly a great deal of autonomy was allowed to local communities to continue their warlike ways. Western students of Albania, taught by Byron and Gladstone to see the Turk as an oppressor, tend to ignore this, as do nationalist Albanian historians trained to regard everything in terms of a struggle for independence against an imperial invader. In the sixteenth century there was a series of wars between Venice and the Turks which Albanian historians tend to paint as nationalist uprisings, but students of Venetian records, led by the great French scholar Alain Ducellier, give a rather different picture.

Venice had been allotted Albania as part of the spoils in the division of the Byzantine Empire after the Fourth Crusade in 1204. She never occupied much of the interior of the country, but at various times in the next six hundred years held several strong points along the Adriatic coast, still being the ruler of Butrint in 1797 when Napoleon put an end to the Venetian republic. Venice's involvement with Albania encompasses the period of Scanderbeg, another difficult problem for the historian. Scanderbeg is primarily a hero of Northern Albania with Kruja as the strong point of his resistance, but there were several campaigns in the East near Dibër, while Lezhë in the West was both the place where he persuaded other chieftains to join the common cause and the place where he died and was buried. He did marry the daughter of the southern warrior George Arianiti, the first Albanian to raise the standard against the Turks, but resistance in the South, apparently under Ottoman control in 1436, was always less strong, and even in the North the mighty but mysterious Dukagjin family provided alternative leadership and a legacy in Albanian history as impressive as that of Scanderbeg and even harder to assess.

Albanian historians tend to ignore these cracks in the facade of Albanian unity, achieved for the first and almost last time in the fifteenth century, since the period after Albanian independence in 1912 has been marked by a series of internal divisions. The communists under Hoxha of course claimed that they had achieved the same goal as Scanderbeg, and in spite of the medieval hero's aristocratic background and devout Christianity praised him without reservation. Western historians have tended to accept this picture uncritically, but there is no thorough objective study of this figure, whose achievements both in war and in diplomacy were clearly considerable. Edward Gibbon shows the unreliability of our main source for the story of Scanderbeg, Marinus Barlettius, who is neither contemporary nor without bias. Gibbon also rather sourly points out that in spite of being a bastion of resistance against the Turks Scanderbeg started life in the Ottoman service and that he found time when defending Albania to fight campaigns in Italy on behalf of the King of Naples.

In fact Scanderbeg was a feudal leader who united other feudal leaders in a fairly successful war against the Ottomans. He received some help from Venice and Naples and gave them help in return, but sometimes he fought against these allies. Local Balkan leaders in the twentieth century changed sides in a similar fashion, and the same pattern can be found in earlier centuries. Scanderbeg comes at the end of a long period after and even before the Fourth Crusade when similar leaders sometimes achieved a precarious independence, sometimes even a nominal suzerainty over other Albanian leaders, but were more often involved in playing one great power against another. In the fifteenth century these great powers were the Turks, Venice and Naples; in earlier centuries, although fortunately not simultaneously, we have the Angevins, the Normans, the Serbs, the Bulgarians and various fragments of the Byzantine Empire, although after 1204 the latter were really only a factor in the South.

Ducellier and to a lesser extent Gegaj have done much to disentangle the complexities of this period, although Ducellier is mainly interested in the coast, and Gegaj is a little too credulous in believing his sources. Albanian historians look at events from the point of view of the Albanians. Their use of the term feudal, fitting in with Marxist orthodoxy, is actually correct, although they have a rather difficult task in keeping a balance between dismissing such figures as Charles Thopia as feudal, unsuccessfully trying to impose an alien rule over his fellow Albanians, and hailing him as an Albanian, a fighter successfully trying to free his country from foreign domination.

In the Middle Ages there is a considerable body of evidence, collected conveniently if not very tidily in *Acta et Diplomata res Albaniae mediae aetatis illustrantia*. Less accessible, less frequent and even less reliable are Slavonic documents. The Priest of Dioclea is a source, if not *the* source, for Northern Albanian history in the period of the Crusades, but this work, hard to find in translation or even the original, has its own agenda. There are of course no documents in Albanian, the first text in that language not appearing until the fourteenth century, the first mention of the Albanian language in the thirteenth, and the first disputed references to Albanians in the eleventh. Because Byzantine and Greek sources are our main guide for the medieval history of the Balkans and because there are no Albanian sources, one risks the charge of being pro-Greek and proSouth in any depiction of medieval Albanian history. References in all languages and their interpretations by modern scholars have to be treated with due caution especially when it comes to matters of ethnic identity. Latin sources, usually connected to the Crusades and the Angevin or Italian occupations that followed in their wake, are not particularly interested in the language spoken by the people whose land they had invaded, Greek, Slav or Albanian. Religion - Slavonic Orthodox, Greek Orthodox and Catholic, with strange heresies like Bogomilism waiting in the wings - was a more obvious and more controversial mark of differentiation. A person was more unlikely to be a member of a number of faiths than to be a speaker of many languages. Kalojan, the greatest ruler of the Second Bulgarian Empire, was briefly during the early thirteenth century master of much of Albania. It is uncertain whether he was of Bulgarian or of Vlach origin, he toyed with adopting Catholicism as opposed to Orthodoxy, and though he proclaimed himself King of Bulgaria and Vlachia, he must have ruled over Greeks, Serbs and Albanians as well. Charles Thopia set up a more boastful inscription near Elbasan written in Greek, Latin and Slavonic. In this he claimed his descent, which was in fact illegitimate, through the rulers of Naples to Louis IX of France. Faced with such complications modern historians from various Balkan countries have tended to use the temporary occupation of parts of the area by a member of their particular race, however dubiously attributed, to justify the claims of that race to rule over great swathes of territory, although Thopia held only parts of central Albania in an uncertain fashion.

Byzantine historians are equally uninformative about ethnic identities. In the eleventh and twelfth centuries Byzantium ruled much of the Balkans, although there were sporadic revolts in different parts of the peninsula. Byzantine rule did not ensure that the whole population spoke Greek; instead contemporary historians are full of information about various races, loyal and disloyal to the empire, confusingly disguising them by antiquarian names like Triballoi for the Serbs. Albanians do not get many mentions. This may be because until the year 1071, which saw the loss of the last Byzantine possession in Italy and a disastrous defeat in Asia Minor, Albania was not the important frontier province it became in the much smaller empire of the Comnenid dynasty. Alternatively we can accept the explanation of Ducellier, which does not fit in with Albanian nationalist thinking. He argues that for most of Byzantine history the Albanians were fairly loyal members of the empire, allowed a good deal of independence but fighting defensive and offensive campaigns against the Empire's enemies when occasion required. A similar state of affairs existed in the time of the Ottoman Empire, although this too does not suit nationalistic thinking. Modern historians, brainwashed into thinking of the Balkans as a mass of different nationalities fighting over boundaries, should remember the medieval Byzantine poem of Digenis Akrites, the frontierman of two races who keeps in Anatolia a fairly fluid border safe for the Byzantines against the Muslim enemy.

In the Balkans the main enemies of the Byzantines were the Serbs and the Bulgarians rather than the Arabs or Turks. Relations between these enemies and the Albanians are a vexed issue with factors like Kosova introducing modern enmities as a complicating factor. Scholars from Serbia and Albania have pored over documents of the Nemanjid dynasty in Serbia to try and establish whether Kosova in the Middle Ages was inhabited by Serbs or Albanians and, needless to say, have reached different conclusions. It is not just Kosova that is a bone of contention. The great Albanian poet Fishta, who fell out of favour in communist times, recounts the struggles on the northern frontiers of Albania between Albanian and Montenegrin warriors. This was in Ottoman times when differences of language and religion clearly divided the two peoples, but similar tribal structures and patterns of behaviour suggest that in the medieval period it would have been hard to distinguish between two peoples so fond of war. The Serbs were certainly the masters of Northern Albania in the fourteenth century and the dominant Balšič family was almost certainly Slav-speaking. The Italian historian Orbini writing at the beginning of the seventeenth century is a fairly good guide to this later period. Earlier the Bulgarian empire under Tsar Samuel had reached the Adriatic at the end of the tenth century, and there is archaeological evidence of a Bulgarian presence in the interior before this. Earlier still Slavonic tribes had swept through the entire Balkans including Albania, as is shown by the evidence of place names.

Since these tribes could not write and left few traces of their presence in archaeological remains, evidence of their presence is provided by a few melancholy and laconic notes from Byzantine chroniclers supplemented by the ecclesiastic lists with the absence or flight of Albanian bishops suggesting the replacement of the Christian population by the heathen Slavs, not converted until

1. Divided Country The North and its History

Cyril and Methodius in the ninth century. Modern historians from both Greece and Albania have played down the extent of the Slavonic invasions, pointing to the survival of the native population and their quick assimilation of the invaders. In the case of Northern Albania there is archaeological evidence of a population that is clearly not Slavonic establishing some kind of civilisation in these dark ages, so lacking in literary texts. This civilisation, known as Komani-Kruja from two principal sites, has been hailed by Albanian historians as the vital link between the ancient Illyrians and the modern Albanians. Western historians, notably Wilkes and Bowden, have cast some doubt on this, suggesting that the Komani-Kruja artefacts, probably Christian, are the work of the Latinised population of the north-west part of the Eastern Roman Empire.

Archaeology is difficult to interpret without literary texts to back it up. In East European countries apart from Romania there is less interest in the Roman past than in the West, and fewer material resources with which to explore this past. In the last sixty years Albanian archaeologists have done a great deal of work with support from the state, but most of this work has been dedicated to Illyrian sites. Recently, however, there has been considerable interest in Roman sites and Roman roads, in particular the route from Lissus to Naissus and the road along the valley of the Black Drin up from Lake Ohrid to Kukes. It so happens that in Procopius' *De Aedificiis* written in the sixth century we do have a text which seems to fit in very well with archaeological discoveries. Procopius says that Justinian fortified and refortified a number of strong points in the provinces of New Epirus, Old Epirus and Dardania. Unfortunately he does not mention the province of Praevalitana, comprising Montenegro and the northern part of our area. Unfortunately too, though there are sites showing refortification and indeed one site, Byllis, which actually has an inscription recording the refortification, in a maddening fashion Byllis is not mentioned by Procopius who does name a series of places, some of them with rather improbable names which scholars have failed to identify, although some efforts are being made to rectify this.

Procopius is not a totally reliable historian since his gross flattery of Justinian in the *De Aedificiis* hardly fits in with his vituperative comments on the same emperor in the *Secret History* - if indeed he wrote the latter work. But Procopius is much more useful for students of Albania than the historians of the Roman Empire in the three centuries preceding Justinian. The admirable Ammianus Marcellinus is concerned with Rome's frontiers, and Albania was not on these frontiers, the disaster at Adrianople in 378 being the result of Gothic pressure in the East Balkans. For information about the later incursions of Alaric and Theodoric in the fifth century we have to rely on the poet Claudian, fragments of Malchus and Jordanes on the Goths. For the so-called Illyrian emperors of the third century we have the fairly worthless *Historia Augusta*. Apart from Diocletian, who came probably from Dioclea in Montenegro, these emperors have nothing much to do with Albania, although some Albanian historians have seized on these later emperors as evidence of Illyrian martial valour. People have been slow to recognise a strong Gothic element in the Balkan melting pot of races.

When we come to the second century Trajan, Hadrian and Marcus Aurelius were all active in the Balkans, although it is odd that Antoninus Pius, in whose reign practically nothing happened, should have been responsible for separating the province of Epirus from Macedonia. Tacitus' melancholy record of disasters on the frontiers and corruption at Rome has little room for the presumably peaceful Albanian territories. In the case of the former Yugoslavia there has been a good deal of work by native scholars and Western writers like John Wilkes to show ways in which members of native tribes became part of loosely constructed Roman *civitates*, but the inaccessibility of Albania and the ideological training of native historians have obstructed this task in the area further south. At the end of the first century BC Albania was an important place in the various civil wars fought in or near its borders, and again the inaccessibility of the country has prevented a totally satisfactory exploration of Caesar and Pompey's inconclusive campaign near Dyrrachium.

1. Divided Country The North and its History

Dyrrachium was part of the Roman province of Macedonia established in 146 BC. The boundaries of this province in the North are uncertain and at the best of times fluid with invading tribes like the Scordisci reaching the Via Egnatia in 119 BC. It is not clear how much of Northern Albania was part of this province or of the province of Illyria further north, itself with fluid boundaries, or of neither. Apart from Scodra and Lissus there are few Roman cities in the North, the fortresses of Gajtan and Sarcia belonging principally to late antiquity. There are Latin inscriptions with Illyrian proper names, suggesting that the people in Northern Albania were brought into the imperial system with a loose tribal structure taking the place of the civic system in the towns, but more work needs to be done on this period. The Romans were after all masters of Albania for over 700 years if we take the final collapse of the Danube frontier in 602 AD as the conclusion and the establishment of the province of Macedonia as the beginning.

Before 146 BC the Romans had been involved in Albania since the year 230 when the activities of pirates with Queen Teuta forced them to interfere in the Balkans. There followed a series of wars against the Macedonians and Illyrians, and for the next eighty years we are fortunate to have two reasonable historians in the shape of Livy and Polybius who between them cover this period fairly thoroughly. Of the two Polybius is the more accurate and more contemporary. His dictum that the historian should visit the places he describes is not followed by Livy, the archetypal armchair historian, although Livy uses Polybius as his main source, and is thus able to fill in some of the gaps in books of Polybius which are missing. F.W. Walbank's commentary on Polybius is better than anything on Livy, although politics made it difficult for him to visit Albanian sites. It was left to Albanian archaeologists to identify such key sites as Dimallium, but some of the places mentioned by Polybius and Livy can only be guessed at. Neither Polybius nor Livy is totally objective.

Nicholas Hammond, the historian of Epirus and Macedonia, did visit Albania before the Second World War, and his reputation was such that he visited certain areas after it. We have pointed out that the North was not his speciality, and sometimes as in placing Uscana in Yugoslavia rather than Albania he is at fault. He is also handicapped by the fact that for the Macedonian period before the arrival of the Romans we are faced with inferior primary sources like Diodorus Siculus. The great Thucydides had a particular interest in north-west Greece, and gives us a few fascinating insights into the Illyrians in the late fifth century. Herodotus has a few gossipy anecdotes, but for most of Illyrian history we are dependent upon the work of archaeologists. It is hard to establish whether the Greek artefacts found in Illyrian cities show a sophisticated civilisation in contact with the Greek world or the occasional piece of trading with the Greek colonies of Dyrrachium and Apollonia. Even in the period after 400 there is still controversy as to whether the Illyrians were a single nation ruled by one king or a motley collection of tribes each with a separate leader. This is a matter of dispute between Hammond and the main Yugoslav historian of the period, Papazoglou.

With so much in doubt, as this short backwards glance at Albanian history and historians has shown, it might seem that the rather longer forward narrative that follows is almost impossible to write. Primary sources are infrequent and unreliable, secondary sources partial in more senses than one. In eschewing footnotes to make this book more accessible to the general reader I may be both falling into and compounding the traps which like Hoxha's bunkers stand at the entry of Albanian territory. Writers repeat statements from other writers, sometimes quoting those other writers as a source in their footnotes. But we then discover that these other writers have no authority for their original statement. Thus it is not true that St Paul visited Durrës. He only tells us that he got as far as Illyricum (Romans 15:19) and this could just mean the frontier. It is not true that Gibbon said that Albania was more remote and unknown than the centre of America. There is no trace of this remark in any of his recorded writings. It is not true that King Zog was the nephew of Esad Pasha although I myself said so in *Badlands*. His mother had the same surname, Toptani, but the connection was a remote one, and Albanians do not place

1. Divided Country The North and its History

much value on maternal lineage. Geographical errors are all too easy in writing about a country where all maps are unsatisfactory. In trying to establish Albania's northern and eastern frontier as it was originally decided in 1913 and finally settled in 1926 I consulted several otherwise authoritative works which frequently disagreed with each other and sometimes with themselves.

Adelante means forward and in order to prevent my forward narrative from becoming embroiled in particular small controversies and a list of the errors of others, I have provided a number of appendices and bibliographical notes. I have also included some maps which have, as the next chapter will show, their own limitations especially where boundaries are concerned. The essential boundary between North and South Albania is roughly the River Shkumbin, but as is the case with the northern frontier it is impossible to keep Northern Albania as a self-contained unit, and the history of Kosova, Montenegro, Macedonia and Epirus will occasionally intrude, especially as there are Albanians in all four areas.

In spite of undermining the work of other historians in the previous pages I am extremely grateful for the efforts of my predecessors, particularly in archaeological matters. The three Albanian periodicals *Iliria, Monumentet* and *Studime Historike* supply essential information. Oddly the area of our study is not particularly strong in Illyrian remains; there are more impressive sites in Southern Albania and the former Yugoslavia, although practical and political considerations may have encouraged Albanian archaeologists - like Adelante Travel - to concentrate on the major tourist sites of the South even though these are less Illyrian and less Albanian. The Archaeological Museum in Tirana like the Historical Museum is an indispensable introduction to Albanian history, but it is a necessary if cruel task to point out that even these museums with their impressive maps, photographs and displays of artefacts have, as we all have, their own limitations.

No visitor to Scanderbeg Square can miss the dazzling facade of the Historical Museum with its portrait of Illyrian warriors, Scanderbeg and partisan heroes and heroines marching *adelante* in a common cause. Inside the museum maps, photographs and impressive inscriptions, some carved suitably on tablets of stone, make the same point. There are notices in not very good French and English to show that Albania has been exploited by the foreign invader. We should not laugh at such notices. French and English museums are not very good at information in Albanian, or very good at concealing chauvinistic pride. Nevertheless we should take exception to this particular portrait of Albania's history. For instance much emphasis is laid upon the great Illyrian revolt against the Romans in AD 6, although in fact this revolt took place in country far to the north of modern Albania. Revolts against the Byzantine and Ottoman Empires are also stressed, although the instigators of these revolts were often not Albanian, and collaboration with these empires by Albanians is overlooked.

Tacitus claimed to write without anger or partisan zeal, although some may think his savage portrait of Roman corruption is full of both. The architects of the historical museum were certainly full of righteous indignation against the foreign powers who had dominated Albanian history, and their creation still demonstrates a lack of objectivity in depicting this history as a series of struggles against the wicked invader. But there is the possibility of a more balanced approach, and curiously this can be seen by looking at what has happened to the museum over the past fifteen years. Here is an update of what I have already partly described in *Badlands*.

Until the collapse of communism in 1991 there were a series of rooms devoted to the struggle against the occupying powers in the Second World War and the achievements of the Hoxha regime subsequently. Under Sali Berisha's government these rooms were closed, and in 1997, with rather unfortunate timing as Berisha had just fallen from power, a new exhibition hall was opened. This was a hymn of hate, possibly justified, against the communists. There was a list of martyrs, tastefully adorned with plastic flowers, and prison cells, less tastefully decorated with plastic blood. There were photographs of religious leaders who had been executed with an obvious preponderance of northern Catholics, although Catholicism is less strong in Albania than either Orthodoxy or Islam.

1. Divided Country The North and its History

Collaboration with the British either after the war when there were attempts to overthrow the communists, or, less excusably, during the war when we were on the same side, was obviously a reason for punishment. The exhibition ended with a picture of the scenes in Scanderbeg Square when Berisha came to power after the elections in 1992.

In 2005, again with rather unfortunate timing as the Socialist Party was just about to be replaced by Berisha, a new exhibition about the war years was opened. Back came Hoxha and his lieutenants, this time as heroes, not villains, and back from the pre-1991 exhibition came the complicated maps of battles, curiously similar to the rather less well authenticated maps of campaigns fought by Scanderbeg. There were, however, redeeming features. British and American involvement was gratefully mentioned. Non-communist fighters against the Germans and Italians like Gani Kryeziu, Abas Kupi and Muharrem Bajraktari received some credit. Of course it is impossible to please everybody, and it could be argued that Germans, Italians and those who collaborated with them get a raw deal in this part of the museum in the same way that the communists are handled harshly in the room depicting events after the war. The abrupt volte-face is a little disconcerting, especially as the period before the Second World War is in another hall, and this has remained untouched since 1991. We got bad marks in 1989 for asking about King Zog's omission from this hall, but he still does not get a mention. These illustrations from modern history show how easy it is to present a distorted vision of the past, and how difficult though important it is to write an objective account.

It could be argued that the most recent addition to the museum gives a more balanced picture of Albania's history, although it is unfortunate that it deals almost exclusively with war. In communist days there was the odd tractor to show Hoxha's agricultural achievements in peace. Nowadays the cause of peace is represented by a bust of the poet Gjergj Fishta and an enormous photograph of Mother Teresa. Even these figures are controversial. Fishta was literally airbrushed out of history after the

Second World War for being a Roman Catholic, for having links with Italy and for, in his epic poem *The Highland Lute*, expressing anti-Slav sentiments. This poem will be referred to in the course of this book. It is, at one level, fiercely nationalistic and should be approved of by the nationalistic school of Albanian historians, but at a deeper level Fishta like his model Homer speaks for humanity in showing the horror as well as well as the heroism of war.

There is nothing remotely warlike about Mother Teresa, but battles have arisen over her reputation. Was she a saint or did she just have a gift for self-advertisement? Was she Albanian, coming as she did from a Kosovar family which had settled in Macedonia, and forgetting her Albanian during her years in India? The latest work on the subject is hardly decisive on the first point, but is insistent that Mother Teresa was Albanian, weakening this case by claiming Albanian blood for Alexander the Great, Napoleon and Kemel Ataturk.

These dubious claims bring us back to war and to our ambivalent title. There are far too many weapons in the National Museum, as if the Albanians did nothing except fight with axes, swords and rifles. Brigand is not a term of praise; it is better than bandit or terrorist, worse than hero or freedom fighter. Balkan too has a mildly pejorative connotation; originally a geographical term to describe a mountain range in Bulgaria it has become associated with small complicated groups squabbling with each other in a distressingly complicated and incompetent fashion. This attitude to the Balkans in general and Albania in particular was very common in the last decade of the twentieth century when the Balkan peninsula did seem to explode into quarrelsome factions. Theoreticians like Todorova explore and deplore this attitude, while pointing out that in Albanian Balkan is a neutral term, and that it like brigand has certain romantic associations.

But this story is not meant to be a romantic one in spite of Adelante Travel and the odd links with British history and literature I have introduced to make a difficult account slightly easier. Owing to current trends in education even British history is a closed book to some, and many of us who studied it did so by opening books that took a strongly nationalist line, teaching us the names and dates of battles that we generally won. History should not be written in this fashion, and as we shall try to show, Albanian history cannot be so written.

2. THE LAND

The landscape of Northern Albania is easier to explain than to explore. A glance at any physical map of the country will reveal a narrow coastal plain and then a series of mountain ranges intersected by rivers. These rivers flow from east to west in the centre of Albania and from north to south in the North, thus reversing the pattern of southern Albania where rivers like the Orilo and Vjose flow from south to north. The mighty Drin starting in Lake Ohrid flows from south to north as far as Kukes where, joined by its tributary the Kosovan White Drin, it bends backwards to flow from east to west. The coastal plain except in the neighbourhood of Tirana and Ourres is narrower than the southern plain of Muzeqe. Another flat area near Shkodër is largely occupied by a lake with the same name, the largest lake in the Balkans. Southern Albania is not an easy land, but in Northern Albania the mountains are higher, harsher and more frequent, the climate colder and wetter. The rivers are more liable to flood, although two of them, the Drin and the Mat, have been tamed in parts and turned into narrow artificial lakes. Because of flooding and steep ravines neither of these rivers nor the Mat's tributary the Fan have been very useful in providing easy routes of communication. South of the Mat sluggish streams like the Erzen and Ishëm do not stretch much beyond the coastal plain, while north of the Drin the steep mountains produce torrents in winter and dry river beds in summer like the Kir and the Proni Thatë (dry torrent).

The Mat and the Fan with their various tributaries water much of Northern Albania, starting in the penultimate range of the country west of the Drin. Branches of the river almost meet the Mat and Fan in the Lurë area, famous for its lakes. The Drin carves its way between the land of the Lurë lakes and the even higher Korab mountain range which acts as Albania's frontier, although both here and elsewhere this frontier has been hard to draw. Near Kukës, where the White and Black Drin rivers converge, the high mountains stop, and this part of the country is easy to enter and leave, making the area one of unusual ethnic complexity. Further north and west the frontier lies well north of the Drin on the crest of a line of mountains known collectively as the Accursed Mountains, Prokletijë, although in the West they are sometimes called together with the district in which they are found, Malësia e Madhe, the Great Mountains.

Other Albanian mountains are not small. Mount Korab in the east stands 2753 metres above sea level, seven metres higher than the highest of the Great Mountains. Even relatively near the coast there are mountains over 1500 metres. Tirana is overshadowed by Mount Dajti, at 1651 metres far higher than Ben Nevis. The coastal plain is gradually getting larger as the rivers flowing rapidly from the mountains push forward alluvial mud, but the marshy nature of this new land does not make it prosperous. The Hoxha regime did a good deal to drain the malarial swamps, but subsequent emigration has destroyed much of the drainage system. In parts of the coastline the land has grown at the expense of the sea by as much as three kilometres in the last five hundred years, and this factor, combined with rivers changing their course, and Hoxha's other achievement of turning rivers into lakes and draining lakes into rivers must be taken into account when discussing the historical geography of ancient, medieval and modern Albania.

The rugged landscape has not encouraged visitors. A map from 1800 confuses the Drilo and the Drin, placing Lake Ohrid in Northern Albania. There were heroic travellers in the early twentieth century who visited parts of the country in primitive conditions which modern visitors would find it hard to endure even if they were allowed to reach them. The communists built a few roads, but discouraged foreigners and private cars. After the collapse of communism the roads collapsed as well, unable to sustain the new burden of traffic or the loss of central control. Standard mid-century works on the geography of Albania like the wartime Admiralty Guide or Pounds's *Eastern Europe* admit that their knowledge of the North is sketchy. More modern guidebooks such as those by Pettifer and Gloyer supply useful information on a few tourist attractions like Orosh and the Lurë lakes, but say little about the land in between. Albanian guidebooks to local areas are now beginning to appear, revealing a creditable spirit of optimism, but an alarming lack of basic infrastructure necessary for the tourist industry. This is a pity because the historian of any country needs to know where places are, what routes people took from one place to another, and the boundaries between different areas.

DRAWING FRONTIERS

We can begin with boundaries, both internal and external. It has already been shown that the coastline has altered considerably in the last three thousand years. Over the last hundred years there have been similar changes in Albania's land boundaries. These have rarely, if ever, coincided with the ethnic frontiers of the area inhabited by Albanians. Albania as a state did not exist until 1912, and the present northern and eastern boundary with the loosely federated Serbia and Montenegro and the totally independent Macedonia owes its existence to what is commonly called the Protocol of Florence signed in December 1913. This drew a slightly different frontier with what was then an independent Montenegro and a Serbia which had recently acquired Macedonia. There then ensued the years of World War and anarchy, during which a number of boundary commissions tried to draw up a definite line of demarcation between Albania and its northern neighbour which had become after the War the Kingdom of the Serbs, Croats and Slovenes, subsequently renamed Yugoslavia. Eventually a new Protocol of Florence, finally ratified in June 1926 in Paris, fixed the present frontier. Between 1913 and 1926 Albania made a few gains in remote mountain areas and in the frontier village of Lin, ironically inhabited by Slav-speakers, but lost a considerable amount of territory near Prizren and Dibër. These two largely Albanian-speaking towns had been awarded to Serbia in 1913, and the 1926 settlement rewarded Yugoslavia with Albanian-speaking villages near them. The year 1913 had left a great many Albanian speakers outside the new state, and 1926 added about fifty thousand more. Only during the Second World War was there any rectification of this injustice, as first the Italians and then the Germans added most of the Albanian territories in Montenegro, Kosova and Macedonia to Albania.

On the other side of the border a small number .of Slav-speakers were left in Albania. In *Badlands* I discuss the Macedonian minority near Lake Prespa, officially recognised as Albania's second largest minority after the Greeks, but only some four thousand strong. Other Macedonian-speakers can be found in Gollobordë south of Peshkopi, but they have no educational rights. Neither do the people between Zapod and Shishtavec who speak a strange Slavonic dialect and are known as the Gorani, as are other Slav-speaking Muslims in Kosova. The only other Slav-speakers are a small group near Vraka, speaking standard Serbo-Croatian. They are recognised as a minority, and have a large handsome new church, but an unfortunate recent history. Slav-speakers in Albania were unpopular because of Kosova, and many from Vraka fled to Montenegro only to discover that people from Albania were unpopular in their new home, and they came back. The famous Albanian poet Mjgeni came from this minority, being like most members of such groups bilingual. A Bosnian settlement at Shijak near Durrës has become largely assimilated, and clearly could play no part in frontier discussions.

As in Southern Albania the political frontier in the North does not coincide with the ethnic frontier, with both frontiers being very difficult to draw. But in the South there are now very few Albanian-speakers in Greece with the predominantly Muslim Chams being expelled after the Second World War and Orthodox Albanians gradually assimilated. There is, however, a substantial and recognised Greek minority inside Albania and of course many Vlachs and Gypsies, although these, described as an ethnic rather than a national minority because there is no national Vlach or Gypsy state, have a status slightly inferior to that given to the Greeks. In the North it is the other way round with many Albanians outside Albania and only a few non-Albanians inside the country, and of these only a very few seem to have minority rights, possibly because of the remoteness of their dialect from the standard language of any national state. The gross unfairness of the border is discussed in Appendix V.

It is, of course, very difficult to establish the exact numbers and location of ethnic minorities. Bilingualism, the exact criteria for determining ethnic identity and political pressure in recording census figures to associate with the majority population are all complicating factors. We have also noted the difficulties in distinguishing ethnic and national minorities. With religion matters ought to be more simple on the grounds that people can and often do speak only one language, but should have only one religion unless they have none. But it is not quite so easy in Albania. In pre-communist times there was, perhaps fortunately, an easy tolerance of other religions and a certain amount of syncretism with crypto-Christianity an obvious factor. In 1968 the official suppression of religion, unfairly blamed as a divisive factor, led to further complications. Some people declared themselves atheists, but religious communities may have felt more drawn together because of the common enemy. It is difficult to find reliable census figures for religious denominations. The maps in the 2003 German demographic atlas are based on the 1960 figures. The atlas also represents religions schematically, each district showing the different percentages of religions, and this is difficult since the boundaries of districts change frequently, as we will show. The same objection applies to the ethnographic map in this excellent atlas, where the Gorani are not shown, possibly because they are not considered an ethnic minority, possibly because of their Muslim religion.

We can, however, divide up Albania into religious districts. There has been in the North a revival of Catholicism and Islam, and new churches and mosques are good signposts, the presence of pigs in a village being a rather cruder indicator. Evangelical Protestantism was more prominent in the South and was a relatively short-lived phenomenon. Muslims are divided in relatively equal numbers between orthodox Sunnis and followers of the more tolerant Bektashi sect. Unlike in the South where there are Albanian, Slav and Greek speakers practising Orthodox

Christianity, religion and nationalism are not confused in the North. There are Orthodox Christians in towns like Durrës and Tirana, and a few through Slav influence on the Macedonian border, but Catholics, Sunnis and Bektashis predominate. Albania's Catholics are to be found in a compact bloc in the north-west of the country and in the district known as Mirditë. The north-east is fairly solidly Muslim as is the district known as Mat. Bektashis outnumber Sunnis in the eastern central area known as Bulqizë.

We have now started dividing Albania into districts, and here the German atlas comes into its own, providing three maps showing the administrative divisions in 1937 when Zog was on the throne, in 1960 when communism ruled supreme, and under the new order in 2002. In Ottoman times Albania was parcelled out between different *sandjaks* and *vilayets*, and the boundaries of these too changed over the centuries. All this is confusing especially for people who have seen less violent changes of regime and get worried about minor alterations of district administration. In England local government reorganisation has tried to keep the balance between administrative convenience and historical sentiment, not always successfully. Ask any Yorkshireman living in the Humberside Metropolitan Authority. Our shires and counties have had a long innings and still carry some weight. It is not quite the same picture in Albania. There are strong, perhaps too strong, local loyalties, involving blood feuds rather than cricket, but the district boundaries have not always been able to control or contain them.

Today there are in Albania 351 communes, 36 districts (*rrethe*) and 12 prefectures (*qarqe*). The communes are usually based on a village, the districts on a town; though sometimes on a geographical district, and the prefectures almost invariably on a large town. In 1960 there were no prefectures but only 26 *rrethe* rather larger than the modern ones. In 1937 there were 10 prefectures and 39 sub-prefectures. In that year in Northern Albania we find prefectures of Elbasan and Durrës, both extending south of the Shkumbin, Tirana, Dibër, Shkodër, and the rather provocatively named Kosova in the north-eastern part of the country. In 2002 we find the same names and roughly the same boundaries except that Kosova has been replaced by Kukës, and there is a new province based on Lezhë. All these names reappear, albeit with smaller territories to control, in 1960 apart from Dibër. Dibër is very confusingly both the name of a town in Macedonia and a district near to this town in Albania. Truthfully the communist authorities called this district by the name of its principal town, Peshkopi.

In view of the marked political differences between the regimes of 1937, 1960 and 2002 it is tempting to see ulterior motives behind these boundary changes. But oddly, though we know that the Catholic district of Mirditë was hostile to both Zog and the communists, it was a prefecture in both 1960 and 2002, as was Zog's own district of Mat. Minor changes of name and boundaries in these and other districts do not seem to have had any particular sinister purpose. The Hoxha regime was, of course, hostile to religion, committed to breaking up the old tribal system, and anxious to create a more urbanised society. It is therefore odd that Catholic Mirditë and Muslim Mat, names of regions with a special tribal and religious resonance, should have been preserved.

The boundary changes must have been confusing. The Gorani inhabitants of the communes of Zapod and Shistavec now belong to the *rreth* of Kukës and the *qarq* of the same name stretching all along the Kosova border. In 1960 the *rreth* was much smaller, its northern half forming the *rreth* of Tropojë. In the Second World War and notionally in the First World War the Gorani were in the same country as their Slav Muslim neighbours in Kosova. Under King Zog Albania was separated from Kosova, but the Gorani in Albania lived in the prefecture of Kosova and the sub-prefecture of Lumë.

Some historical continuity can be found in the extreme north-west of Albania where there are communes called Kelmend, Kastrat, Shkrel, Shala, Shoshi and Pult. All six names reflect tribal districts marked in Edith Durham's map in *High Albania*, although there are no precise boundaries in this map. Pult's origins go back to the medieval bishopric of Pulatum, Kastrat reminds us of Scanderbeg, and a fortress Clementiana is mentioned by Procopius in the sixth century AD. All this seems to show a touching faith in antiquity, but the tribal system of a hundred years ago, though not totally dead nor dying, is hardly alive and kicking. It is also extremely confusing for the modern visitor. Modern maps of Albania still show tribal districts, elaborately worked out by, for instance, Durham and the 1945 Admiralty Guide, but these are probably not relevant to a study of Albania today, and only partially relevant at the times when they were composed. In particular, as Margaret Hasluck noted in her rarely studied book and still unpublished notebooks, there is a difference between the extreme north of the country, where there are still small tribal areas like Shala and Shoshi, and further south where there are much larger areas like Mat and Mirditë. These are not encompassed by one single tribe, although in the first half of this century they achieved unity under one powerful leader. In the north-east there are tribes like the Hasi and Krasnich, but these names have lost much of their resonance as the tribes have lost much of their power, since the border with Kosova passes through their territory. To the west the territories of the Hoti and Gruda were given almost in their entirety to Montenegro.

The territory of Mirditë, with its heavy rainfall and shortage of fertile land, is a confusing pattern of mountains and inaccessible, poverty-stricken small valleys bisected by the surging River Mat, nowadays dominated by massive hydroelectric schemes. Although there is ample archaeological evidence of early human settlement, the region was of little interest to the colonists of antiquity, except for the evidence of Roman copper mining in and around the modern town of Rubik. Rubik was also important in the medieval period and prior to the Ottoman invasion saw the construction of the outstanding Church of Shen Ndout. The Mat river valley track running from Rubik to the Adriatic coast near Lezhë, ancient Lissus, was for centuries the only usable means of transport for wheeled vehicles; otherwise the Mirditë interior could only be reached on horseback or by mule. In the communist period other mines were opened up, often worked by forced or prison labour, including the notorious prison mine at Spaç in the Fan river valley.

Mirditë brings us almost but not quite to the Drin river to the north and east. On the eastern side near Kukës is a district called

Lumë. This is where the Gorani live, but the British drew on a certain amount of tribal loyalty among Albanians here during the Second World War. North of Mirditë there is the administrative district of Pukë, full according to Durham of small tribes with interesting names like Berisha, but not particularly interesting in previous periods of Albanian history. The district is poor and inaccessible although a major east-west route across it seems to have existed in most eras.

North of the Drin we can conveniently divide the country into three sections. North of Shkodër are the Great Mountains, subdivided into the tribal communes. South of Shkodër in a rather confusing area of rivers with changing courses there is a small area known as Zadrimë. To the east crossing the Catholic-Muslim boundary we are in Tropojë. This is a less mountainous region. There is a town called Tropojë, but the main centre is Bajram Curri, previously known as Kolgecaj. South of Tropojë is a district rather vaguely known as Has. This rough division is, of course, a very simplified picture. There are some revealing other names for small areas. Close to Shkodër just north of the Drin we find Postribë, a good Latin name for across the bank. Further along the Drin we find Nikaj-Mertur, the name of two tribes, in Edith Durham's time famed for their savagery. Some have seen a Latin root in Mertur. South of Nikaj-Mertur used to lie the village of Dushman, now drowned under an artificial lake. This was the name of a tribe in Durham's time and the name of a contemporary of Scanderbeg. Some have claimed to find the name in Procopius. An even more confusing and interesting name is Dukagjin. This is used as a collective name for most of the northern Catholic tribes. It was the name of a sub-prefecture in King Zog's time including the eastern section of this Catholic area. More bafflingly it also is used to describe a small area south of the Drin and a general name to describe the whole of the land north of the Drin. Dukagjin is, of course, the name of the powerful family, contemporary with Scanderbeg, whose influence is as important as that of Albania's greatest historical figure, but more mysterious.

ROADS MODERN AND ANCIENT

Scanderbeg by his leadership and Lek Dukagjin by his laws united a country which geography had divided into the small areas we have described. There were and are, of course, roads leading from one district to another, and the location of these roads is very important in history. Unfortunately as with the boundaries the story of Albania's roads is a difficult one. In England with the Fosse Way and Watling Street we tend to think of roads as having a long history, following obvious routes along straight lines which the Romans had set down. As a small boy I lived at the side of a straight road near the small Kentish town of Edenbridge, and my father patiently explained to me that it was an old Roman road, even taking me to a place where some zealous antiquary had excavated the original pavement at a point where the modern motor road had diverged from its ancestor. I remember thinking the Roman road, admittedly a minor one, vastly inferior to the modern B road.

In Albania there is roughly the same pattern of modern roads following ancient routes, but there are marked differences. For a variety of reasons parents during the Second World War living near the great Via Egnatia which bisected Albania in Roman times are unlikely to have given the same history lesson as my father. But modern tourists allowed into Albania in the 1970s travelling along the main road from Pogradec to Elbasan were invited to inspect a stretch of the Via Egnatia, part of a Roman A road near the major road of Albania. Modern improvements to this motor road seem to have made the two roads diverge, and an inspection of the Via Egnatia in 2000 involved a long and difficult drive from the main road along tracks little better than the rough path along which I found paving stones which indicated the Roman road. Unlike in Central England where Watling Street and the Fosse Way traverse flat lowlands the roads which the Romans heroically carved out in the Balkans had to cross high mountains. Modern roads built for motor traffic do not cope with these mountains in the same way, and it is thus rare to find the straight Roman roads coinciding exactly with their modern equivalents. The Romans did not know about hairpins.

The barbarian invasions and the forces of nature did not improve the condition of these Roman roads, although we do hear of early invaders like Theoderic in 395 AD moving along them. In Byzantine times Alexius Comnenus advanced along the Via Egnatia, but retreated by a more difficult route. His Norman adversary Bohemund marched from the coast to Lake Ohrid on a road which appears neither on ancient or modern maps, based on the River Devoll. One of the leading crusaders came along the coast and found it very difficult, although the road from Shkodër to Durrës is now Albania's best road. The campaigns of Scanderbeg against the Turks and vice versa involved marches between Kruja and Dibër again on neither ancient nor modern itineraries. Under the Ottomans, as we can see from archaeological evidence, some old Roman roads were restored with slight divergences for new bridges and stopping places. Traders, very often Vlachs, crossed by a variety of routes from the interior to the coast, but there was less need for traffic between north and south.

Imperialism is a dirty word, but empire builders like the Romans and Ottomans needed more than dirt tracks to hold their empire together. Mussolini's imperial ambitions lasted less long, but it was the Italians who built the modern motor roads which, sadly battered, form the basis of Albania's transport system today. Under the communists, private transport was prohibited, and the all powerful state ensured that the roads were kept in reasonable order for essential public traffic. In the past twenty years melting snows in spring and sudden storms in autumn have wrought havoc on carriage ways quite incapable of dealing with a vast increase of motor vehicles. Local authorities, with insufficient funds and a not totally unblemished record in avoiding corruption, have tried to repair and improve, often making the roads even slower in the process.

Warts and all, Northern Albania's modern roads do give a rough idea of the main routes in all periods of history. There has always been some way of proceeding along the coast from Shkodër to Durrës, the absence of harbours making progress by land preferable to a sea voyage. The other routes marked in the schematic Peutinger Table, drawn up probably in the fifth century AD, are the Via Egnatia and the road from Lissus (Lezhë) to Naissus (Nis). The route of the former roughly following the River Shkumbin has been traced. Unlike its modern equivalent it is on much higher ground than the river which in many places is an obstacle rather than an aid to a smooth passage, flowing through ravines, being the recipient of precipitous torrents and liable to seasonal flooding. Medieval and Ottoman travellers would seem to have followed Roman rather than modern lines. The road from Lissus to Naissus has never been exactly traced. Here the river with which the road has to contend is the Drin. This was tamed in the time of Enver Hoxha for much of its course to form an artificial lake, providing electricity and an alternative mode of transport with a ferry boat capable of taking cars. Before the war the Italians seeing the Drin flowing through such difficult country decided to build a road well to the south passing through the small town of Pukë and not crossing the Drin until Kukës. Dervla Murphy managed to survive this route on her bicycle, although she met some human hazards.

More than a hundred years ago Edith Durham got on better with the inhabitants of Northern Albania, but travelled by a different and more difficult road from the coast to Kosova. She did not go through Pukë. There are no Roman remains so far verified near this town, and it may be wrong to link it with the name Ad Picaria, which appears in the Peutinger Table, or the name Pacue mentioned by the sixth-century geographer Hierocles. Attempts to link the name to Publica Via may also be fruitless; there is an alternative explanation for the name in the Greek word *Pevke* for a pine tree of which there are plenty near Pukë. There is before Pukë on the way from either Shkodër or Lezhë or both a good Roman site at Vig with a good Roman name, foreshortened from Vigilium, a watch tower, although this particular fort seems more likely to a fortress guarding a road than a station on the road.

After Ad Picaria the Peutinger Table gives Crevenium and Gabuleo. Crevenium is usually associated with Vau Spasi, where Edith Durham crossed the Drin, and Gabuleo with the site of old Kukës, now submerged beneath the lake and thus concealing any archaeological remains. Those at Vau Spasi are just visible, and though it is difficult to get to the site it is possible to see from nearby roads that are just viable good straight lines passing close to remains of forts at Kostur and Helshan to the two passes near Letaj where the present frontier lies. Alternatively one could proceed along the Drin to Kukës and then in another straight line along the route of the modern road to Prizren. Albanian archaeologists suggest quite reasonably that as in modern times and in the age of Edith Durham so in the Roman and late Roman era there were alternative routes in this stretch of the Lissus-Naissus road.

The Peutinger Table does not take any account of this possible divergence, nor does it give any hint of a fourth major route, that along the valley of the Black Drin from Kukës to join the Via Egnatia. This route certainly existed in late Roman, medieval and Ottoman times as remains of forts, bridges and even traces of the actual road attest. It is an important route for history. In the sixth century Slav invaders used it as they pushed southwards, bypassing Northern Albania where the roads were more difficult. In the fourteenth century, proceeding in the opposite direction the Ottomans used it to reach Kosova long before they had subdued Albania. Twentieth-century atlases still marked it as a major road, and Robert Carver in 1995 travelled in some trepidation in a minibus from Peshkopi to Kukës. I was unable to persuade a tough taxi driver to make the reverse journey in 2005.

To get to Peshkopi from Tirana one starts on the road to Shkodër and then diagonally down the Mat river to Burrel and Bulqizë. This and another route up the Fan river to a point east of Pukë conclude our list of modern roads, but the two last named diagonal roads are of little relevance to most of Albanian history. In Ottoman times it is clear that there were a number of different east west routes. The Dibër road is still a landmark in Tirana like Oxford Street in London, and is still marked as a major road in some atlases, although disappointingly it is in very poor condition, and even more disappointingly turns out to go by a different route from that of the old Dibër road that existed in the first half of the twentieth century.

It was, however, on the new Dibër road that I realised why Northern Albania, so divided by rivers, mountains and bad roads, with its different religions, boundaries and such a reputation for barbarity and blood feuds, is still a unity. We travelled slowly down a terrible road for three hours to the small village of Bizë. This is about sixty kilometres from Tirana and the same distance from the Macedonian border. In the Second World War the British had dropped parachutists here, and after the war was over continued to use Bizë as a landing ground for Albanian agents to overthrow the Hoxha regime. Such agents were almost always caught, and it is a moot point whether this was due to the clever but disloyal Kim Philby getting word to the Albanian authorities that an attack was imminent, or loyal but stupid English officials choosing to launch an attack from a well tried but expected quarter. Bizë lies on a desolate plateau, and one can see its suitability as a landing ground. A ring of bunkers and a nearby barracks both now derelict show how Hoxha was prepared.

Bizë is close to Tirana and yet remote from it. It is also in spite of appearing to be in the middle of nowhere very suitably placed as a launching pad from which to move in several different directions. It is on the Dibër road. The Erzen rises a few kilometres west, and a similar distance east we meet tributaries of the Drin. Tributaries of the Mat leading northwards and of the Shkumbin leading southwards almost meet at Bizë, and indeed there are roads near Bizë leading to Burrel in Mat and Elbasan on the Shkumbin. So it is possible from this central point to obtain access to many seemingly self-contained areas, as the British and Hoxha realised, and Northern Albania is more unified than it seems. The Dibër road is also a reminder of the same country's diversity. On the way from Tirana, one can and we unwisely did, plunge down from the rough high road to an even rougher track passing through the villages of Shënmeri, Shëngjerj and Shëngjin, reminders of Albania's Christian past in a largely Muslim, area. If we had pushed on a little further we would have reached the Gollobordë Mountains with their Slav minority. Gollobordë is in the *qarq* of Bulqizë, a centre of the Bektashi sect with impressive *teqe* or holy places.

This is a chapter about geography rather than literature, which perhaps never receives its fair due for its role in determining national and regional identities and differences. It so happens that in Gjergj Fishta, who lived between 1871 and 1940, we have a writer who encompasses Northern Albania's unity and diversity. This is fortunate. It is unfortunate that he writes in the Gheg dialect, and has only recently been translated into English. More unfortunately he was considered persona non grata by the Hoxha regime for being a Catholic priest, vaguely sympathetic to pre-war regimes and the Italians, thus promoting tribal feudal anarchy directed against fellow workers in Slav countries. In fact Fishta's great epic poem *The Highland Lute* is almost as fiercely nationalist as was the Hoxha regime, and is a useful if not very precise guide to Northern Albania. Most of the names of the districts mentioned above appear in his poem, although most of the action takes place in Montenegro. Rather sadly, the names Hoti, Gruda, Plava and Gucia form a recurringly melancholic line, and this is not just a reflection of Homer, but a complaint against the way in which these territories had been lost by Albania. But in the struggle to regain them from Montenegro and regain some liberty from the Turks - a difficult balancing act - other Albanian tribes and districts, from the east as well as the west, from Central Albania as well as the north, Muslims as well as Catholics, are all mentioned. There are polite references to the family of King Zog and the Doda family of Mirditë, both prominent in the period around independence, although hardly in harmony with each other or with post-war Albanian thought.

Fishta gives a portrait of a united Northern Albania determined to foil the efforts of the Great Powers to award part of its territory to the Montenegrins and the efforts of Turkey to re-establish control over the fiercely independent tribes. He wavers, sometimes a little uncertainly, between these two aims, as he also wavers between events in 1878 and in 1912, in both of which years Albania lost territory to Montenegro. The communists blamed Fishta for anti-Slav prejudice and not saying enough about fighting for freedom against the imperialist Ottoman oppressor. In fact Fishta is remarkably chivalrous to Montenegrin warriors, and if he makes his Albanian heroes ally with the Turks, this would seem to coincide with the facts of history. The same may be said of an apparent glorification of war. Albanians and Montenegrins sought honour in battle, as did Homer's Greeks and Trojans, but neither Fishta nor Homer are warmongers. Hoxha, in any case with his heroic rendering of the Partisan struggle, could hardly blame Fishta for the occasional piece of sabre rattling. Nor could Hoxha blame Fishta for his fiercely nationalistic views in which not only Scanderbeg plays a part, but earlier less well known and less successful shadowy figures emerge. Apart from Pyrrhus, Leka (Alexander the Great) and Naim Frasheri not many of Fishta's fighters for Albania come from the South, and the first two of these are rather dubious Albanians. But there are plenty of Illyrians in Fishta. Teuta and Bardyllis, Agron and Pleuratus, two otherwise unknown Illyrian names Hila and Clinic, and poor Gentius defeated by the Romans are all mentioned. Thus well before Hoxha the Albanians were reclaiming their Illyrian past, difficult though it is to disentangle the story of this past from nationalist prejudice.

3. THE ILLYRIANS, 1200-230 BC

'Why, lady, this is Illyria.' The shipwrecked Viola in *Twelfth Night* asks the name of the country on whose shores she has been wrecked, and the answer that it is Illyria is presumably meant to reassure her. Travellers like to know where they are. But neither in ancient or medieval or modern times has there been much reassuring certainty about where Illyria or the Illyrians could be found.

Shakespeare who gave Bohemia a sea coast was the last person to ask, although in making his Illyrian town ruled by a duke he makes it seem like a Venetian possession on the Adriatic coast. When Napoleon conquered Venice he called this part of his empire in Dalmatia the Illyrian provinces. An Illyrian movement in the former Yugoslavia, whose borders in the twentieth century were roughly equivalent to those of the Roman province of Illyricum, was started in the nineteenth century by Slavs seeking independence from Turkey and from Austria who had been awarded Napoleon's Illyrian provinces in 1815. The Albanian claim to be the descendants of the ancient Illyrians, noted in Fishta's poem, was subsequent to the Illyrian movement in Yugoslavia, although it was more justified. The South Slavs, though clearly different from the ancient Illyrians, did live in areas inhabited by these people. The Albanians, though in some sense the same as the Illyrians, also lived partly in areas inhabited by Illyrians, although inconveniently they dwelt as well in areas inhabited in ancient times by other races like the Dardanians and Epirotes. This creates difficulties for the study of Kosova and Southern Albania, but fortunately for our study Northern Albania seems to have been almost exclusively inhabited by the Illyrians in ancient times and Albanians in the modern era.

The ancient Greeks briskly dismissed all who did not speak Greek as barbarians. They vaguely divided up these tribes into Illyrians in the north-west of the Balkan peninsula and Thracians in the north-east while adding a few more colourful tribes like the Scythians north of the Danube. Meanwhile in the central belt of the Balkans there were the Macedonians and Epirotes in an ambiguous position, halfway between the sunny shores of the Mediterranean and the grim northern mountains, halfway between Hellenism and barbarity. Inconveniently for a number of countries, notably Albania and the present state of Macedonia, the dividing line between barbarism and semi-Hellenism bisects the modern state. In the case of Albania there are two such bisections: that between Epirotes and Illyrians roughly along the River Shkumbin, and an even rougher dividing line along the Black Drin between Macedonians and Illyrians.

The first division, discussed in *Badlands*, need not concern us. Epirotes except in the time of Pyrrhus rarely advanced north of the Shkumbin. Illyrians more often made aggressive moves southwards, but that does not turn Epirotes like Pyrrhus into Illyrians. North of the Shkumbin there was clearly a permanent Illyrian presence extending well north of the present frontier of Albania. To the east the position is more problematic. Since there is very little of Albania east of the Black Drin, the demarcation line between Macedonians and Illyrians might not seem to matter, but large numbers of Albanian-speakers live beyond the Drin in Western Macedonia and Kosova, and this is an area in which we find neither Illyrians nor Macedonians, but Dardanians. This people plays a large part in Illyrian history, most notably between 400 and 100 BC in the Macedonian and Roman wars. Dardania survived like Epirus as a name for a small province in the reorganisation of the Roman Empire at the end of the third century AD. In spite of their remoteness in time the Dardanians have been used to prove or disprove Albanian claims to lands beyond the Drin. Unfortunately the evidence to show that the Dardanians were or were not Illyrians is inconclusive. We can discount arguments that the word *dardhe* (pear) in modern Albanian proves their link with the Illyrians or that Homer and Virgil who call the Trojans Dardanians prove their links with the eastern part of the Balkans and thus the Thracians. The Dardanian king Bardylis is sometimes called Illyrian, and the Illyrian king Monunius is sometimes called Dardanian, but our sources for both characters are late and unreliable. A helmet inscribed in Greek with the name Monunius has been found near Lake Ohrid, maddeningly just outside both Dardanian and Illyrian territory, although well within the area of both races' incursions. Archaeological evidence suggests that north-eastern Albania was really a Dardanian area, and this is not surprising given the easy access to Tropojë from Kosova over low passes. The Dardanians do not solve the problem of Kosova.

Much of our evidence about both Dardanians and Illyrians comes from Roman sources. The Romans only entered Albania towards the end of our period, and deservedly will receive a whole chapter to themselves. In general they get today a bad press, being perceived as brutal imperialist philistines very different from the cultured, freedom-loving Greeks. But they did not dismiss all non-Latin speakers as barbarians, and they did show some curiosity about and tolerance towards the peoples they conquered. They differentiated the Dardanians from the Illyrians on account of the savage habits of the former, involving cave dwellings, tattooing and a strange love of music. The Yugoslav scholar Fanula Papazoglou contrasts these bizarre habits with the behaviour of the more civilised Illyrians. These, she suggests, were better organised, unified under a single monarchy in the period before the Roman conquest, more amenable to Greek influence, and more readily subservient to Rome. This praise of Illyrians may seem surprising from a non-Albanian scholar, but of course Papazoglou is anxious not only to disassociate Illyrians from Dardanians, but also Illyrians from Albanians.

Rome entered the Balkans almost by accident in the late third century BC and fairly quickly established a protectorate over the Greek colonies at Dyrrachium and Apollonia. This protectorate was extended to include some Illyrian tribes in the hinterland of the archaeological sites of Durrës and Pojan. The distinction between Greek citizens of these two cities and others is likely to have been blurred in the previous century, as numismatic and epigraphic evidence suggests a strong, even commanding Illyrian presence in them. Earlier literary evidence suggests a division between superior Greeks and inferior Illyrians. In between 229 and 168 BC there were three Illyrian and three Macedonian wars, all of which Rome won. Polybius, Livy and Appian give detailed accounts of these campaigns, and Albania for the first and almost the last time in its history receives a detailed commentary from major historians, although modern commentators on these historians are still in some doubt about the topography of the campaigns they describe. Nor do the historians of Rome give a great deal of information about native Illyrians, and both Livy and Polybius can be accused of a certain amount of bias in, for instance, invariably making the enemies of Rome the instigators of all the wars Rome fought.

In spite of this bias it is to Rome that we owe our best account of Illyricum and the Illyrians, and we therefore have to carry our account of this province and people beyond 200 BC. By 168 Rome controlled the coastline of Albania and in 146 incorporated most of the country into a large Balkan province called Macedonia in which Illyrians must have been a powerful minority. There were still plenty of unconquered Illyrians both around Lake Shkodër and further north. It is not exactly clear when or why Rome established a separate province of Illyricum. This was the province which was allotted to Julius Caesar in 59, but he decided to go to Gaul instead. At some stage between 146 and 59 Rome decided to link its conquests among the Illyrians along the Adriatic into a province. We hear of campaigns against the Delmatae, who have given their name to Dalmatia. One of these campaigns according to Appian was to punish the Ardiaei and Pleraei, presumably based in Montenegro, for their attacks on Roman Illyria. Another expedition was mounted according to Livy against the Delmatae for attacking Illyrians, allies of Rome. On the other hand in 118 Lucius Caecilius Metellus led a campaign against the Delmatae with the sole and successful aim of being awarded a triumph. For the next seventy years Roman control over the Illyrians extended only over the coastal areas. Many Illyrians both in Yugoslavia and Albania lay outside the boundaries of the provinces of Macedonia and Illyricum.

Julius Caesar and his family were much involved in Illyrian affairs. Caesar's campaign against Pompey near Dyrrachium in 48 BC was in the province of Macedonia, but in Illyrian territory. The future emperor Augustus was studying in Apollonia when Caesar was murdered. After some difficult campaigns along the Via Egnatia Caius Octavius and Mark Antony divided the empire between them. As in many other divisions the boundary was fixed in Albania at Shkodër. Presumably the line north of Shkodër was equivalent to the boundary, as yet not formed with any certainty, between the provinces of Illyricum and Macedonia. This boundary was to last a long time, but it started life with some difficulty. Octavius conducted some arduous campaigns in the north of Illyricum in 35 BC, while Antony in charge of Macedonia sent Asinius Pollio, the patron of Virgil, to subdue the rebellious Parthini near Elbasan in 39 BC. With another surge towards the Danube in 27-6 BC, led by Marcus Crassus, son of the triumvir, after the battle of Actium Octavius and Rome seemed secure, and thus Illyricum with its boundaries roughly equivalent to those of Yugoslavia was confidently declared a senatorial province. Such confidence was premature. An Illyrian revolt well away from Albanian territory in 6 AD took the future emperor Tiberius three years to suppress, and at the end of this revolt Illyricum was divided between Pannonia in the north and east, clearly a difficult area, and the more peaceful Dalmatia in the south and west along the coast.

Illyricum and the Illyrians still survived. St Paul announced in his epistle to the Romans that he had visited the borders of Illyricum, which presumably counted as a geographical expression. Pious commentators assure us that this reference shows us that St Paul visited Dyrrachium, but probably it means that he got no further than the Macedonian frontier somewhere in north-western Greece. Yet, if not pacified by St Paul, the Illyrians were fairly peaceful in the first two centuries of the Christian era. In the third century they proved to be the saviours of the Roman Empire by providing a series of soldier emperors who resisted barbarian invasions across the Danube. The last of these, Diocletian, a powerful persecutor of Christians, was probably born at Doclea near Podgorica in Montenegro. He gave the name Illyricum a new and complicated life. He divided the Roman Empire into four dioceses, and one of these gigantic dioceses was named Illyricum, stretching from the Danube to Crete. This diocese was divided between two prefectures with the northern half known as Dacia and the southern half as Macedonia. Prefectures were further subdivided into provinces, one of which, roughly corresponding to north-western Yugoslavia, was confusingly called Illyricum. Albania was divided between the provinces of Epirus Vetus, corresponding to southern Albania and a bit of northern Greece, Epirus Nova, which took up the centre of modern Albania as far as the Drin, and Praevalitana comprising Albania north of the Drin and a good deal of Montenegro. All these provinces were part of the diocese of Illyricum, but Praevalitana unlike Epirus Vetus and Nova formed part of the prefecture of Dacia rather than Macedonia. So did Dardania, occupying Kosova and, ironically, part of modern Macedonia.

These divisions did not last very long, although the boundaries established had important consequences. Diocletian had intended to divide in order to rule, but his greater successor Constantine united the Roman Empire again only to divide it again in a different fashion between his sons. In the latter half of the fourth century the Goths became a serious threat and decisively defeated the Romans at the Battle of Adrianople in 378, an event that has rightly been seen as the end of Roman Illyricum. Theodosius united the Empire again, but there were now large settlements of Goths in the Balkan peninsula. At his death he created a further and final division of the Empire with Shkodër being once again at the demarcation line between East and West. The exact boundary between the East Roman Empire under Honorious and the West under Arcadiius is hard to determine, and in any case was rather academic as Goths were very active in both empires. Thus Alaric and his Visigoths were first settled in Epirus before moving west to sack Rome in 410 and settle eventually in southern France and Spain. At the end of the fifth century Theoderic the Ostrogoth was well ensconced near Dyrrachium before he too moved to Italy, which had already together with western Illyricum passed from Roman control. It would seem that Praevalitana together with the Illyrian provinces north of it became part of the West, and thus temporarily came under Gothic control. Significantly Praevalitana is not mentioned in Procopius' list of Justinian's buildings in the Balkans, although Justinian, who came from Dardania, still in the eastern part of the empire, did recover in the part of the sixth century all the territory ceded to the Ostrogoths.

In Justinian's time Illyricum had become a geographical expression. It is mentioned as such in Procopius' account of Justinian's wars, as indeed is Praevalitana, lurking under the name Praekalis. Other Byzantine historians use it vaguely, though not very frequently, after the time of Justinian. Following the Slav invasions Illyricum had finally passed out of Byzantine control, and historians like Theophanes would not really be in a position to know whether this area was any longer inhabited by Illyrians. At the beginning of the eleventh century Basil the Bulgar Slayer recovered for Byzantium the whole of the Southern Balkans, and we do find archaising writers like Anna Commena using Illyricum to apply to both the area around Dyrrachium in which her father fought and to the area further north now inhabited by Slavs. Byzantium had to contest Illyrian land not only with Slavs, but with invaders from the West, of whom Venice was the most persistent. And so back to Shakespeare where Duke Orsino presumably ruled one of the Venetian outposts along the Adriatic, some of them in Albania. By the end of the sixteenth century the only Venetian possession in Albania was Butrint which, although it would make a magnificent site for a production of *Twelfth Night* with its lagoon and its theatre, is the least Illyrian site in Albania.

The above pages are a rather long answer to a second question Viola might have asked, namely, 'Where is Illyria?' This question is indeed hard to answer. It is much easier to answer a third question about the whereabouts of the Illyrians. Clearly the Illyrians inhabited most of the former Yugoslavia and Albania for the period between the alleged date of the Trojan War in 1200

BC and the battle of Adrianople in 378 AD. The exact borders of Illyrian settlement are a little blurred on the northern, southern and eastern sides, possibly on the western too if some tribes in southern Italy like the Messapians can be reckoned to be Illyrians. Archaeology and our literary sources concur in acknowledging a broad swathe of Illyrians stretching along the coast and for a considerable area inland from northern Croatia to the middle of Albania. One of these sources, the Elder Pliny, slightly confuses the issue by calling one of the many Illyrian tribes the true Illyrians. Tantalisingly for Albanian and Yugoslav historians anxious to claim the Illyrian heritage, this particular tribe, the *Illyrii proprie dicti*, are delicately poised on the borders of Albania and Montenegro. But in fact Pliny's information is of little use in settling ancient or modern ethnic boundaries. The Graeci, a small group living in southern Italy, have given to a nation a name which everybody but the Greeks recognises. The Greeks both now and in antiquity have called themselves Hellenes, originally the name of a small tribe in Thessaly. So too the Illyrians from small beginnings became in a way a great nation, although they in their tribes like the Greeks in their city states never really became a united nation in antiquity. Occasionally, as in the war against Troy or against the Persians, the Greeks achieved a mythical or ephemeral unity.

Attempts to portray at any rate the southern Illyrians as united in the period between 400 BC and the Roman occupation owe something to myth, and the unity achieved was very fragile. On the other hand well before the Trojan War and well after the Persian Wars at the beginning of the fifth century we can talk with a certain amount of confidence about Illyrians living in what would become Yugoslavia and Albania.

In Neolithic times there is evidence of a people engaged in hunting, stock rearing, farming and fishing at certain sites in Northern Albania, notably Blaz in the Mat valley. The Bronze Age lasting from 1900 to 1200 BC has left remains that are witness to war and trade. The principal sites of this area are found in the south at Maliq and Pazhok, but important discoveries have been made in a cave at Nezir also in Mat. Objects found in Albania show similarities with discoveries in the former Yugoslavia and have led to the rather crude hypothesis of a proto-Illyrian culture covering most of the Western Balkans. The same pattern is found in the Iron Age beginning around 1200 since in northern and central Albania there are many tumuli containing iron weapons, rich jewellery and some rather poor pottery. These sites are scattered all over the country with some concentration on the Drin and Mat valleys. They show continuity of occupation often from Bronze Age times to the era of the Macedonian and Roman invasions, and have been used by the Albanian archaeologists who have excavated them to prove that the Illyrian ancestors of their countrymen have been there and in most of the former Yugoslavia since time immemorial.

In spite or because of archaeological discoveries old certainties about Balkan history in the pre-Classical period have been eroded. In Greece it used to be thought with evidence both from archaeology and literary sources that the land of the bronze-using Mycenaeans was invaded by the iron-using Dorians around 1100 BC, both races speaking Greek. Nowadays we are less confident about the Dorian invasion, although clearly there was some kind of collapse in civilisation towards the end of the second millennium, and there was a change from bronze to iron. In Albania without any literary evidence we cannot be sure of any kind of invasion, or know how the Bronze Age Illyrians related to their Iron Age successors or how both groups can be linked to the parallel groups further south.

Again it used to be widely assumed that both Illyrians and Macedonians were Indo-European peoples and therefore distantly related to each other. The decipherment of Linear B as a primitive form of Greek and the presumption that Albanian was the descendant of ancient Illyrian were used to prove this point, since Albanian is clearly an Indo-European language. Some have even sought to prove that either Mycenaeans or Dorians or both were really Illyrians who became civilised, citing as evidence similarities in burial patterns and the blood feud, common to Aeschylus and

Northern Albania. But confidence in the Indo-European myth like that in the Dorian invasion has been weakened if not broken. We can, however, be fairly certain that such Illyrian speakers were the sole inhabitants of Northern Albania apart from the Greek colonists of Dyrrachium and some Dardanians near Kosova between 1200 and 200 BC.

This is a long period of continuous occupation by the Illyrians, but individual Illyrian tribes may not have lasted so long in the same place. The power of these tribes waxed and waned in the same way as we know Greek city states were sometimes powerful, sometimes insignificant, Argos and Thebes being useful examples, and even Sparta and Athens being sometimes humbled. But these cities remained in the same place, whereas some tribes may have moved their abode, or even been nomadic or semi-nomadic. Most of our knowledge about Illyrian tribes comes from people writing in the period after the Roman invasion. Scylax is an exception, but he concentrates on the coastal districts and is demonstrably inaccurate. The later Scymnus is also concerned with the shore. Strabo may be drawing on the sixth-century Hecataeus. He is honest about the difference between the deserted landscape of his day and the Illyria of the past. Pliny gives more information about Yugoslavia than Albania, although some evidence of continuity is provided by the fact that he shows how Illyrian tribes were tamed into Roman *civitates*, a typically Roman adaptation of the tribal structure which did not involve the founding of city states to which such tribes were unsuited. Of the historians Polybius and Livy are better at naming tribes and towns than placing them in exact locations. Appian clearly blots his copybook by confusing Illyrians with Epirotes, and he is not very helpful about individual tribes. There are complications about tribes in different places having nearly identical names, and about some tribes being sub-divisions of others.

In spite of these difficulties Balkan and Western historians have produced maps recording a number of Illyrian tribes, and these show a good deal of uniformity. Balkan historians have tended to err in stretching Illyrian power too far, an inconvenience

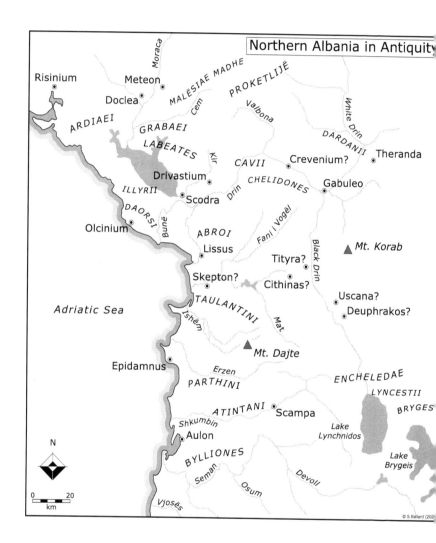

Northern Albania in Antiquity

Risinium

Meteon

Doclea

ARDIAEI

MALËSIAE MADHE

PROKETLIJË

Moraca

Cem

Valbona

White Drin

GRABAEI

LABEATES

DARDANII

Theranda

Kir

CAVII

Crevenium?

Drivastium

CHELIDONES

Gabuleo

ILLYRII

Scodra

Drin

DAORSI

Bunë

Olcinium

ABROI

Fani i Vogël

Black Drin

▲ Mt. Korab

Lissus

Tityra?

Skepton?

Cithinas?

Uscana?

Deuphrakos?

Adriatic Sea

TAULANTINI

Ishëm

Mat

▲ Mt. Dajte

Epidamnus

Erzen

PARTHINI

ENCHELEDAE

LYNCESTII

ATINTANI

Scampa

BRYGES

Shkumbin

Aulon

Lake Lynchnidos

N

BYLLIONES

Semañ

Devoll

Lake Brygeis

0   20
km

Osum

Vjosës

© S.Ballard (202

when we are faced with a tribe with a long name living in a small area, or vice versa. My own map is heavily dependent upon the work of others, but requires some explanation. South of the Shkumbin, and thus not in our area, we have Bylliones, appropriately near Byllis, and the Dassaretae near Korcë. These tribes bordered on people of Epirotic origin and dubious ethnicity, the Chaonians and Molossians, and the Dassaretae, possibly the same as the Dexari. Also in the area of the great lakes, Lyncestis, with its appropriately named tribe the Lyncestii, was in the time of Philip and Alexander definitely Macedonian. In what is now northern Macedonia and Kosova, spreading into Tropojë, we have already discussed Dardanians, again not definitively Illyrian, although playing an important part in Illyrian history. Even more problematically along or near the course of the Black Drin lived the Pirustae and Encheledae. The former tribe figures in the campaigns of 170 and 169 BC when Perseus and the Romans took and retook the town of Uscana, more probably in the Dibër area than in central Macedonia. This would place the Pirustae in a kind of buffer zone between Dardanians and Illyrians, perched on the mountains which at present form the boundary between Albania and Macedonia with a foot in both camps. The trouble with placing the Pirustae in the Dibër area is that there is not then a great deal of room for the Encheledae or eel men who are associated both with the lakes and a district much further north and west around Budva in Montenegro. Possibly we have here an example of one tribe displacing another. Alternatively the Encheledae may have been transhumant, travelling along the length of the Drin in search of summer or winter pasture or even of eels or fish.

The same problem arises with the Atintani or Atintanes who seem to appear just north of the Shkumbin in Cermenikë, near Tepelenë in southern Albania and the Pindus Mountains. Vlachs today can be found in or near all these three areas, and in former times would think nothing of making the long journey between them. On the other hand it is odd to find the Illyrian Atintanes so far south in Epirote territory, and the Roman protectorate to which they belonged would have had rather a strange shape if they had lived in southern Albania or the Pindus. They were rather uncertain members of the protectorate, being detached from it both by the Ardiaean kingdom and the Macedonians; this particular form of disloyalty again does not fit in with a southern domicile.

The Parthini living along the Shkumbin had like the Atintani a mixed history of loyalty to Rome. They flirted with Macedon during the First Macedonian War, may have been under the rule of the Ardiaean king Pleuratus at the end of the Second, but fought against Gentius in the Third Illyrian War. They were still restive in the period before the war between Antony and Octavian. North of the Atintani and the Parthini we have the Chelidones or snail men occupying Mirditë, while the powerful and long lasting Taulantini ruled over the coastal plain close to Dyrrachium at most stages of its independent history. There is a problem about what happened to the Taulantini in the third century. This list covers Albania south of the Drin apart from a minor tribe, the Abroi, makers of mead. North of the Drin we find the distant and savage Autiaratae and then in rather crowded fashion near the coast the *Illyrii proprie dicti*, of whom we hear little, the Ardiaei, powerful enemies of Rome, and, subservient to this tribe, the Grabaei, probably in Montenegro, and the Cavii who appear briefly in the Third Illyrian War and have been placed near Crevenium one of the stations in the Peutinger Table, probably to be found at Vau Spasi west of Kukës. There are also the Labeates around Lake Shkodër, hard to distinguish from the Ardiaei.

Clearly this list has its imperfections. It is compiled from sources very often writing after our period of a thousand years, in which many changes must have occurred. Appian talks in connection with Dyrrachium of the Bryges and the Liburnians, who lived much further north, but writing in 150 AD about Homeric times he can hardly be trusted. Scylax and Scymnus also mention the Bryges.

With the snail men and the eel men we are back at the beginning of this period in the mythical landscape of Homer who lists among Troy's allies the proud Hippomolgoi, drinkers of mares' milk. Myth is rarely a good basis for historical geography. Nevertheless our rough map of ancient Northern Albania does correspond in certain features to the way in which the land has divided itself throughout the ages, with the coast often controlled by foreign powers, large powerful entities in Mat and Mirditë, and smaller groups in the wilder North occasionally asserting themselves like the Ardiaei in the third century BC and the Kastrioti in the fifteenth century AD. With the exception of the Dushman family, not very important supporters of Scanderbeg, and the modern and fairly insignificant Dushman tribe there are almost no plausible links between the medieval and modern groups in Northern Albania, and it is therefore inherently unlikely that there should be any connections between ancient Illyrian tribes and their medieval Albanian counterparts. There is a longer period of time between the Illyrians and the late medieval Albanians than there is between Albanians in the time of Scanderbeg and those in the time of King Zog, and we still have to discuss the problem of the link between Illyrians and Albanians.

QUESTIONS OF ANCESTRY

Before embarking upon this vexed question we should perhaps consider why Albanians should be so keen to prove their Illyrian ancestry. This wish, as we have shown, is not confined to the communist era. Among other European nations it is only the Greeks who are keen to go back to the days of Homer to prove their undoubted claim to the land of Achilles and Agamemnon. The Italians are proud of Ancient Rome, but the French do not worry much about the Gauls any more than in England we boast of Boadicea and our Celtic heritage. In Romania they call their sons Trajan, but Slav nations in the Balkans cannot go back more than fifteen hundred years. It seems in a way strange that almost the last nation in Europe to achieve a separate identity as a nation state should be so emphatic in claiming that it was the first nation to occupy the territory of that state. Of course Albania, so often occupied by foreigners, for this reason felt obliged to state and perhaps exaggerate the priority of Albanians. The absurdity of trying to redraw modern frontiers by looking at ancient boundaries, or of insisting that ethnic purity can survive the vicissitudes of history in a much invaded area is not confined to Albanians. But there can be no doubt that the Hoxha regime, having fought against the Italians and Germans, and then having quarrelled with almost every other country, felt particularly obliged to stress the Illyrian connection as a means of uniting a divided nation against external enemies. It is due to this sense of obligation that Albanian archaeologists have done excellent work in excavating Illyrian remains. This work, however, has been slightly marred by an insistence on continuity both backwards so that Albanians talk of Illyrian Stone Age sites and forwards so that medieval sites, slightly less eagerly excavated, are supposed to contain artefacts showing links between the ancient Illyrians and modern Albanians.

The chief link in this chain is the Albanian language. We have a language that has survived in a remote area, derived neither from Greek or Latin, dominant languages in the Illyrian era, nor from Slav or Gothic, races that intervened between the end of ancient Illyricum and the first mention of Albanians. It possibly survived through the competition of these more dominant rivals as well as through remoteness and a certain independence of spirit. Loan words from these rivals and from Turkish, common syntactical features with other languages, notably Romanian, and a common Indo-European base make Albanian rather different from Basque which has probably survived for much the same reasons. The Welsh with only one competitor and not all that remote would probably stress their independence as the major factor in the relative prosperity of their language.

Of course, language is not the only factor in ethnic continuity. The large Sinhalese-speaking population in Sri Lanka, occupied in the past four centuries by Portuguese, Dutch and British colonists, have a very mixed ancestry as their physical features show. Other cultural features like churches, cricket and proper names make the same point. Colour, caste and even Christianity are factors inhibiting mixed marriages in Sri Lanka, whereas such influences were not present in Albania for invading Greeks, Macedonians, Romans, Goths, Slavs, Byzantines, Normans, Venetians or Turks. On the other hand anthropological studies would probably establish a good deal of genetic continuity in Northern Albania as it has among the Gaelic-speakers of Connemara. Tribal law in the Albanian mountains has strict rules guarding against the marrying of cousins on the father's side, but there are practical obstacles like remoteness and the blood feud in the way of marrying outside the tribe, and a tribal system, not normally present in Western European minorities, is a strong argument to suggest in Albania some kind of ethnic continuity.

When we come to language there are difficulties. Few traces of Illyrian survive except in place names and proper names. Resemblances between Albanian names (Genc) and Illyrian names (Gentius) are not proof of linguistic continuity but of a wish to prove this continuity. There are Illyrian names for villages, rivers and mountains as there are Slavonic and Latin names, but visitors arriving at Dover in Kent, Dubrovicum in the land of the Cantii, do not assume they have reached a Celtic- or Latin-speaking land. The Russian philologist Georgiev has exposed some worrying features in the relationship between Illyrian and Albanian, well summarised by the American historian of the Balkans, J.V. Fine.

Fine notes that Albanian has few loan words from Greek, and that loan words from Latin show links not with the Romance languages of Western Europe nor the Dalmatian dialect once spoken along the Adriatic coast, but rather with the speech of the East Roman descendants of Latin, namely Romanian and Aromanian or Vlach. This is odd in view of the fact that the Illyrians were certainly active in coastal areas where they came into contact with the Greeks and later the Romans. The marine terminology of Albanian is derived from other languages, and this suggests that the Albanians were not a nautical people, unlike the Illyrians who terrified even the Romans by their mastery of the sea. Links between the sound system of ancient Illyrian, as conjectured from place names, and modern Albanian are hard to find. There is a gap of about five centuries between the last genuine mention of Illyrians and the first authentic reference to Albanians. During these centuries, it is argued, a new Indo-European race could have entered Albania. They would have arrived at the same time as the Slavs, though different from them. They would have come from the Danube area, and this would explain the links between Albanian and Romanian, reinforced by meeting Latin-speakers in Albania, in the same way as the Franks met Latin-speakers on the Rhine and in Gaul. French shows few traces of the language of the ancient Gauls because this language had vanished by the time the Franks arrived. In the same way, it is argued, Illyrian would have vanished after seven hundred years of Roman rule which began earlier and finished later than in Gaul.

These are strong but not irrefutable arguments. As a Slav Georgiev is not totally unbiased. Northern Albania is not like the pleasant hills and plains of France. In the rugged Pyrenees a pre-Roman language did survive. Latin was the official language of Northern Albania, but contact with Western Latin was overshadowed by more lengthy contact with the East Roman Vlachs in medieval times. In the South the official language was Greek, and this would have driven out Illyrian and possibly Epirote with the Albanians not really arriving until the end of the Byzantine Empire. This explains the absence of links between Albanian and ancient Greek.

These counter arguments give the Albanians half their cake but not all of it. If we are to play the absurd game of apportioning territory to different nationalities according to which race reached that territory first, then Albanians, even if they are descended from the Illyrians, have a relatively poor claim to Southern Albania, not Illyrian in ancient times, and not Albanian until the later Middle Ages. Northern Albania was Illyrian in ancient times, as was most of the former Yugoslavia, but in the early Middle Ages long before the Albanians had reached the South, Yugoslavia was overrun by Slavs, leaving only Northern Albania relatively untouched by alien influences, although even here the Illyrian Albanians had to compete with Latin-speakers, the ancestors of the modern Vlachs. We will later discuss the relationship between Illyrians and Vlachs in connection with the so-called Komani-Kruja culture, a name used to describe a number of artefacts found in sites scattered through Northern Albania which native scholars maintain show a link between the Illyrian civilisation and their Albanian descendants. Western historians are more sceptical, and think that these remains are more likely to be associated with the Latinised remnant surviving in Northern Albania. Such a thesis would not, of course, contradict the theory that the Illyrian language is the ancestor of modern Albanian, or that Illyrian speakers survived in the fastnesses of the north, living through difficult times without difficulty in concord with the Vlachs, with whom they moved southwards in the fourteenth century.

On balance the Albanian claim to be the descendants of the Illyrians is a justified one, and we should be grateful to this claim for much recent archaeological work in Albania. Unfortunately there is a dearth of literary evidence, and without this evidence archaeology is hard to interpret. Most of this literary material deals with the South, as Greek historians, marginally interested in the Epirotes and Macedonians, tend to relate the dealings of the Illyrians with these races. A pattern emerges in which the Illyrians were strong in the first half of the fourth century until first Philip and then Alexander got the better of them. Alexander's successors and then Pyrrhus were also powerful in Southern Albania, and the creation of Hellenistic cities like Byllis and Amantia with impressive amphitheatres should not be attributed to a sudden surge in Illyrian strength. In the north the transition from sites that were fortified as a place of refuge to proper urban centres engaged in trade took place later, and there are fewer of them, although Lezhë and Zgerdesh, supposedly the Albanopolis marked on Ptolemy's map, qualify as real towns, being situated in reasonably accessible places.

Rather different is the Illyrian site of Rosunjë near the town of Bajram Curri. Though a bleak and windy place in winter and fiercely hot in summer Bajram Curri lies on a large plateau formed by the River Valbona. But the Illyrian fort is tucked away on the side of a mountain, only reached with some difficulty. Clearly this was a place of refuge. Likewise Gjaitan near Shkodër has intensive fortifications, but little inside them apart from a few rough sheds. The climate in the north is more suited to livestock rearing than to agriculture, and this again fits in with refuge sites rather than trading centres. Of course Illyrians did trade with Greek colonists, as can be proven by a number of objects that must have come through Epidamnus. There are also a number of artefacts made in imitation of the Greeks, although it would be an exaggeration to talk of a Greek-Illyrian culture.

From Polybius writing in the second century we form the impression that Illyria was an aristocratic society with chieftains ruling over a free peasantry who fought for them - probably in a not very disciplined fashion. Richly endowed burial sites suggest this. Polybius was writing about a time when Illyrian society had coalesced into large tribes, and even, though this is disputable, into one loosely organised kingdom, but his picture of local chiefs ruling over a small area owing allegiance to larger units does correspond to the nature of Albanian society throughout the ages. Almost certainly this was the pattern of Illyrian life before they enter the pages of history. Herodotus mentions Illyrians in a vague fashion covering the whole of the north-western Balkans. Thucydides is more precise, and we are fortunate that Greece's most accurate historian should have been interested in the northern frontiers of the Greek world.

As was once widely taught, one of the causes of the Peloponnesian War was a quarrel between Corcyra (an ancient Greek city on present-day Corfu) and Epidamnus, the Latin Dyrrachium, the Albanian Durrës. There was an internal dispute in the latter town with the ruling oligarchs seeking support from the Illyrian Taulantini against a democratic faction which then sought support from Corcyra. Later Corcyra itself was riven by a terrible civil war described in some detail by Thucydides who also discusses campaigns in north-western Greece where Epirote tribes played an important part.

After the incident at Epidamnus we next hear of Illyrians on the other side of Albania in an episode connected with Brasidas, the great Spartan general whose defeat of Thucydides in the campaign of Amphipolis in 424 BC led to the historian's exile. Prior to Amphipolis Thucydides mentions Brasidas helping Perdiccas the King of Macedonia in his struggles against Arribiaios ruler of the Lyncestians in the Ohrid area. Perdiccas had hoped for some help from Illyrians, but these had changed sides, and Brasidas with some difficulty extracted the Macedonians from an awkward situation, in the process rallying his troops with a powerful speech on the nature of the Illyrians, a fierce opponent but an undisciplined one. This speech is, of course, the work of Thucydides rather than Brasidas who was the historian's adversary at Amphipolis. It is rather as if Rommel was the ghost writer for Montgomery. Nevertheless this speech and the incident that led to it is a useful reminder of the fact that at the end of the fifth century the Illyrians appeared to be pressing southwards in a rather disorganised fashion. It may be the case that the Illyrian tribes from their northern strongholds had always been eager to expand southwards, and it is just coincidence that first Thucydides, then some rather inferior historians like Diodorus, record these movements lasting until the rise of Philip and Macedon.

Some modern Balkan historians do see a leap forward in Illyrian power at this time, shown by the improvements in urban life and caused by the Illyrians uniting under one king. It is true that we hear of a number of Illyrian kings like Bardylis who fought Philip, his son Kleitos who fought Alexander, Monunius and Mytilus who used coinage from Dyrrachium and finally Agron and his successors who fought the Romans with a base in Northern Albania. It is true that with the exception of the Ardiaean royal house who were active in Roman times, we do not know to which tribe these kings belonged. Our sources merely call their subjects Illyrians, while the coins just state the title king. One king who is merely the King of the Illyrians in our sources is clearly not the King of all the Illyrians, this being Kleitos who fought Alexander at Pelion in alliance with Glaukias,

King of the Taulantini. The latter was a powerful and long-lived ruler, intervening in the affairs of Epirus at the end of the fourth century, but clearly he was not king of all Albania. It is true that in Epirus and Macedonia strong kings like Philip and Pyrrhus did establish strong central monarchies at this time, but there is no real evidence for Illyria following suit. Although historians have seized upon the Illyrians to promote unity among the Albanians, they are not really an advertisement for this unity.

In the fourth century Dionysus of Syracuse briefly ruled over most of Southern Albania as did Pyrrhus at the beginning of the third. In an age where Greek city states were no match for rulers of big kingdoms like Philip of Macedon it is not surprising that Epidamnus and Apollonia should appear to have lost their independence to these monarchs and in between them to Macedonia under Cassander. In the third century after Pyrrhus we find Monunius and Mytilus in control, although the evidence, numismatic and literary, is not very clear about the nature of this control or where these kings come from. In the hinterland of the Greek colonies the Taulantini after Glaukias seem to fade away, although Monunius and Mytilus may have belonged to this tribe. Matters become much clearer with the intervention of Rome, a city state which had turned itself into a nation, on the whole friendly to city states resisting domination by other nations.

4. ROME,
230 BC-235 AD

Only 65 kilometres separate Albania from Italy. The Adriatic, in spite of the odd squall, has never proved much of a deterrent to people crossing in either direction. Greek colonists in the eighth and seventh centuries BC, the Athenian expedition to Sicily in the fifth, and Pyrrhus of Epirus in the third made the journey from east to west without difficulty. In the other direction there is only a brief invasion by Dionysius of Syracuse in the fourth century, but the Romans soon redressed the balance. In spite of its unpromising coastline for modern shipping, Albania was often invaded from the west. In the last century of the Republic Rome's armies frequently landed there to fight Rome's enemies or each other. Normans, Venetians and Mussolini followed in their footsteps, although with less success and less effect.

We tend to think of the Romans as a land power, but they had won the First Punic War after a series of sea battles and had been rewarded with Sicily as their first overseas province in 241 BC. Sicily, like southern Italy, gained after the wars with Pyrrhus in the previous generation, was inhabited by Greeks, and thus Rome's collision with the Greek world was almost inevitable. This collision resulted in three Macedonian and three Illyrian wars between 230 and 168, all of which Rome won, as she also won the Second Punic War which lasted from 219 to 202. This was no small achievement, and Livy and Polybius are hardly neutral in recording this achievement. Hannibal was a formidable opponent, but in the Eastern sideshow Rome had some advantages. Opposition came rather spasmodically from two quarters. There were the native Illyrians and the kingdom of Macedon under Philip V and Perseus who reigned in succession from 221 to 168. The Illyrians were hardly united among themselves, and were the traditional enemies of Macedonia, although occasionally these old foes formed an alliance. In fighting Philip and Perseus the Romans received some help from Greek city states and confederations like the Aetolian League. In Albania some tribes came over to her side, and Dyrrachium and Apollonia, which had lost a good deal of independence to Dionysius, Pyrrhus and perhaps to Illyrian overlords like Monunius and Mytilus, seemed to welcome Roman protection.

Thanks to the full narratives of Polybius and Livy, it is fairly easy to trace what happened in the six wars. Questions of topography are more difficult. It is also hard to determine the rights and wrongs of the various conflicts. Our historians are on Rome's side, although this does not prevent them from recording her mistakes, defeats and even acts of cruelty like the enslavement of the unfortunate Molossians in 168 BC. Her opponents are generally shown as undisciplined and treacherous. There are questions about the extent of Illyrian unity under King Agron and his successors, and there is doubt as to whether this monarchy came from the Ardiaeian or Labeates tribe. In general Polybius and Livy, supported if occasionally contradicted by Appiah, Dio and minor historians, give the impression that Rome became involved in the Balkans almost by accident, and that she acquired territory reluctantly and with the acquiescence of the local inhabitants. Later invasions from Italy did not follow this pattern, although two of the most infamous of such invasions, that of the Crusades in 1204 and of Mussolini in 1939, had some spurious pretext for their action.

The pretext for the Roman invasion in 229 BC was that the Illyrians under Queen Teuta, widow of King Agron, were conducting piratical raids on Roman shipping. An envoy sent to complain had been murdered. The centres of this kingdom which we will call the kingdom of the Ardiaei were the districts around Lake Shkodër and further north the Gulf of Kotor. From these admirable bases the Illyrians had conducted raids as far south as the Peloponnese and had recently captured Phoenice in Epirus. But they were no match for the Roman army and fleet. Based on Apollonia the Romans relieved Dyrrachium which was under siege, attacked some Illyrian coastal towns, including the unknown Noutria, and eventually forced Teuta to come to terms in 228.

A treaty was made preventing the Ardiaei living in Montenegro and Albania north of the Drin from proceeding south of Lissus with more than two ships. Corcyra, Dyrrachium and Apollonia together with a number of Illyrian tribes in central Albania came under the protection of Rome. Her military might had thus secured the southern Adriatic and established a useful base in the western Balkans. Perhaps these achievements, masked by the pretext about piracy, were the objects of the exercise, although the acquisition of the protectorate does not seem to have been particularly calculated or brutal.

The major victory in the First Illyrian War as in the First Punic War was won at sea. The Roman consul Fulvius had set sail for Corcyra, which had been captured by the Illyrians under the command of Demetrius. He was the ruler of Pharos, the modern Hvar, an island in the Dalmatian archipelago, coincidentally and confusingly next to another island also called Corcyra, the modern Korkula, and also close to the Greek colony of Issa, the modern island of Vis. Demetrius betrayed the Illyrian cause and surrendered the garrison of Corcyra to the Romans. He presumably also brought some ships to the Roman side, and since the Romans had sent a further army under Postumius Albinus they now had superiority by land and sea. They advanced in an amphibious operation along the coast to the heart of Teuta's kingdom north of Shkodër. Polybius says there was a battle at Noutria, and Dio says the Romans suffered some losses at a hill called Anution. These are probably the same place and possibly Gajtan. Eventually the Roman juggernaut reached Issa, which was also under siege from the Illyrians who however gave up and retreated to a place called Arbo. This sounds promising for a student of Albanian history, but cannot be identified; it seems unlikely that it is the northern Dalmatian island of Rab, called Arbe by Constantine Porphyrogenitus.

The narratives of Polybius and Appian, both written from the Roman standpoint, suggest an Illyrian realm of uncertain loyalties stretching by sea from one Corcyra to the other, but with uncertain frontiers inland. Appian is clearly in error in thinking that this realm included Dyrrachium and Apollonia. He allows independence to Issa, and makes an appeal from this island an even more praiseworthy reason for Roman intervention. We do not know how far Ardiaean control extended before 228 in central Albania over tribes like the Parthini and the Atintani, or what form this control took. There is doubt as to whether the Atintani lived east of the Parthini or south. The former seems more probable. In that case the Roman protectorate, established in 228, would seem, like the dominion of Charles of Anjou, to have encompassed Albania's coastal plains with upland tribes in the vicinity owing some kind of loyalty. Further north, Demetrius was put in charge of most of Northern Albania, while the Ardiaei under their infant king Pinnes were left along the Montenegrin coast. Fairly soon Demetrius, by marrying Triteuta, the mother of Pinnes, became master of this realm as well.

Like many ruling families in Albanian history the royal house of Agron appears to have been rather dysfunctional. It is odd that Teuta should rule the roost after her husband's death, only to be replaced by the confusingly named Triteuta who gave the kingdom very rapidly to her opportunistic new husband, Demetrius. We hear little about, and feel rather sorry for, the infant Pinnes. A more permanent figure is Scerdilaidas, involved in raids in Epirus before the Roman arrival and still present as Rome's ally at the end of the First Macedonian War twenty years later. He is usually assumed to be the brother of Agron, since his son Pleuratus, another Roman ally, has the same name as Agron's father.

Because of his loyalty to Rome Pleuratus ended his life ruling a fairly large area encompassing most of northern and central Albania as well as Montenegro. It is not clear how much of the realm had been ruled by Agron before the first Illyrian War or Demetrius before the Second. What had happened to the Taulantini, once the rulers of the coastal plain? Agron is said by Polybius to be the most powerful of the Illyrians, presumably more powerful than Monunius or Mytilus, although they, possibly Taulantinians, had issued coinage from Dyrrachium. Probably Agron and later his widow had a firm base among the Ardiaei, and tribes in central Albania had owed to them a loose form of allegiance, easily transferable to Rome. Demetrius, deprived by the Romans of this allegiance, would seem to have turned his attention further south.

By the terms of the treaty of 228 the Illyrians were debarred from advancing south along the coast. According to our sources it was the breach of this agreement which led to the Second Illyrian War. Rome was not yet involved in the war against Hannibal, and either Demetrius was extremely unwise, or our sources have misrepresented the case in Rome's favour. Possibly Demetrius who seems to have had his eye on the main chance was intriguing with Macedonia by seizing strong points south of the Roman protectorate like Dimale, which Livy calls Dimallium. Thanks to Albanian archaeologists we can place this strong point at Krotinë in the mountains between Byllis and Berat, useful for dominating routes south to Epirus, east to Macedonia and a threat to the Roman protectorate in the plain to the north and west. It is possible that Rome's attack on Dimale may have been a pre-emptive strike to avoid any danger from Macedon since this fort as well as the Parthini and the Antinani lay blocking the route from Macedonia to the Adriatic.

After Dimale the Romans advanced to Pharos where they easily defeated Demetrius forcing him into exile with Philip of Macedon. Rome's three wars with the Illyrians appear very one-sided affairs. The Romans imposed the same restraints on Illyrian advances by sea as in 228. In 218 Hannibal crossed the Alps, and in 216 the leader of the Roman army against Demetrius, Aemilius Paullus, was defeated and killed at Cannae. Rome's weakness seemed a good opportunity for Philip to extend his power westwards, and he sent a fleet to the Albanian coast, but this beat a hasty retreat upon a false report that the Romans were crossing the Adriatic. Scerdilaidas was also active first in piratical raids along the coast, but then in alliance with Rome he attacked Macedonian forward bases in Dassaretis. These attacks seem to have been hit and run affairs, as Philip quickly recovered control of this area. In 215 Philip, now formally at war with Rome, made a treaty with Carthage, whereby Macedonia would have been granted the Roman protectorate.

Another naval campaign in 214 ended in total disaster for the king, but he persisted and succeeded in detaching some Illyrian tribes from the Roman alliance. In 213 or 212 he captured Lissus, but the Ardiaei under Pinnes remained loyal as did Scerdilaidas. Philip's march across the mountains of Northern Albania to the coast was a considerable feat, although Polybius' account is not very informative about the route he took. Most roads from Macedonia to Lissus pass through narrow passes. Rome allied herself with the Aetolian League and became involved with the longstanding dispute between Macedon and the Greek city states. Illyrian allies of Rome acted as a distraction, but Polybius and after him Livy are more interested in Greece than in Illyria, and unfortunately at this point in his narrative there is a lacuna in the manuscript of Polybius. It is tantalising that Dassaretis and Uscana, important places in this and subsequent Macedonian wars, situated in eastern Albania or its borders, should have been mentioned in Book 8, now extant only in fragments, but that we do not know the context in which they are mentioned, nor are we certain of exactly where Uscana is (see Appendix I).

Livy is an inadequate substitute for Polybius. His narrative with its main concentration on the Punic War in Spain, Italy and eventually North Africa is partial in more than one sense when it comes to dealing with the Balkans. He mentions the initial disaster to Philip in 214, the naval campaign against Apollonia and the forced return by land across central Albania to Macedonia. There is no report of the successful attack on Lissus, but in 210 Philip attacks Apollonia by land and devastates what are rather vaguely called the nearer parts of Illyricum. In 208 Philip is at the Nemean Games, behaving disgracefully with the wives of leading citizens, while the Aetolians though defeated are proposing terms under which Atintania is given back to the Romans and the territory of the Ardiaei to Pleuratus and Scerdilaidas. These two had presumably lost territory south of the Drin but were still active north of it, spreading rumours that Philip had been killed in 207 and together with other northern tribes like the Thracians threatening Philip's plans for Greece. In 206 after the peace with the Aetolians we hear of restlessness among the Parthini, presumably against Philip and of the Romans besieging Dimale. The peace of Phoenice gave the Parthini, Dimale and two unknown towns, Eugeniium and Bargullum, to Rome, while Philip kept Atintania.

What Livy does not show, either through laziness or partisanship, is that Philip after capturing Lissus became the effective ruler of Albania from the Drin down to Lakes Ohrid and Prespa for about eight years. The Ardiaean kingdom lost territory south of the Drin, the Romans lost their protectorate, and further south Philip like Demetrius before him occupied places like Dimale to guard his new possessions and to harry the Epirotes and Aetolians. No wonder the two latter were anxious to broker a peace, especially as Pleuratus and Scerdilaidas were not above the odd bit of harrying themselves, although they too were signatories to the peace of Phoenice, a place which Scerdilaidas had visited under rather difficult circumstances twenty-five years before 205. Pinnes seems to have vanished.

Phoenice restored the boundaries that had been established after the two Illyrian Wars with the three main players, the Romans, the Ardiaeans and the Macedonians in roughly the same positions, although the Macedonians had made some gains in the east. But as had happened after the two Illyrian Wars the terms of the treaty of Phoenice were more honoured in the breach than in the observance. Our sources say that Philip continued to interfere in Greek affairs. Rome may have wanted to strengthen her position in Illyria. War broke out in 200. Roman and Macedonian armies marched and countermarched across southern Albania while in the north Pleuratus now reigning alone remained loyal, offering help to the Romans. When Philip was decisively defeated at Cynoscephalae in 197 Pleuratus was rewarded with territory which Polybius says rather sourly he had done nothing to deserve. According to this author, whose narrative is now restored to us, this territory consisted of Lychnis and Parthus which both sound like towns. (Livy says Lychnidus and the Parthini, which sound like districts.) It seems improbable that the Romans should hand over the territory of the Parthini, on their side in 205 and before and after Philip's occupation of central Albania an integral part of the Roman protectorate, being situated very close to Dyrrachium. It is much more likely that Parthus is a town like Lychnis in the Ohrid area. Thus the Romans hoped to insert an Illyrian wedge between their protectorate and Macedonia. Philip after his defeat wisely kept away from Illyria, though he did fight against the Dardanians, and Pleuratus, whose mother came from north-western Greece, was allowed to plunder Aetolia, but gained no further territory.

Like Banquo's descendants the Ardiaean monarchs seem shadowy figures, although Scerdilaidas and Pleuratus with Roman propaganda behind them sound fairly sturdy. Indeed, Polybius in spite of his harsh remarks about Pleuratus' rise to power acknowledges him to be the greatest of the Kings of Illyria. In the age of the Hellenistic monarchies succeeding Alexander the Great petty monarchs liked to be called greatest among the great, but Pleuratus who, as far as we know, made no attempt to earn any high titles, does have some claims to distinction. Thanks to the Romans he ruled over most of Northern Albania in addition to the centre of Albania and parts of Montenegro. Thus Pleuratus ruled over an area greater than any other Illyrian or Albanian ruler either before or after him. Pyrrhus' realm extended further south, but not much further north than Epidamnus, and he was probably not an Illyrian. Scanderbeg had little power north of the Drin, and he was constantly threatened by the Turks from the east and south. Nor was he absolute ruler over his loose confederacy. King Zog and Enver Hoxha controlled modern Albania, a country smaller in area than the kingdom of Pleuratus.

In spite of his achievements and the fact that unlike Scanderbeg, Hoxha and Zog he handed over his kingdom to his son, Pleuratus does not receive much recognition in Albanian history. The name, shared with Agron's father and son and probably the brother of the next king Gentius, is clearly common in Illyrian but unlike Agron and Gentius (Gene) is not used by modern Albanians probably because Pleuratus collaborated with Rome. Gentius did not. Fishta, who was also accused of collaboration with a new Roman empire, calls Gentius poor, and he does seem to have been unfortunate. He ended up in a Roman triumphal procession with his sons appropriately called Pleuratus and Scerdilaidas, his wife Eteuta and half-brother Caravantius. Another brother, called Plator, possibly a variant of Pleuratus, had been killed by Gentius in a dispute over the hand of Eteuta, possibly Eteva, a Dardanian princess. In addition to this difficult family life, Gentius had problems in keeping his kingdom intact. He had lost control of the Delmatae along the Croatian coast. During the war with Rome the Daorsi and Cari, rather vaguely situated in the north, revolted against him and other tribes, notably the Taulantini, and cities, notably Ulcinium and Risinium in Montenegro, were granted exemption from tribute by the Romans because they had taken Rome's side in the very one-sided contest between Gentius and the Roman praetor Lucius Anicius Gallus which only lasted thirty days in 168 BC.

Gentius had been tempted into revolt against Rome by bribery from Perseus, the last King of Macedon with whom Rome had been at war since 170. It is clear from the account of the campaigns of this war that Gentius had lost control over the valley of the Black Drin between Kukës and Ohrid, as this was where Roman and Macedonian armies captured and recaptured various garrison towns. Some place these towns further east in the modern state of Macedonia, but the main base of the Romans was at Lychnidus, previously handed over to Pleuratus, and the Pirustae who lived along the Albanian and Macedonian border were another tribe to be rewarded with freedom from tribute, presumably because they too had deserted Gentius.

After the two wars had ended there were triumphs. That celebrating the victory over the Illyrians was a smaller affair than the Macedonian triumph, as Illyrian resistance had not been very fierce or united. There were also settlements. The kingdom of Macedonia was divided into four republics with notional freedom for each republic, and Illyria into three. Savage reprisals were taken against the Molossians in Epirus, but the Illyrians got off fairly lightly. Arrian says that the Romans destroyed seventy Illyrian cities, but this seems a confusion with Epirus, although Strabo refers to the desolate condition of both areas. Before Rome's double victory it is clear that boundaries were not hard and fast affairs. Uscana changed hands three times in the brief Third Macedonian War. It would have been difficult to establish from the members of the Pirustae or the Parthini what kind of loyalty they owed to what great power at any time in the first sixty years of our period, and thus a map of the country is hard to draw.

The position is not much clearer in the next hundred years. Polybius abandons us, and Livy's epitomiser is not very helpful. We know that the experiment of dividing Macedonia into four republics did not last very long, and that in 146 BC Rome rather brutally annexed the whole of the southern Balkans and incorporated this large area into the province of Macedonia. This too had fluid boundaries. We do not know how far north of Dyrrachium it stretched. Periodically barbarians from the north broke through as far as the Via Egnatia, constructed in the last third of the second century BC. Even in the first century BC our more plentiful sources refer to the difficulties of governing Macedonia, an enormous province, from which Achaea (Classical Greece) and Epirus (north-west Greece and southern Albania) had to be detached.

Further west the problem of delimiting boundaries is even more difficult. We do not know the frontiers of the three Illyrian republics set up at the end of the third Illyrian War. A rough guess would put them around Lissus, around Scodra and around the bay of Kotor in Montenegro. The text of Livy is not very certain. We know that there were urban settlements in these places from accounts of the Maceddnian and Illyrian war, although Scodra only enters history in the time of Gentius. We do not know how far inland the republics went or how far they incorporated previous tribal divisions. Nor do we know when the three republics comprising most of Northern Albania lost their nominal independence and became part of the province of Illyricum. This is first mentioned when it was awarded to Julius Caesar in 59, but must have been regarded as Roman territory if not formally established as a province before this date. The three republics cannot have lasted very long, their position threatened by and threatening the Roman presence on the coast being satisfactory to neither party. In Macedonia the four republics were abolished after a failed revolt in 146, and the same year probably saw the collapse of the southern Illyrian republic. We know of an uprising by the Ardiaei and Pleraei in 135.

Further north Rome continued to wage war against Illyrian tribes along the Adriatic coast, notably the Delmatae who have given their name to Dalmatia. Against this tribe in 119 the consul. Lucius Caecilius Metellus - from a family used to triumphal honours - is alleged to have fought a war in order that he too could celebrate a triumph. There were further campaigns against the Delmatae in 78-6. Control over Illyricum was exercised in rather a vague fashion either by the proconsul in charge of Macedonia or from Cisalpine Gaul, annexed in 121. The latter province was a long way from Albania, and even nearby Macedonia was not exactly a safe haven for Roman rulers with various proconsuls finding it literally a graveyard for their ambitions. Nevertheless Rome exercised some kind of control over most of Albania in the century before the Battle of Actium in 31 BC.

This century saw not only a series of campaigns in the Balkans and Asia Minor by Roman generals against Rome's enemies like Mithradates and against each other, but the first great flowering of Roman literature. It is therefore disappointing that references to Northern Albania in classical sources are meagre. Cicero travelled in Greece and Asia in 79 and 78, but that was before he began his letters. He was Governor of Cilicia in 51-50, but made the journey there by sea, as did many voyagers from Rome to the east. In his exile he was in the Balkans, but his thoughts were on Rome and himself, and he says little about Dyrrachium and his journeys between there and Thessalonica. The campaign near Dyrrachium in 48 is described by Caesar in military terms, and we hear little of how the native inhabitants reacted to the legions trampling over their land. Armies need food, and the provision of this food must have cost these inhabitants dearly. It is small wonder that the Parthini revolted after Philippi.

The Parthini lived near the Via Egnatia which played a prominent part in the Philippi campaign. The lands further north were less affected by this and previous campaigns, as there were no such roads from Lissus or Scodra, and the rough tracks from these places led nowhere as Rome did not control the central Balkans. Before Actium Octavius had himself conducted campaigns against tribes in what was later Yugoslavia between 35 and 33 BC, the Delmatae being apparently unsubdued. After his defeat of Antony he proceeded in a series of campaigns conducted by his generals to carry the imperial frontier to the Danube with the result that all Illyrians were under Roman control, and a province of Illyricum, roughly equivalent to the modern Yugoslavia, was formed, as we have shown.

In between 6 AD and 9 AD there was a serious revolt in this province, successfully if brutally put down by the future Emperor Tiberius. The centre of this revolt was far away from Albania in the plains of the Danube, but as a result of it Illyricum was divided. Some of Albania north of Scodra became part of the relatively peaceful p ovince of Dalmatia along the coast, separated from the more dangerous inland province of Pannonia. Further east the campaigns of Crassus, son of the triumvir, in the early years of Augustus' reign had advanced the frontier to the lower Danube, but a separate province of Moesia is not firmly attested until 44 AD, Crassus' conquests being initially attached to Illyricum.

Crassus had finally subdued the Dardani in Kosova and parts of Albania and Macedonia. Thus the Dardani became attached to Moesia. Under the early Roman Empire the small area we have called Northern Albania was divided between Moesia, Dalmatia and Macedonia. Later these large provinces were to be further subdivided with the result that we have the much smaller provinces of Praevalitana, Epirus Nova and Dardania between them covering Northern Albania, Kosova, Southern Montenegro and Northern

Macedonia. These smaller provinces, largely if not exclusively inhabited by Albanians today, were obviously more exclusively Illyrian. The exact boundaries between the original large provinces and the later small divisions are difficult to determine, although the Drin and Shkumbin probably bounded Epirus Nova. These boundaries are important when we come to the fourth century AD when there were divisions between the East and West Roman Empire. As in the brief partition between Antony and Octavian, Scodra was an obvious frontier post, but the rugged mountains above it made a boundary very hard to draw.

DIVIDE AND RULE

Divide et impera. It is easier to discuss the ways in which Northern Albania was divided and redivided by the Romans than it is to discuss the manner in which the area was ruled both in republican and imperial times because we have so little evidence. We have mentioned the silence of our literary sources. There are not many Roman sites in Northern Albania. It is unfair to blame Albanian archaeologists working in difficult terrain with limited financial resources for their failure to unearth their Roman heritage. It is true that in communist times Illyrian sites were more of a priority. It is true that in Albania as in other Balkan countries there are only a few people trained in the classics ready to enthuse schoolchildren, amateurs and local authorities to explore and preserve Roman buildings. Northern Albania's geography did not encourage the creation of towns or the construction of roads to link these towns. Its climate did not favour the building of villas with agricultural plots to support them. In Britain Roman villas are predominantly found in the flat south-east, Roman towns along roads like the Fosse Way and Watling Street were built and used by the legions that were stationed in Britain. Northern Albania was more like Scotland which the Romans never conquered, but was at any rate guarded by legions on the Roman wall. For most of its existence after 168 the only legions in Albania were those tramping along the Egnatian Way and other southerly routes engaged in military campaigns elsewhere.

It is odd that Britain, almost the last Roman province to be conquered and the first to be abandoned, and almost the province remotest from Rome, should be so plentifully supplied with towns like Deva and Eboracum, Chester and York, both in the inhospitable north, connected to the south by famous roads. In contrast Northern Albania, so close to Italy, so easily conquered, with a climate that at any rate allowed the growth of the vine, is very short of Roman towns and roads. We do not know when the route from Lissus to Naissus was built (see Appendix II). It appears in the Peutiger Table, probably of the fourth century, but not in the earlier Antonine Itineraries. It is tempting, as Wilkes does, to ascribe it to the impressive period of Roman road construction that followed Tiberius' campaigns. These resulted in a network of roads from Salona, just north of Split, for which there is epigraphical evidence. We have no such evidence for when the road from Lissus to Naissus was built, except that it precedes the fourth century. Nor do we know exactly where this road went, nor where the stations, marked on it, Ad Picaria, Crevenium and Gabuleo, can be found. There is a case for saying that Crevenium is Vau Spas, and Gabuleo Kukës, both sites being submerged under the flooded River Drin. The distances marked on the Pentinger Table suggest that there may have been alternative routes from Albania into Kosova in Roman times as in modern times, and that Ad Picaria should be sited not at Pukë but near the Roman fort of Vig, the road making a sharp bend in order to work Lissus as well as Scodra into the route towards the interior.

Along the coast the Peutinger Table marks a road more or less along the lines of the modern road with stations at Cinna north of Scodra and Pistium south of it. Livy may in a passage where the text is suspect mention Pistium, but there are no archaeological records of either town. Thus the map of Roman Northern Albania begins to look rather empty if we insist on the double qualification of a site attested by ancient sources and by modern discoveries. There is Zgerdesh, which not improbably has been identified by Pettifer with Albanopolis named by Ptolemy. In the north-east of the country there is the Illyrian citadel of

Rosunjë near Bajram Curri which has Roman remains of the Classical period. This is well away from the Lissus-Naissus road, but the plain of the Valbona is an obvious place for a settlement. Along the course of the Drin between Kukës and Kosova we find sites with Roman remains at Pezë and Bardhoc lying close to one obvious branch of the Lissus-Naissus road, and further south the sites of Bushat and Grazdhan along a route which is not shown on the Peutinger Table but which must have existed close to the Black Drin valley. In both these areas there are many more late Roman forts, but the location and purpose of these forts belong to the history of the next period.

Archaeology may reveal more facts about the history of Northern Albania in Roman times. The dearth of sites and the absence of roads suggest that the Romans left this barren part of their empire fairly neglected, as it furnished neither reward nor danger. In contrast the former Yugoslavia, with its network of Roman roads starting in Salona (modern Split) and the evidence of Pliny about tribes being tamed into *civitates*, even though these states may have lacked a central town, seems to have been Romanised fairly rapidly. Montenegro, although its terrain is as rugged as Northern Albania, had two established Roman roads along the coast and along the Zeta valley, important sites like Doclea and Meteon, mentioned by Livy, and Roman colonies settled at places like Olcinium and Butua which have preserved their Roman names in Ulcinj and Budva. So too have Dyrrachium (Durrës), Scodra (Shkodër) and Lissus (Lezhë), but these seem to be the only Roman colonies in Northern Albania. We do not know what happened to towns mentioned by Livy and Polybius in the east like Uscana, Oaeneum and Draudacum, probably in the Drin valley, Bassanium eight kilometres from Lissus or towns associated with Gentius' campaigns north of the Drin.

In Southern Albania there are more cities like Byllis obviously inhabited throughout Roman times. There are also villas. The landscape of Northern Albania is not really suitable for agriculture, and therefore small farms attached to such villas would not have worked. Illyrians in Northern Albania seem in pre-

Roman times to have preferred livestock rearing to the growing of crops, and Roman rule is unlikely to have altered this pattern. The Romans may have been less enthusiastic about the other major Illyrian occupation, fighting, although they could have harnessed the warlike qualities of the Illyrians by making them auxiliaries in their armies and navies. Such auxiliaries would be rewarded with Roman citizenship and gradually in the first two centuries of our era we find evidence of Illyrian leaders being incorporated into the Roman administrative system, taking Roman names. But though conquered earlier than Gaul the climate of Northern Albania made such assimilation difficult.

In the second century AD under four emperors, Trajan, Hadrian, Antoninus Pius and Marcus Aurelius, the Roman Empire was peaceful and secure. Gibbon speaks eloquently about the prosperity of this age. He is equally contemptuous about the emperors who succeeded Marcus Aurelius like the brutal Conmodus, the effete Elagabulus and the gigantic Maximinius, the son of a Goth, whose accession in 235 marks the end of this period in Illyrian history. We shall see the changes between the third and second centuries in the following chapter. The terminating date of 235 is a convenient one for introducing the Goths, although there are other interesting dates in this period. The edict of Caracalla in 217 gave Roman citizenship to all inhabitants of the Empire. This should have hastened the process of assimilation between Romans and Illyrians. The arrival of the Goths, who in 251 defeated and killed the Roman Emperor Decius, brought a new and discordant element into the equation, and made assimilation more difficult. Finally 229 marks the end of the history of Cassius Dia, not a historian of the first rank, but a great deal better than our sources for the second half of the third century. This is unfortunate as this was a period when Illyricum in general and North Albania in particular underwent important changes as it ceased being a quiet backwater and became, as it did in the period described by Livy and Polybius, a centre of military activity.

5. GOTHS, SLAVS AND BYZANTIUM, 235-1018

The third century was a bad century for the Roman Empire. Our imperfect literary sources record a series of short reigns by incompetent emperors unable to cope with the barbarians menacing the Rhine and Danube frontiers. Gibbon waxes eloquent on the eccentric inadequacy of these rulers, although external factors played their part in bringing the Empire almost to its knees. In the last quarter of the century there was a recovery. Stronger emperors generally originating from the legions based on the Danube succeeded in containing the Gothic menace. The last of these so-called Illyrian emperors was Diocletian who ruled either alone or with partners from 284 to 305. He reorganised the Empire, creating smaller provinces, taxing these provinces more harshly, and overseeing the defence of such provinces with this increased revenue on a different basis. His reforms were carried on by Constantine the Great, who ruled over the whole of the Empire from 323 to 337. Constantine like Diocletian was a divider as well as a ruler, but under his rule and that of his successors from his family in the first half of the fourth century the Goths seemed to have been tamed. But in 378 with the Empire once more divided there was the disastrous Battle of Adrianople in which the Emperor Valens lost both his life and his army in a defeat which was even more catastrophic than that in which the Emperor Decius was killed by the Goths in 271.

This is the picture which ancient historians, ranging from the deplorable *Historia Augusta* to the admirable Ammianus Marcellinus have painted for us, and there is no reason to doubt its essential truth. We could argue that Constantine who converted himself and his empire to Christianity gets an unduly favourable press from pious apologists, although Diocletian, the persecutor of Christians, also receives due praise from historians, ancient and modern. Jordanes, the historian of the Goths, has been shown to be too dependent upon oral myth, but he too supports the thesis that the Gothic tide flowed, then ebbed, then flowed again in the years between 238 and 378. In Albania modern historians have perhaps been too anxious to turn into Albanians the agents of Rome's recovery, the Illyrian emperors ruling in the latter half of the third century. Most of these were based on Sirmium, now Srem Mitrovska in northern Serbia, an obvious place for a defensive bastion against the Goths since the middle Danube is the place where an enemy would try to break through. Sirmium is a long way from Albania, almost further away than Rome to which there was a good road from the central Danube. Thus the Illyrian emperors apart from Diocletian, who was probably born at Doclea in Montenegro, have little to do with Albania, although it is interesting that Albanian archaeologists have discovered a number of late fortifications on or near the course of the Drin river which fit in with the pattern of decline before the Illyrian emperors, a recovery under Diocletian and Constantine and a subsequent decline at the time of Adrianople. They also fit in with the administrative and military changes that took place in Eastern Europe during the third and fourth centuries.

In 271 the Emperor Aurelian wisely abandoned the province of Dacia, and the Danube became Rome's official frontier as it had been in the first century AD. Obviously this frontier was breached before and after Aurelian's move, and large numbers of Goths entered the Roman Empire, sometimes being allowed in as *foederati* pledged to fight for the Romans rather than against them. The main concentrations of Gothic settlement were in northern Bulgaria, whereas in the west Aurelian moved many settlers from what is now Romania to new homes in northern Serbia and this area became known as Dacia. These moves of population may not seem particularly relevant to Albania, but they would have meant a dilution of the Illyrian element in the population of what is now Serbia with the arrival of large amounts of people of Latin speech and Gothic blood. It is, of course, an odd paradox that though there are now a few Romanian-speakers south of the Danube their main concentration today is in the last Roman province to be conquered and the first to be abandoned, and this is a warning against using ethnic geography of past ages as an explanation or justification of ethnic geography today.

More relevant to Albania are the major reforms of Diocletian and Constantine. It was actually Gallienus (258-268) who had initiated the military changes by strengthening a mobile field army even if this meant weakening the legions on the frontier. Such a policy brought about victorious campaigns against the Goths by Gallienus and his successor Claudius, given the title Gothicus for his defeat of the Goths at Naissus. Diocletian and Constantine carried on this process again with some success, although the historian Zosimus sourly blames Constantine for accelerating Roman decline by neglecting the frontiers in this way.

Whatever the merits of this change in military organisation it does explain the presence of several late Roman fortifications. Because the frontier was so fragile the Romans needed to defend it in depth. Although they could generally rely on holding Sirmium, most of the thickly forested land north of Naissus was fairly insecure, and it was this town, probably the birthplace of Constantine, which became the focal point of Roman defences. From Naissus one major route led to Constantinople following the route of the much later railway line. The Orient Express used to pass through both Srem Mitrovska and Nis on its way to Istanbul, following the same path as legionaries who tramped from Sirmium to Naissus and Constantinople or vice versa. This route and the Via Egnatia are the most prominent thoroughfares in the Balkans. But there were other routes which have fared less well in modern times. There was a road from Lissus to Naissus which appears in the Peutinger Table which can be dated before the fifth century. This is difficult to trace exactly and almost certainly involved alternative routes. Much easier to trace, although not appearing in the itineraries, is the route connecting the road from Lissus to Naissus along the Drin valley where there is an impressive line of Roman forts, of which that at Grazdhan near Peshkopi is the largest.

It is difficult in the light of present archaeological research to determine the exact purpose of these forts. Were they military outposts or civilian refuges? Were they built for the advantage of the ruler or the ruled, always a difficult question to ask of governments in any century? In the heyday of the British Empire it used to be assumed that the *Pax Romana* existed to bring peace to Rome's citizens rather than prosperity to its rulers. Rebecca West, a great admirer of Diocletian and British rule, though not so keen on Hitler, Mussolini and the Ottoman Empire, was ambiguous about empires. Now political correctness demands that we are totally opposed to them. A *via media* suggesting that Roman buildings along the Drin valley were established both for the oppressor and the oppressed is possibly appropriate in this discussion about roads.

In addition to their military reforms and to their attitude to Christianity Diocletian and Constantine are important in Albanian history for other reasons. Diocletian, who ended his days appropriately in Split, divided the Roman Empire. The boundary between East and West was not a fixed or lasting one, but it had permanent effects. The division between Catholic Croats and Orthodox Serbs has its origin in Diocletian's reforms. The Muslims in Bosnia live in the borderlands of this religious faultline. In Albania there are more Muslims, but we still have Ghegs and Tosks, Catholics in the North and Orthodox believers in the South. Diocletian cannot be blamed for these religious divisions in view of his persecution of Christianity, but he did create new administrative divisions. These, however, have contributed little to the history of modern Europe, whereas the major division between East and West is important.

The boundaries of the provinces set by Diocletian in Northern Albania probably followed natural features. Although the southern frontier of Epirus Nova was south of the Shkumbin, the Drin was its obvious northern limit. In this case parts of our fairly small area would be in three other different provinces, Macedonia, Dardania and Praevalitana, with a tiny fragment north of Shkodër in Dalmatia. Dalmatia belonged to the prefecture of Italia, the other four parts to the prefecture of Illyricum, split between the dioceses of Dacia (Praevalitana and Dardania) and Macedonia

(Macedonia and Epirus). All very confusing like the *vilayets* and *pashaliks* of the Ottoman Empire, lines on the map which were constantly changing with little real significance for future history.

What was more significant for the immediate future of Northern Albania in Diocletian's day was the smallness of the provinces, each of which had an array of military and civilian officials to be supported. Most bureaucrats - and Diocletian was a great bureaucrat - work primarily for the benefit of the bureaucracy. Taxes would have to be raised. The question whether the forts of Northern Albania were for the benefit of the ruler or the ruled can perhaps be answered by looking at the *Notitia Dignitatum*, a useful if slightly baffling document giving a list of Roman officers in the various sections and subsections of the Empire. Interestingly it only mentions one inferior legion stationed at Scampa (Elbasan), and this small military presence might suggest that Northern Albanian forts were primarily for civilian purposes, but quite a lot had happened in the century between Diocletian and the *Notitia Dignitatum*.

Diocletian's provinces had a longer life than the elaborate system he had devised for ensuring the succession in each half of the Roman Empire. His subordinates, all of Illyrian origin, did not follow the rules of this system, but fought each other to gain total power. One of these successors, Licinius, left an inscription on the fort he had built at Paleokastër in Southern Albania, and one wonders whether this and other forts were built against rivals for the Roman throne rather than external enemies. The presence of Roman forts on either side of the Drin, a long way from the boundary of the Empire, but on or near a provincial boundary, suggests provincial governors looking after their own.

DIVIDED LOYALTIES

Especially in Northern Albania, placed in the centrefold of the Empire with its provinces belonging to three dioceses and two prefectures, it must sometimes have been difficult to know to which Caesar or Augustus a particular province owed its loyalty. Constantine the Great solved the problem by defeating Licinius and all other rivals, but he too divided his empire at his death between his three sons. The last emperor of his line was Julian the Apostate whose campaign in the East with its tragic outcome might seem to indicate that the Gothic danger was over. A new dynasty, the descendants of another Illyrian, Gratian, was in control at the time of Adrianople with the feeble Valens ruling in the East and his more energetic nephew Gratian in the West.

The disaster of Adrianople was caused by the poor treatment of the Goths at the hands of Roman officials. These Goths had been allowed to settle in northern Bulgaria by Constantine and had remained loyal to his descendants. Valens dissipated this good will, unwisely did not wait for reinforcements from Gratian, and lost his life and two-thirds of his army at Adrianople. The situation was saved by another strong emperor, Theodosius. Unlike Diocletian and Constantine he was not of Balkan origin, but like them he had a powerful influence on the history of the region, acting both as a uniting and dividing force. He was the last person to rule both halves of the Empire, twice journeying from East to West against usurpers who had risen against the house of Gratian into which he married. Eventually with both his brothers-in-law murdered by the usurpers he took control himself. His success in the West was won with the aid of the Goths in the East whom somehow in the dark days after Adrianople he had brought over to his side. As a Christian Theodosius, in spite of acts of great cruelty like a massacre at Thessalonica, gets on the whole a good press from ancient and modern historians. The orator Themistius is fawning in flattery, Zosimus, a muddled historian at the best of times, is less favourable. As a pagan he is not impressed by Theodosius' piety and he blames him like Constantine for administrative reforms that achieved little. In particular Zosimus attacks the separation of military and civilian duties in each province which we find recorded in the *Notitia Dignitatum*.

This document suggest that Theodosius was not quite so successful as Themistius indicates in bringing about peace in the Balkans. He had campaigned in the Balkans, but had been defeated. The *Notitia Dignitatum* seems to show that the military losses suffered at Adrianople had not been made up, or if they had, only by employing the Goths whom we find fighting for Theodosius in Italy, having settled in the Balkans. Unfortunately our sources are not very precise about the location of these settlements, cloaking them under old-fashioned names like Thrace, Macedonia and Illyricum. But a strong Gothic presence in Northern Albania is more than likely in the years after Adrianople just as it is almost certain after the invasion of Alaric, the sacker of Rome.

After Theodosius there are no more strong emperors until after a century we come to Anastasius and Justinian, again both of Illyrian stock. In the reign of Theodosius' namesake and grandson, who ruled in the East from 408 to 450, his ministers at least performed a powerful service to the Empire by building the gigantic walls which are still visible today protecting Istanbul. Asia Minor, Syria and Egypt, all wealthy provinces, were unthreatened by the Goths, and, protected by walls and wealth, the emperor of the East was fairly safe, at times even offering help to the West where various provinces were picked off one by one by different barbarian tribes. The situation in the Balkans even before the death of Theodosius appears to be rather similar to that in the West except that Constantinople was nearer and that twice the problem was solved by dispatching Goths settled in the Balkans to a new home in the West.

Our sources for Alaric's exploits both in the West and the East are unsatisfactory. Zosimus is weak on chronology, being confused by Alaric's two incursions from the Balkans into Italy. Marcellinus Comes, although probably coming from Illyria, is singularly terse in describing events of the fourth and fifth centuries. Claudian, a Greek writing in Latin, a poet writing history, is more effusive, but he is an unashamed partisan of Stilicho, the barbarian power behind the throne in Western Europe, and his geography is weak, perhaps not helped by the fact that certain geographical names do not scan. Other historians provide trivial details such as the story in Procopius that when Honorius the Western Emperor heard that something was amiss with Rome, as there was when Alaric sacked it, he thought his messengers were referring to his favourite hen.

We would be more interested to know the nature and location of Alaric's occupation of some area in the western Balkans and his appointment to the chief military command of a place not very helpfully entitled Illyricum, which might encompass any area from Istria to Epirus either in the Western or Eastern Empire and probably in both. Confusion about the whereabouts of Alaric and his Goths, ravaging Greece from 395 to 397, invading Italy in 401 and 407 from a base somewhere in between, does not diminish the probability that there was a large Gothic presence in the western Balkans in the whole of the period between the Battle of Adrianople and the sack of Rome. It is likely that this presence was not a very comfortable one for the previous inhabitants. We hear of rape and pillage in the march through Greece, and the sack of Rome was not as civilied an affair as some modern historians have made it out to be. On the other hand, restless and warlike as Alaric's warriors were, they are unlikely to have moved lock stock and barrel to Aquitaine from where they subsequently moved to Spain. In Spain the Visigoths learnt a kind of Latin, although a pre-Latin language survived in Basque. The same kind of thing probably began to happen in Albania.

Following Alaric the history of the Balkans is less exciting. Attila the Hun made two invasions. He was a more savage opponent than the Goths, being able to take fortified cities like Naissus which he destroyed in 445. Like others he was distracted from the Balkans by the prospect of prizes in the West, and his hordes do not seem to have penetrated into Albania. Under pressure from the Huns, Goths continued to move south of the Danube, and by 473 we hear of two groups of Goths in the eastern Balkans, both led confusingly by a leader called Theodoric. Our main historian of the Goths, Jordanes, derives his information from Cassiodorus who served at the court of Theodoric the Amal when he later ruled Italy, and is biased in his favour and against Theodoric Strabo with whom the Amal was engaged in a complicated three-way struggle as the Byzantine Emperor Leo tried to play one set of Goths against the other. Fortunately we have the fragments of another historian Malchus, who describes the interesting campaign which led Theodoric to Dyrrachium.

Theodoric had marched from Stobi to Heraclea (modern Bitola) both of which he had sacked. The inhabitants of the latter town fled into the hills. Theodoric had presumably learnt the art of taking cities from the Huns, since he originated from the Danube basin. His campaign along the route of the Via Egnatia does not suggest that the Roman forts were much use as military defences against an invading army or as a refuge for civilians. Scampa was deserted. Dyrrachium fell owing to a ruse by Sidimund, a presumably Gothic inhabitant of the area who had persuaded its citizens that Zeno had surrendered the city to Theodoric. In fact what Zeno had offered Theodoric was Pautalia, the empty plains of eastern Kosova. But while Adimantius, Zeno's envoy in these matters, had failed to dislodge Theodoric from Dyrrachium, his general Saturninus, the military commander of Illyricum, was more successful in swooping down behind Theodoric's baggage train and capturing it. He would seem to have done this from a strong point south of the Via Egnatia, and this is perhaps rather disappointing since if he had come from further north, he might have found a use for the forts along the Drin.

These forts and some along the Via Egnatia may not have contained Alaric, Attila or Theodoric, but would have ensured the presence of some Latin-speakers in Northern Albania. Malchus' account gives hints of a substantial Gothic population. The Gothic army travelled with women and children. Sidimund's residence suggests that Goths remained after Alaric. The empty fields of Pautalia would seem to show a diminution of the Illyrian element in the population of the Balkans, but this would have survived in less accessible areas, retreating out of trouble into the mountains like the inhabitants of Heraclea, presumably a mixed bunch of Latin-, Greek- and Illyrian-speakers and the inhabitants of Dyrrachium, where Theodoric's Goths joined an already diverse collection of races.

Theodoric did not stay long in Dyrrachium. In a strange parallel with Alaric he too moved to Italy. The Goths and Byzantium often seem to be involved in a curious dance with the former winning the battles and the latter winning the peace. Theodoric's campaign against Odoacer in Italy was entirely successful, although the exact status of his realm, officially recaptured for Zeno, was uncertain. So too are its boundaries. The division between the East and West Roman Empires had never been exactly fixed. Alaric's position on both sides of this empire shows this uncertainty. Even today there is confusion in the coastal area between Dubrovnik and Shkodër and in the high mountains behind them about ethnic, religious and political boundaries. In the time of Theodoric there were no maps, frontier posts or statistics to record boundaries, and almost certainly as in the case of Alaric Theodoric left some Goths behind in Northern Albania.

Such a Gothic presence receives confirmation from two unlikely sources. One is Procopius, the author of the anecdote about Honorius' hen. In his work *De Aedificiis* he gives a magnificent account of buildings and rebuildings by Justinian in the Balkans (see Appendix III). He gives little evidence of such work in Northern Albania and this suggests that even when Theodoric moved to Italy the Goths still had nominal control over this area. Much later than Procopius, but uneasily rubbing shoulders with him in our appendices, we find the first Slav source of this area, the Priest of Dioclea, talking about Goths as well as Slavs in his history of Northern Albania and Montenegro. Boundaries in this area have always been difficult. In recent times Albanian-speakers living near Ulcinj have been subjected to Venetian, Ottoman, Austrian, Yugoslav and finally Montenegrin control. It can be of little comfort to these people that in the fourth and fifth centuries the boundary between East and West Illyricum, subsequently the boundary between the Eastern and Western Roman Empire, passed near their town. Illyricum was a bone of contention between East and West even before the Battle of Adrianople which, as we have shown, by removing swathes of the Balkans from Roman control made the distinction rather an academic one.

In the sixth century the East Roman Empire recovered.

Anastasius, a native of Dyrrachium, started the recovery. By fortifying his native city he guaranteed that it would remain a bulwark of Byzantine power for centuries. Almost certainly he was at least partly responsible for a major rebuilding operation in Albania and elsewhere in the Roman Empire attributed by Procopius to Justinian. Anastasius was succeeded by Justin, an elderly Illyrian peasant who had risen through the ranks, and Justin was succeeded by his nephew Justinian who recovered much of the Western Empire. In so doing he overstretched the resources of the realm, and the last great Illyrian emperor of Rome, in spite of his superficial successes, did far more damage to Roman rule in the Balkans than any of his predecessors. Procopius as well as offering lavish praise for Justinian's aggressive advances in his account of the Gothic and other wars is even more flattering about his defensive measures in rebuilding and building in the Balkans and elsewhere. In *The Secret History* he is less complimentary, rightly laying Justinian open to the charge of leaving his empire vulnerable to invasions from the north.

As on previous occasions in Albanian history archaeology supports literary evidence, but does not give the total picture. Justinian's list of fortifications in Epirus Nova and Dardania is an impressive one, but it is difficult to verify. Without literary evidence archaeological finds are hard to interpret. One wonders what future archaeologists would make of the bunkers littering the landscape of Albania if they had no written sources to mark this particular folly of the Hoxha regime. Our literary sources give little due to the purpose of fortification in the fourth century and the refortification in the sixth of the Albanian strong points along the Drin and Shkumbin valleys. They do show that they both failed to stem the wave of Gothic and Slav invasions. The bunkers were equally unsuccessful.

Unlike the Goths who moved on to the West and the Huns who made lightning raids before returning north of the Danube, the Slavs after initial sporadic raids in the sixth century established settlements in the seventh which have lasted to this day. Unfortunately this invasion was largely unchronicled and archaeology, though it does show some kind of breakdown at the end of the sixth century, cannot show where and how the Slavs displaced the native inhabitants, speaking Illyrian, Latin, Greek or Gothic. There are a few Byzantine and Western sources recording in melancholy fashion how the Slavs occupied the whole of the Balkans as far as the Peloponnese, but unlike in the case of the Goths where we have plenty of written records of activity in the Balkans, the Slavs ushered in a real dark age.

This period lasts from the seventh to the ninth century, when Byzantine authority began to re-establish itself in the Balkans, coinciding with the rise of the Bulgarians. This rise is well documented, especially towards the end of our period when some of the campaigns between Byzantium and Bulgaria were fought in the neighbourhood of Dyrrachium, which appears to have withstood earlier Slav onslaughts until briefly falling victim to an attack by almost the last Bulgarian emperor, the mighty Samuel. For the earlier attacks by the less organised Slavs we can only conjecture what happened. The Slavs appear to have moved in undisciplined hordes. There is some suggestion that they were subservient, as their slave like name indicates, to a superior non-Indo-European race, the Bulgars in the East Balkans, the Abars in the West. Even the Croats and Serbs may not be entirely Indo-European. Lacking leaders and impervious for some time to Christianity and education, they were different from the Germanic tribes who in Eastern Europe had become unreliable allies of the Empire and in Western Europe took over the administration and language and fairly soon the religion of Rome. Modern historians debate whether this takeover was painless or brutal, using the literary evidence available. The presence of this evidence suggests that civilisation was not totally annihilated. In Britain where the Angles and Saxons, unlike the Goths, Vandals, Franks and Lombards, had had little exposure to Roman civilisation or Christianity the invasion was clearly brutal and hard-fought with Romano-British chieftains like King Arthur putting up good resistance but eventually having to leave most of the land to the invader whose language prevailed. Neither

Britain nor the rest of Western Europe quite fits the pattern of the Balkans. We have no written records, and this suggests some kind of annihilation. We do not hear of any heroic resistance even in legend. Albania had to wait nearly a thousand years to find its King Arthur in Scanderbeg. Thus Western European analogies are not very helpful.

What we do find in the Balkans is the survival of languages, both native in the case of Albanian, and imperial in the case of Latin and Greek, and this calls for some comment. Clearly the Slavs arrived in great numbers, leaving evidence of their presence in place names and the collapse of building activity in well-studied sites like Butrint. Clearly these vast hordes would not be interested in barren mountains such as those of Northern Albania and would press on to sunnier plains. This would explain the survival of Albanian as a language in places bypassed by the Slavs. Elsewhere in the Balkans people along the coast would flee from the invader to safe retreats on nearby islands. Albania is less well provided with such refuges. There is evidence of the Bishop of Lissus retreating to Sicily, and the Komani-Kruja site in Corfu shows that some people were lucky in their escape. But for most of the Illyrian inhabitants of Northern Albania and the few legionaries remaining in Justinian's scattered and useless forts there were only the hills into which to flee, as had happened in the days of Theodoric at Heraclea. And in these hills a Latin-Illyrian civilisation survived, as witnessed by the Komani-Kruja culture, to emerge as Albanians and Vlachs in the second millennium. The language and the religion of this culture remains uncertain. Most graves face east, but with bishops absent abroad the mountain flocks cannot have been too versed in theological or linguistic niceties.

Another place where refugees could shelter was Dyrrachium. Anastasius' walls were a good defence against attacks from the land, and his reinforcements could arrive by sea. Byzantine rule survived in southern Italy after Justinian's reconquest and it would make sense as well as be quite easy to preserve an outpost on the other side of the Adriatic. There is no evidence to suggest that Dyrrachium passed out of Byzantine control between the invasion of Theodoric at the end of the fifth century and the time of Samuel at the end of the tenth. In both cases the invaded gained access through treachery rather than assault. It is true that in succeeding centuries the city changed hands many times in bewildering fashion, but these conquests were at the hands of more sophisticated enemies than the primitive Slavs, who over the years must have established a modus vivendi with the inhabitants of Dyrrachium in the same way as Illyrian tribes traded earlier with Epidamnus. Earthquakes and plagues in Justinian's reign must have reduced the population, and at the end of the eleventh century Anna Comnena reports that the city only occupied half the area of the Greek colony. But unlike Epidamnus Dyrrachium did extend its rule into the interior, and long before the eleventh century a Theme (province) of Dyrrachium had been established.

This theme certainly existed in 856. It has been plausibly argued that it was founded by the Emperor Nicephorus who reconquered much of Greece for the Empire before meeting a nasty death at the hands of the Bulgarian ruler Krum, who made his skull into a drinking vessel in 811. Nicephorus' campaigns against the Bulgarians were conducted in the eastern half of the Balkans, and there seems no reason to suppose they carried him as far west as Albania at this stage. Initially the theme would have been confined to the coastal strip. At the beginning of the tenth century the archbishopric of Dyrrachium only had four sees, Alessio, Kruja, both easy to locate, Chounavia and Stephaniaka, less easy but assumed to be near the coast, although some think Stephaniaka may be Peshkopi. Writing in that century Constantine Porphyrogenitus is a mine of information about themes and people in the Balkans, but is not very precise about exact boundaries. He does clearly distinguish Dyrrachium from the Theme of Nicopolis (southern Albania and Epirus) and the territories of Duklja, Tarunja and Zahumlje to the north. In the east the Drin and the mountain ranges behind it provide a natural frontier, but the Byzantines are unlikely to have stretched their authority so far except in times of great strength. Constantine's grandson Basil II at the end of his reign had reached this boundary, and had gone beyond it to make the *zupans* or heads of the tribal territories acknowledge his authority, but at one stage had lost contml even of the town and Theme of Dyrrachium to his great adversary Samuel.

We get some kind of information about boundaries from three other sources. There is a further list of bishops in the Dyrrachium see at the end of the tenth century. The see has been extended to include Berat and northwards to take in Dioclea, Bar, Ulcinj, Shkodër, Polati and Drisht. Of these the first three are now in Montenegro. Polati is probably to be placed in the northern mountains of Albania where Edith Durham knew of the church of Pilot, and it and Shkodia with nearby Drisht may have been part of the Theme of Dyrrachium. Ecclesiastical boundaries may not coincide with political boundaries, and medieval boundaries certainly do not coincide with modern ones, but clearly there was some expansion of the Dyrrachium Theme in the tenth century.

There is further evidence for the northern boundary in *The Chronicle of the Priest of Dioclea* (see Appendix IV). Writing in the twelfth century, this author has a mythical account of the founding of Dioclea by a figure called Pridimir. Pridimir is allegedly the great great grandfather of the historical John Vladimir, active around the year 1000. The list of districts under Pridimir's four sons may correspond to the territory of Dioclea at some stage between 900 and 1200. Ulcinj is not in Dioclea nor is Bar, even though the Priest has a special axe to grind in promoting the claims of the church of this latter town to be an archbishopric. A further ecclesiastical complication that may make the Priest unreliable in his account of previous centuries is that in his time there were three Churches at work in the area, the Catholic, the Greek Orthodox and the Slavonic Orthodox, but the Slavs were mainly heathen until the reign of Tsar Boris of Bulgaria, who extended Bulgarian rule and Slavonic orthodoxy over Macedonia and Southern Albania towards the end of the ninth century. Boris toyed with the idea of becoming part of the Catholic Church, but eventually settled for a Bulgarian Church based on Ohrid. The

Priest would seem to show Bar and Ulcinj politically attached to Dyrrachium, while the list of bishops would indicate that Dioclea was attached ecclesiastically.

Boris' son Symeon was an even more formidable enemy of Byzantium than Krum. His real ambition was to become Emperor of Byzantium, and he nearly succeeded. Like Krum he fought mainly in the East Balkans, but he campaigned against the imperial rulers of the West, and must have encroached upon the Byzantine realm, since we hear that in a rare concession he handed back thirty *castra* (forts) in the Theme of Dyrrachium. It would be interesting to know where these *castra* were. Paul Stephenson, who has done considerable work on the defences of Dyrrachium, locates some of them in the immediate vicinity of the town, and draws our attention to the usefulness of these fortifications in the time of Alexius Comnenus. But Alexius was facing a possible invasion from the west, and he would have used fortresses near Dyrrachium either as an inner ring or outer ring of defence against an army coming from Italy, as both Robert Guiscard and Bohemund came. In the tenth century Byzantium still held Apulia, and if Symeon had captured major fortresses like Kruja or Lezhë we would have heard of the loss, in the same way as we know about the loss of Durrës to Samuel. Therefore most of Stephenson's forts cannot be those given back by Symeon, and we must look elsewhere for their location, the obvious place being along the line of the Drin where we have previously found a series of late Roman encampments. Boundary changes naturally occur at boundaries, and so by a roundabout route with certain logical leaps we have made the frontier of the Theme of Dyrrachium more or less coincide with the frontiers of the area we have designated as Northern Albania, although the theme would extend south of the Shkumbin before meeting Nicopolis.

Northern Albania, as we have shown, is now inhabited almost entirely by Albanians with tiny pockets of Slav-speakers. It is the South which has Greeks and Vlachs as well as a few Slavs. In medieval times there were many more Slavs in both the Themes of Nicopolis and Dyrrachium. In the former as in the rest of

Greece these were gradually Hellenised over the centuries. It was rather different in Dyrrachium and its theme. In the town there would be plenty of Greek-speakers. Greek was the language of religion and administration, but there would be other nationalities who would eventually predominate.

FAMILY INTRIGUES

We can illustrate the ethnic complexity of Albania around the year 1000 by considering the history of one person who lived there and took part in the stirring events which suddenly brought into the news what had hitherto been rather a backwater in the Byzantine Empire. Agatha, a good Greek name meaning good, was the daughter of John Chryselios, a leading citizen of Dyrrachium. Chryselios, too, looks Greek, although modern Slav historians call him Hrisilic and the Priest of Dioclea calls the family Cursilius. There are vague hints of Vlach in the ending of this name, and it is possible that Agatha may be a translation of a name beginning with Dobro of which we find plenty in this period. The coincidental resemblance of this person's name to that of the English crime writer Agatha Christie draws attention to some of the more lurid features of the tenth-century Agatha's story. She came from a large dysfunctional family, linked by a series of strange happenings punctuated by sudden deaths, and it requires considerable powers of detection to discover what happened.

Agatha was married to Samuel, Tsar of the Bulgarians. We learn this from Michael of Devol's additions to the manuscript of Skylitzes, one of the two main sources for this period. The other is the Priest of Dioclea. Both are unsatisfactory, especially in chronology. We do not know when Agatha married Samuel or whether she was the mother of all his children. Samuel and his three brothers David, Aaron and Moses, started a revolt in either 969 or 976 or possibly both, and Samuel must have been born around 950. In the late 980s he was active in the western half of the Balkans and it is to this period that modern historians attribute the loss of Dyrrachium to Samuel. Our ancient sources do not mention this event, although a recent inscription attributes it to neglect by the authorities in the city failing to keep their communications open. At about the same time, Samuel conquered Dioclea, and here the Priest of Dioclea is full of information about the romantic story of the young ruler of that country, John Vladimir, being captured by Samuel, imprisoned in Prespa, but rescued by the king's daughter Kosara. The young couple were forgiven by Samuel, who put John Vladimir in charge of Dyrrachium. The same story appears in Skylitzes, but on this occasion the name of the daughter is given by Michael of Devol as Theodora, although some scholars think that this is a mistake and that the young princess was the daughter of Theodore, the brother of Agatha, still related to Samuel, but less directly. This suggestion would make sense of the chronology as Samuel would have had to marry very young to have a nubile daughter in the 980s. There is also the fact that the name Kosara is fairly like Chryselios or Cursilius, and it would thus make sense if she were the daughter of a male member of the family.

However, the next episode in the family's history causes more doubt about the reliability of these sources. In the 990s Samuel attacked Thessalonica and captured Asot Taran the son of the governor there, a man of Armenian origin. Again a daughter, this time called Miroslava, fell in love with the young prisoner, and again Samuel allowed them to marry. This was a mistake as Asot intrigued with the Byzantines and his wife's mother's family and fairly soon the Chryselioi handed back Dyrrachium to the Byzantines. This is dated by Lupus Protospatharus to 1005, but others would place it earlier following Samuel's disastrous defeat at the River Spercheios in 997. Of course, the strange resemblance between the stories of Miroslava and Kosara/Theodora is suspicious, especially as in both cases Samuel unwisely handed over Dyrrachium to his new sons-in-law. The Bulgarian ruler does not appear to have been lucky in his in-laws, as Dyrrachium would seem to have been betrayed by Agatha's father, brother and son-in-law acting in concert. Such treachery was not uncommon in the wars between Samuel and Basil, with local leaders changing and rechanging sides according to the fortunes of war. Nor regrettably in Albanian history is it unusual for members of the same family to be on different sides. This is true of Roman times, the Second World War, and even the age of Scanderbeg whose nephew went over to the Turks.

There was more family treachery after Samuel's death. He was succeeded by his eldest son Gabriel Radomir, but suborned by the Byzantines. John Vladislav, Samuel's nephew, killed Gabriel and also John Vladimir, the husband of Kosara, before himself dying before the walls of Dyrrachium, terrified according to the Priest of Dioclea by the apparition of the murdered John Vladimir. John Vladislav was the son of Samuel's brother Aaron, killed by Samuel probably because he was too friendly to Byzantium. The Chryselioi escaped this fate and became part of the Byzantine aristocracy, as indeed rather surprisingly did the family of Samuel and Aaron. John Vladimir became a saint whose tomb near Elbasan can still be seen.

This happy ending to a sad story does not help us with two problems. The Chryselioi were clearly leading citizens of Dyrrachium before and after 1000, but their official position is not exactly clear. Agatha's father and brothers handed over the city according to Skylitzes in order to be made Byzantine patricians. Later the Priest of Dioclea talks of a Cursilius in Dyrrachium helping the Byzantine cause and he is called a *toparchus*, like a *proteuon*, a vague title belonging to a ruler. Clearly the Cursilius family had great influence in Dyrrachium, and this makes it more likely that they were local people rather than a family imported by Samuel to keep control of the city. This does not of course solve the problem of the ethnicity of the Chryselioi or their exact status in Dyrrachium, *proteuon* and *toparchus* being terms used at different times under different regimes.

It does not help matters that not only is the ethnicity of Agatha and her family in doubt, but we are also not sure about Samuel himself. In addition to the dispute about whether Samuel should be considered a Bulgarian or Macedonian, there are theories that he might be an Armenian or even a Vlach, possibly beginning life as the son of a local ruler, a *comes*, with some kind of allegiance to Byzantium. His father-in-law would seem to have begun and ended life in this position. The campaigns of Samuel and Basil bring Northern Albania to our notice for the first time since Roman times. It seems at first sight disappointing that with their confused chronology, muddle about names and emphasis on a few noble families who were always changing sides that we can form little idea about how the people of Northern Albania lived in what in England was the Anglo-Saxon era. But the story of Samuel, and his relatives does show that it is a mistake to think of these years in crude nationalistic terms - barbarian Bulgars against Byzantine Greeks. Local chieftains speaking a variety of languages changed sides frequently with little in the way of nationalist, religious or even family loyalty or prejudice to stop them, and their followers shared their destiny. In a way this has been the pattern of the whole of Albanian history, although Albanians would disagree, preferring a picture of gallant natives struggling against imperialist powers and oppressive foreign invaders. This picture is a little more plausible in our next chapter, when we do have an imperial power, Byzantium, for the first two centuries, then a series of foreign invaders in the next three, and we do have our first mention of Albanians, although except in the case of Scanderbeg the record of resistance by these Albanians is not very impressive.

6. ALBANIANS AND ANARCHY, 1018-1500

When Basil the Bulgar Slayer died in 1025 he left the Byzantine Empire in a stronger condition than it had been since the days of Justinian. It is true that in less than fifty years the combination of Basil's weak successors and two enemies against which he had not fought, the Turks and the Normans, drastically reduced the size of the empire. In the East and the West, thanks to the Arab conquests, Basil's empire had never approached the frontiers reached by Justinian's armies, but in the central Balkan region the Danube frontier threatened by the Slavs even in Justinian's reign and lost to them very rapidly afterwards was kept more or less intact for nearly two hundred years after Basil. Albania, especially under the strong Comnenid dynasty in the twelfth century, remained a Byzantine bastion, although Dyrrachium was threatened and occasionally taken by the Normans or independent generals. The Fourth Crusade of 1204 brought about a disastrous change, and until the Ottoman conquest at the end of the fifteenth century Northern Albania knew many masters, or, on an alternative reading, no masters.

In beginning a new chapter half way through the period of Byzantine domination which lasted almost as long as Roman or Ottoman rule I am trying to show a fundamental difference between the nature of Byzantine rule before and after Basil's triumphs. After the defeat of Samuel in spite of the feebleness of Basil's successor, Byzantium had control of the old Via Egnatia and could thus reach Dyrrachium and Albania by land. These territories became much more connected with the capital and were no longer an isolated fragment. With the loss of Bari, the last Byzantine fortress in Italy in 1071, Albania emerges into the limelight as an important place on the frontier. For both reasons our area is mentioned in literary sources, and we hear for the first time of Albanians although initially in a rather tentative fashion.

After 1204 references to Albania become much more frequent, although political history and geography become much more complicated. Bulgarians, Serbs, Latins, Venetians, Angevins and various Greek successor states competed for fragments of the Byzantine realm before the fourteenth century when the Ottomans arrived to make a more permanent claim. Native Albanians may periodically have achieved some kind of independence in these three hundred years, although not until the time of Scanderbeg was there any kind of Albanian unity, and even he ruled a confederation rather than a state. Indeed, though the historiography of Albania in this period is very different in this chapter from that in the last with an embarrassing variety of sources replacing guesswork and hypothesis, this history of the average Albanian in the tenth century is not all that dissimilar from that of his or her counterpart in the twelfth and fourteenth centuries. Dyrrachium was in the first period an isolated theme, in the second an important frontier province, and in the third hotly competed for by various successor states, but outside the town life in the mountains of Northern Albanian probably did not change very much.

Albanian nationalist historians are reluctant to accept that as in Roman and Ottoman times so in the pre-Byzantine, Byzantine and post-Byzantine eras, most inhabitants of Albania paid nominal allegiance to the ruling authority. It was, of course, difficult between 600 and 900 and between 1200 and 1500 to know who the ruling authority was. Such historians are on firmer ground in referring to the period from 1025 to 1500 as the feudal era, as it seems a characteristic of Albanians in all ages to owe their first allegiance to their tribal leader, leaving the tribal leader to choose which major ruler to follow - a confusing and difficult task in the anarchy after the Fourth Crusade. Albanian geography favours tribal divisions, and makes national unity more difficult than in Serbia or Bulgaria. It is hard to disprove Ducellier's thesis that the Albanians were on the whole loyal to Byzantium and had problems in achieving unity or adjusting themselves to the new order after Byzantium had collapsed.

6. Albanians and Anarchy, 1018-1500

There were revolts against Byzantine authority in Albania during the eleventh century, but they do not seem to have been led by Albanians. In about 1035 Duklja became independent under a ruler called Vojislav. The Priest of Dioclea calls him Dobroslav and makes him a cousin of the martyred John Vladimir. The same source, always anxious to boost Dioclean power, says that he extended his rule over much of Northern Albania. Byzantine efforts to drive him out failed, as armies based on Dyrrachium were unable to achieve any success in the mountains. In 1040 Peter Deljan, claiming to be the son of Gabriel Radomir, started a revolt in distant Belgrade, and even briefly took Dyrrachium after getting rid of a rival called Tibromir. Imperial incompetence in this area prompted a revolt by an able Byzantine general, George Maniaces, and it is in connection with this revolt that we first hear of Albanians, since he appears to have had Albanian troops in his army both in Italy, from where he started his revolt, and in his journey along the Via Egnatia. Doubt has been cast on the ethnicity of these troops. Maniaces was killed near Salonica, and the Dioclean revolt was suppressed with the help of Alusianus, the son of John Vladislav who had killed both Gabriel Radomir and John Vladimir. This replay in the 1040s of events after Tsar Samuel's death shows how fragile loyalties were, and how they were based not on ethnic consciousness but rather on political expedience. Although the historian Atteliates talks of Albanians among the troops of Maniaces, there is little sign of any of them taking charge of their own destiny. Of course, Byzantine sources like Atteliates are principally interested in Byzantium, while the Priest of Dioclea does not look much further than Duklja.

Duklja survived the revolts of 1040 and 1043 unscathed. Alusianus got rid of Gabriel Radomir's alleged son but not the family of his father's other victim, John Vladimir. Vojislav did not share the fate of his sainted predecessor but he had a difficult family. His five sons disputed the succession at about the same time as the rebellion of Maniaces. Eventually Michael prevailed and achieved some kind of rapport with Byzantium, marrying a Byzantine princess. The boundary between Duklja, which gradually came to be known as Zeta, and Byzantium is likely to have remained fairly flexible during this period. Ecclesiastical rather than secular authority might be a guide, but the Priest of Dioclea has his own axe to grind in these matters, and archives from the Vatican show some vagueness about Catholic interests in this part of their jurisdiction. The year 1054 marks a decisive break between Constantinople and Rome. Michael of Duklja, to show his independence from Byzantium, had himself crowned by the Pope and we can begin fairly talking about the Catholic population of Northern Albania for the first time.

Michael died in 1081. His son and successor Constantine Bodin was less successful. Captured by the Byzantines, possibly on two occasions, he had difficulties with outlying parts of his kingdom and with members of his family, a recurring nightmare for Slav rulers. He should have prospered because Byzantium, attacked on all sides and with a throne disputed by various generals, was at a low ebb. But a widespread revolt in 1072 led by a Slav nobleman proved a failure, and Bodin joining the rebels was defeated and captured. Alexius Comnenus prevailed over various rivals based in Dyrrachium and became Emperor of Byzantium in 1081. He was tested in Albania by the invasion from Italy of the Norman Robert Guiscard, forcing Alexius to retreat through narrow passes in what his daughter calls Albanian territory. But Alexius, a wily diplomat, caused trouble in Italy, and Robert was forced to retire from Dyrrachium which he had temporarily occupied. Led by Robert's son, Bohemund, the Normans returned first as rather uncertain allies in the First Crusade of 1097 and then as enemies again in 1107. Alexius was too astute to lose control of Albania, giving Bohemund distant Antioch instead, and with a series of fortresses surrounding Dyrrachium he began to protect this vital western boundary.

Alexius' son and grandson, John and Manuel, continued to strengthen Byzantium's position. The Adriatic was guarded with Venetian help. Duklja lost its independence after a complicated civil war in the reign of Alexius and became more and more subservient to Byzantium. Manuel did much to strengthen Byzantine power in the north-west Balkans. Native chiefs or *zupans* were allowed a good deal of independence provided that they acknowledged Byzantine supremacy. Duklja differed from the *zupans* in having a large Albanian and Catholic element in the population. Further south, Dyrrachium with its strong line of inland fortresses was a regular theme of the Byzantine Empire, with its governor, very often a member of the imperial family, one of the key figures in the realm. There were Latin-speakers in Dyrrachium and Greek-speakers throughout the province. There were also Albanian-speakers, and when Byzantine authority collapsed the area was known as Dyrrachium and Albania. In Duklja, not under direct control, there were fewer Greeks and more Latin-speakers with the presence of the Catholic Church and almost certainly vestigial Vlach elements. Further north and east there were Slav-speaking *zupans*. The Byzantine Empire was a multi-ethnic entity, and after nearly two hundred years of Byzantine rule Northern Albania in the year 1175 seemed to be settling down as a regular province of this empire.

In that year Manuel Comnenus fought and lost a disastrous battle against the Turks at Myriocephalum. As with the equally decisive Battle of Manzikert in 1071 there were, after this tragic and unnecessary defeat, a series of short reigns by weak emperors, and this time there was no Alexius Comnenus to take control. Bulgaria and Serbia became and remained independent. In 1204 Constantinople itself was taken in the Fourth Crusade. Byzantium still had two and a half centuries of existence with Greek forces recapturing the capital in 1261 and reaching the Adriatic, again towards the end of the thirteenth century. But Northern Albania, which had been distantly loyal to Byzantium for most of the two preceding centuries, was never to be Byzantine again. Instead we have a series of ephemeral empires which made conflicting claims on the shifting loyalties of the Albanian tribes, and these began to emerge as distinct entities in this confusing period. There was a Greek state based on Arta in Epirus and another based on Nicaea in Asia Minor. It was the latter which captured Constantinople and, swallowing up the Despotate of Arta, ruled Southern Albania for a time, but neither state made much progress north of the Shkumbin. The Bulgarian or Vlach state under its most powerful ruler John Asen II got as far as the Adriatic, and he declared himself in 1230 to be the ruler of the Albanians among other races, but after his death in 1241 Bulgarian power declined, and it was the Serbs under the Nemanjid dynasty who held control over Northern Albania for the second half of the thirteenth and first half of the fourteenth centuries. The death of Stephen Dušan in 1355 brought about the collapse of this empire, as his successors were unable to withstand the Turks whose overwhelming advance was only challenged by Scanderbeg in the fifteenth century. From the west a small principality was carved out along the coast, first by Manfred of Sicily and then by Charles of Amjou, but claims by the house of Anjou to have an Albanian empire should be discounted.

Religious as well as secular loyalties were strained after the Fourth Crusade. Even before it there was a strong Catholic presence in Northern Albania. Powerful monarchs like Kalojan, Stephen Dušan and even the Byzantine Michael Palaeologus made overtures to the Pope. The latter's subservience to Rome meant the defeat of the obviously Catholic Charles of Anjou, because the Sicilian Vespers resulted, Michael was confirmed as ruler of the Southern Balkans, and Angevin rule in Albania and elsewhere became nominal rather than real. Dante has his Western and Catholic loyalties firmly entrenched. He puts both Charles and Manfred in *Purgatorio*, promotes Charles' grandson, Charles Martel, and Manfred's remote ancestor Robert Guiscard to *Paradiso*, and makes the Pope occupy a prominent place in *Inferno*.

The average Albanian, like the average reader of Dante, is likely to have been more confused in his or her loyalties. We have seen how in the time of Basil II local chieftains suddenly switched sides, almost certainly on the grounds of personal expediency rather than ethnic loyalty. Under the Comneni we know that the great military barons were awarded great tracts of land on condition that they promised armed troops to serve the Empire.

These grants, known by the oddly theological name of *pronoia* (it means forethought), seem to have been an important part of Byzantine fiscal and military organisation, although our records of *pronoias* are much less full in the great days of Manuel Comnenus than in the precarious reign of Michael Palaeologus. By the latter's time the Latins had arrived, and started dividing up the Balkan peninsula. The Peloponnese formed a feudal division of the Latin Empire, and we know that in the late thirteenth century, the time of Michael Palaeologus, the Peloponnese was divided into feudal baronies, each with their feudal castle and presumably with sub-feudal lordships owing similar loyalties, although here history becomes a little more obscure as eventually the whole of the Peloponnese reverted to Byzantine rule.

This record of feudal arrangement is not available in Albania, and such an arrangement would not seem to have been suitable. There may have been *pronoias* in early Byzantine times. The family of Chrysellus, the father-in-law of Samuel, and the Arianites who helped Basil II may have been *pronoia* holders. We do not hear of any such local leaders after the collapse at the end of the twelfth century, although the revolt in Bulgaria is supposed to have been provoked by the refusal of the Byzantine authorities to grant a *pronoia* to the Asen brothers. With less territory to grant, Michael Palaeologus was fairly lavish with bequests of feudal territories, as was Charles of Anjou with even less to bequeath. The Serbs and even Venice appeared to adopt the *pronoia* system which the Ottomans adapted more economically to create their *timars*, rewards given for outstanding service in their expanding empire in return for further if limited military obligations.

As will be seen later, the *timar* system never really worked in the Northern Albanian mountains. Even in the plains near Dyrrachium the *timars*' predecessors, the Byzantine *pronoias*, technically like *timars* non-hereditary, and the feudal fiefdoms passed down from father to son were impossible to operate, mainly because the ruing power changed so rapidly. In the Peloponnese we do know that there was an elaborate system of minor and major barons owing loyalty to the Prince of Achaea

Medieval Northern Albania

Moraca
MALËSIAE MADHE
PROKETLIJË
Valbona
Cem
White Drin

BALSIĆ
Budva
Lake Shkodrës
Bar
Balzë
Drisht
Shkodër
Kir
Bunë
Ulcinj
Lezhë

SPANI
DUSHMAN
DUKAGJIN
ZAHARIA
KASTRIOT
JONIMA
Drin
Fani i Vogël

Approximate boundary of direct Ottoman rule in 1431

Mt. Korab

Orosh

Adriatic Sea

Kruja
Stellush
Dibër

Ishëm
Mat
GROPA
Svetigrad?

Black Drin

THOPIA
Mt. Dajte
Erzen

Dyrrachium

ARIANITI
Shkumbin

Lake Ohrid

Lake Presp

N

Avlonya
MUSACHI

Seman
Osum

Devoll

Approximate boundary of Byzantine theme of Dyrrachium in 10th Century

0   20
km

Vjosës

© S.Ballard (2

who owed loyalty to the Latin Emperor of Constantinople, and that Charles of Anjou, who at one stage aspired to be Prince of Achaea and Latin Emperor, tried to establish a similar regime, but by the time his grandson started listing Albanian feudal barons the Angevin claim to Albania was as shadowy as some of their other claims such as Jerusalem. Albanian rulers in the centre of Albania had a longstanding record of loyalty to Byzantium, but unfortunately there were two Byzantine states to contend with. *Pronoia* holders had plenty of opportunities to change sides, and did so. Bulgaria under John Asen was only a factor for a short time near Dyrrachium as was Serbia under Stephen Dušan, while Serbian rule in the North lasted much longer, but was never likely to have been very demanding. Oddly it is Venice, officially granted most of Albania after the Fourth Crusade, and still nearly three centuries later battling it out with the Turks, which is linked with a difficult grant of Albanian *pronoia* to the Jonima family near Shkodër.

AN ALBANIAN NATION?

These facts should be borne in mind in connection with the claim that around the period of the Fourth Crusade Albania established its first independent state under the rule of Progon and his two sons Dimitir and Gjin. This first princely dynasty since the royal house of the Ardiaei who fought with and against the Romans had a shorter but equally chequered existence. In the year 1216 an otherwise unknown Gregoras Camonas sent a letter to Demetrius Chomatenus in Ohrid asking if he could marry the widow of Dimitir the brother of Gjin, after being previously married to and divorced from the daughter of Gjin. Chomatenus said he saw no objection to this slightly inbred, but not actually incestuous, marriage thus indicating that Camonas was not actually of the same bloodline as the family of Progon. His second wife was well connected, daughter of a Serbian king and a Byzantine princess, and he himself is addressed as *pansebastos sebastos*, a complimentary royal title, while Progon is simply called *archon* or ruler. Previously in 1208 we find the Pope corresponding with Dimitir, this time rather bafflingly described as *judex* or judge. Finally there is an inscription issued by Progon proudly displayed as evidence of Albanian independence in the Tirana museum.

Even Ducellier is impressed by this dynasty. After establishing quite correctly the existence of an Albanian ethnic group loyal to Byzantium in the eleventh and twelfth centuries, he seems unduly anxious to show that this group almost became a nation at the beginning of the thirteenth. But in fact there is no evidence that the Albanians even temporarily threw off Byzantine hegemony. Progon as *archon* may have been a Byzantine official or a *pronoiar*. The term *sebastos* originally reserved almost exclusively for members of the imperial family appears to have been debased in the thirteenth century. Loyalties were clearly stretched after the Fourth Crusade, and it is hardly surprising to find Progon's sons communicating with the Pope and the Archbishop of Ohrid or marrying into the Byzantine and Serbian royal family. Kruja as a vital strategic point had been granted tax exemptions by Manuel Comnenus and these were renewed after a century by Michael Palaeologus when the ruler was known as Golem, possibly related to previous rulers, although there is no evidence to prove this.

So much for Albania's second royal family. Progon, Gjin and Golem are good Albanian names, and one can understand why Albanian nationalistic historians have been keen to honour their names in the same way as they honour Gentius and Teuta. Other dynasties like the Arianiti, the Thopias, the Musachi, the Balšićs and the Kastrioti play a much more prominent part in medieval Albanian history for a much longer time than the family of Progon. But with the exception of the Kastrioti who arrive rather late on the scene, conveniently based in Kruja, these families disqualify themselves from being true Albanians by their foreign connections. The Musachi fled to Italy, where one wrote a boastful account of his grand connections. Charles Thopia claimed like a previous Musachi to be the ruler of Albania, but he based his claim on his illegitimate descent from Charles of Anjou. The Arianiti, leaders of the first revolt against the Turks and with marriage connections to most families including that of

Scanderbeg whose wife was an Arianiti, ended up in Italy with daughters given the names of Classical Greek heroines. It is possible, though not certain, that David Arianites, a general of Basil II, may be a member of this family thus giving the Arianiti, a name that sounds as it belonged to the whole of Albania, a long life. Both the Musachi and the Arianiti belong to the South, and the Thopias to the Centre. In the North the two great families were the Dukagjins and the Balšićs. The former left the sinister legacy of the Kanun of Lek Dukagjin and the latter, although occupying Northern Albania with their capital at Shkodër, also ruled over Montenegro. The Balšićs only come to notice with the collapse of the Nemanjid kingdom of Serbia at the end of the fourteenth century; before that time their realm was either directly ruled by the Nemanjids or by a sub-kingdom corresponding to the old realm of Duklja with some kind of independence under a ruler related to the royal family.

In the nineteenth and twentieth centuries this area was disputed between Albanian and Montenegrin tribesmen, then divided by language and religion. Kosova faced similar disputes and divisions. The Slav states gained after various peace treaties far more territory than they deserved, and it is perhaps worth mentioning that for most of medieval times the area of their maximum claims was largely ruled by the Slavs, although inhabited by both Slavs and Albanians. The religious issue is complicated as Stephen Nemanja, the first crowned, was so crowned by the Pope. This so shocked his brother Sava that in 1219 he succeeded in making Peć a patriarchate, and there is some evidence for Catholicism being in difficulties during this period. The connection with first Manfred and then the house of Anjou should have helped the Catholic cause, but, as we have shown, rule from the West was more nominal than real.

Venice lost Dyrrachium by 1214 to Michael Ducas, vaguely and illegitimately related to the Comneni. Though technically granted rights over Epirus in 1204, Venice did not recover Dyrrachium until 1392. It is uncertain whether the Bulgarians for all their boasting ever captured the city. Michael's half brother Theodore had ambitions to extend his Greek kingdom further east. He had a great triumph in capturing in 1217 the ruler of Constantinople, Peter Courtenay, who had rashly ventured along the Via Egnatia to claim his throne, but Theodore was defeated by the Bulgarians at Klokonitza in 1230. Albanian chieftains probably switched loyalties from the Greek rulers of Arta to the Bulgarians at this point. In 1246 the rulers from Nicaea conquered Salonica, and the realm of Theodore, which had once stretched from Dyrrachium to Adrianople, was reduced to Greek Epirus and Albania south of the Shkumbin. Even this realm was reduced when Manfred in 1257 first conquered and then was given as dowry a section of the Albanian coast. The Nicaean cause in contrast was in the ascendant, under Michael VIII Palaeologus defeating Michael II of Epirus in 1259, reconquering Constantinople in 1261, and finally seeing off the threat from Charles of Anjou in 1282.

Once again Byzantine rule in Europe stretched from the Adriatic to the Black Sea, but it was a sadly diminished realm both in the north and in the south. Serbia was gradually extending its power southwards, the Despotate of Epirus still maintained a precarious existence, and Michael Palaeologus' son and successor Andronicus II had a disastrous reign, losing practically all the empire's Asian possessions to the Turks, and engaging in a futile civil war with his grandson Andronicus III. At one stage Dyrrachium would seem to have been taken by the Serbs, but Charles of Anjou's son Philip of Taranto still claimed it as the capital of his shadowy Albanian kingdom, issuing pompous and meaningless instructions to his feudal Albanian lords as if he owned the place. In one last flash in the Byzantine pan Andronicus III took the Despotate of Epirus. He also suppressed a massive Albanian incursion from the north, but unfortunately with the aid of Turkish troops. The younger Andronicus died in 1341, and in 1348 the Serbs under Stephen Dušan conquered the whole of Albania and northern Greece.

The Nemanjid dynasty in some form or another ruled Northern Albania for about two hundred years. Six generations of the descendants of Stephen Nemanja came to the throne, usually with some difficulty as they had to fight off the claims of rival brothers, sons, fathers or uncles. The fighting was not pretty. Stephen Dečanski, who ruled from 1321 to 1331, was blinded on the orders of his father, strangled on the orders of his son. He started to build a church at Dečani, now a Serb island in a Kosovan sea, then a monument to the piety of the Nemanjids that contrasts oddly with their bloodthirsty history. Younger brothers like St Sava, the founder of the partriarchate at Peć, and his namesake and nephew preferred the service of God to worldly ambitions. Stephen Nemanja retired to a monastery voluntarily, while his grandson Stephen Uros I was forced into monastic retirement by a revolt of his son. Other sons and brothers were given minor kingdoms to rule as appenages, and Zeta including Northern Albania became just such an appenage. Unfortunately with its important history Zeta was not always loyal to the main Serbian state. Stephen Nemanja's son Vukan quarrelled with Stephen the First Crowned and it needed St Sava to reconcile them. Vukan's son George ruled Zeta for a short while. Stephen Dečanski gave Zeta just such an appanage to Stephen Dušan with fatal results.

Stephen the First Crowned was so crowned by the Pope. Four generations later Stephen Dušan considered acknowledging papal supremacy, although all over southern Serbia and Kosova there are a host of Nemanjid tributes to Orthodox faith. There are no such buildings in Northern Albania, and this is an indication that our area retained its Catholic faith and presumably and possibly consequentially the Albanian language. Stephen Dušan aspired to become Emperor of Constantinople and to rule over a multi-ethnic, multi-faith empire as the Byzantine Empire had been, but his early death in 1355 led to the rapid collapse of his realm which split into a series of squabbling lordships. In Northern Albania it was the Balšič family who took over, but though they reigned for four generations they were not nearly as powerful as the Nemanjids and can hardly pass muster as a heroic Albanian family, being Slavs, fighting other Albanians and subservient at various times to Serbs, Turks and Venetians.

Balša Balšić was a petty nobleman in the time of Dušan. We do not hear of his family until 1360. It is difficult to establish the exact boundaries of their realm and that of the Slav tribes, notably the Crnojeviči to the north and the Albanian rulers to the west and south. They began life as vassals of Dušan's son and at the time of the Battle of Kosova in 1389 they acknowledged the suzerainty of the Serbian Prince Lazar. George Balšić, grandson of Balša, was captured by the Ottomans in 1392 and forced to surrender several cities including Shkodër. His cousin Constantine with whom he had quarrelled was installed by the Ottomans as Governor of Kruja. In 1395 George abandoned Ottoman suzerainty in favour of Venetian and handed over Shkodër and Drisht which he had captured to his new overlords. He presumably held onto some territory in the interior as he had fought successfully against the Dukagjins, but just as the Balšić family were uncertain who their real overlord was, so too those nominally under their rule must have been uncertain about any loyalty to the Balšićs. Possibly the Dukagjins and the Thopias had more authority. Lek Dukagjin's Kanun may reveal an attempt to impose law and order, albeit in a rather brutal way, and Charles Thopia's claim to be descended from the Kings of France, though conceited, does suggest a genuine wish to assert his own control instead of being subservient to foreign power. The times were extremely unsettled. Brigandage was rife, hard to distinguish from the wars between petty dynasts. People moved from the plains to the mountains to avoid trouble, but then found the mountains inadequate to support them and had to return to the plains for plunder, creating trouble again. It is about this time that families began to gather together to support each other, thus forming the tribal system of Northern Albania as opposed to the feudal families of the medieval period.

George Balšić's father and uncles had converted to Catholicism. His son Balša III, who succeeded him in 1403, reconverted to Orthodoxy since his mother was a Serbian princess. The Turks were temporarily out of the picture after the Battle of Ankara in 1402 and the civil war which followed it. Balša revolted against the Venetians, but then having toyed with acknowledging Serbian suzerainity reverted to the Ottoman cause, now on the mend after the death of Timur. He had married a member of the Thopia family and for a time by juggling the Ottomans, the Serbs, the Venetians and his fellow Albanians he managed to keep his realm fairly intact. But he died without a male heir in 1421 and left his kingdom to be fought over by the major powers with the resurgent Turks as the obvious winner.

The Ottoman invasion of Northern Albania came in three waves. After the decisive Battle of Marica in 1371 they were masters of the eastern Balkans and found few to stop them in the west. Tzar Lazar of Serbia tried and it is now generally agreed that at Kosova in 1389 he fought a draw with the Turks and lost his life in the process. His son continued to rule in Serbia, but as the vassal of the Turks in the same position as George Balšič. At this stage direct rule over the western Balkans was not contemplated by the Ottomans, although there was plenty of interference by them in Albanian affairs. Ankara and the disputed succession after this battle provided a check to Ottoman progress. Mehmed I, the eventual winner in the Turkish royal family battle, practised in general a peaceful policy among his Balkan subjects and neighbours, but he took Gjirokastër and Vlorë.

By 1430 under Mehmet's more aggressive son Murad the whole of Central and Southern Albania was in Turkish hands after a second wave of invasion and a register was made of the timars in that area, many of them in Christian hands. To the north there were leaders like the Dukagjins and Kastrioti, who were vassals of the Sultan. There then followed Scanderbeg's gallant revolt in which the whole of Albania rose up against the Turks.

SCANDERBEG

Before analysing the story of Scanderbeg, which seems a fitting conclusion to an untidy chapter, it might be as well to examine the register for the *sandjak* of Shkodër, which the Ottomans prepared in 1485 to mark their conquest of Northern Albania. This is interesting for a number of reasons. It shows, as will be explained in the next chapter, that the *timar* system never really worked in

Northern Albania. There is a large area in the mountainous north which simply does not appear in the register. This black hole extending from Gusinjë in the north to Nicaj-Shalë in the south and from Selce in the west to Dragobi in the east shows that either these mountain districts were unsubdued, or possibly that they were uninhabited, either temporarily or permanently, or that their inhabitants had won special privileges for guarding mountain passes. There are a surprising number of Slavonic names which increase the further one gets from Shkodër. This can be explained by the existence of a Slavonic scribe, although it is perhaps revealing that while the *sandjak*'s borders reach roughly the present linguistic border between Slav and Albanian, the Albanian names are largely to be found within the present political frontier.

Scanderbeg at any rate is indubitably Albanian. In fact he is the Albanian, brave and resourceful, holding his people together as he won battle after battle against the superior numbers of a foreign foe. His presence dominates Albanian history as his huge statue dominates the central square of Albania's capital. But writing about him is difficult. We are dependent on one main source, the florid Latin narrative of Marinus Barlettius, written a generation after the death of his hero. The book is not easily available in Latin or in translation. Historians of the Ottomans like Critobulus support Barlettius' facts but omit the extravagant praise. Students of the Classics can admire the echoes of Livy in Barlettius, and the archaising way he calls Albanians Illyrians, but we are not, as with Thucydides or Tacitus, dealing with a historian whose principal interest is the truth. Nor can we expect much truth from the flattering but rather despicable records of Naples, Venice and the Papacy who used Scanderbeg for their own purposes.

Clearly Scanderbeg was a commander of genius, winning a series of victories against impossible odds. His forces were inferior in numbers, but Scanderbeg was a master of tactical surprise, working wonders with guerrilla attacks. Turkish cannons wreaked havoc on the thickest walls, but the natural defences of Kruja's rocks were better than walls. The standing armies of the Ottomans were superior in quality as well as quantity to the feudal levies that Balkan and Western powers pitted against them, but Scanderbeg was an inspiring leader, uniting the various Albanian chieftains by the force of his personality and by a series of marriage alliances. Yet he was more than once betrayed, even by his own nephew. He was more adroit than the Balšičs and his own father in keeping a balance between the Turks and rival Western powers. But he was clearly better as a warrior than as a diplomat, as a tactician than a strategist, and like his predecessor Pyrrhus to whom he rather tactlessly compares himself he won many battles without actually winning the war.

Gibbon in his sceptical, cynical way is fairly contemptuous of Barlettius and by implication of Scanderbeg's achievements. For Albanian nationalists Scanderbeg can do no wrong since he united his people, fought a mighty foreign foe and received scant help from other untrustworthy countries in exactly the same way as communists claimed they had won the Second World War. His aristocratic birth and staunch attachment to Catholicism were forgotten by Hoxha's historians. Acts of treachery against him were matched in modern times. A more detached approach would suggest that unlike the victorious Partisans Scanderbeg was fighting a losing battle and that his death at Lezhë was perhaps fortunate, leaving his reputation unsullied but his realm virtually conquered.

Lezhë was in a way a fortunate place to die as it had been the scene of the congress which had apparently united the disparate Albanian chieftains in their fight against the Turks. It has, like Kruja, been turned into a shrine to Scanderbeg and to Albanian nationalism. Both in 1444, the date of the initial congress, and in 1468, the year of Scanderbeg's death, Lezhë was in Venetian hands, but worshippers at the shrine are not reminded of this fact. Kruja with its massive natural defences makes a better shrine, and one can understand how the Albanians year after year managed to entice huge Turkish armies to besiege the town, picking off the enemy by surprise raids until winter set in and the Turks had to march back to Macedonia. Eventually after Scanderbeg's death

Kruja was starved into surrender, but by that time the Turks had occupied most of Albania and had installed their own fortresses at places like Elbasan. Earlier Scanderbeg with powerful defensive positions at Svetigrad near Dibër and at Berat had tried to prevent the Turks invading from the east and the south, but he lost both these strongholds, suffering two rare defeats in the process.

Another place where the Albanians were defeated was at the fortress of Ballsh near Shkodër, although here Scanderbeg was not in charge of the defence and it was not the Turks but the Venetians who seized the fort. Scanderbeg's wars against Venice rather dent his reputation as the hero of Christendom as in a way do his campaigns on the side of his other patron, Naples, in the 1460s fought not in his hard-pressed native lands but across the Adriatic in Apulia. Contradictions like this show how difficult it is to write history in black and white terms, but we must eventually come down on the side of Scanderbeg. He is a better patron saint for Albania than St George for England. The original St George was a Cappadocian entrepreneur of dubious morality with no connection to England and little connection with Christianity. In contrast, Scanderbeg fought valiantly and brilliantly for the Christian faith and for Albania. Epic songs and stories recount his valour particularly against his last major adversary, Balaban Pasha. It is true that Homer is no guide to history and Gibbon would have noted, as historians of the Hoxha era failed to note, that Balaban was both an Albanian and a member of the working classes. He was the son of a peasant on the Kastriot estates. There is a good story of how Scanderbeg sent him as a gesture of contempt in one of the courteous parleys of medieval warfare a hoe and a ploughshare.

If Balaban had been successful he would no doubt have given a tract of land somewhere in the Ottoman Empire, perhaps in his native Albania, and he is an indication that with the death of Scanderbeg the old order was bound to change. Of the main chieftains of Albania in the fifteenth century some fled to Italy, some turned Turk and were absorbed into the Ottoman administration as Scanderbeg himself almost had been. Such leaders would not have been given land in Albania, as they might attempt to arouse old loyalties against their new masters. As has already been pointed out, except in the solitary case of the Dushman family there seems almost no continuity between the feudal lordships of the Middle Ages and the still archaic tribes which existed in the time of Edith Durham and Hasluck. The feudal families have vanished, but the tribes still give their names to districts in Albania today. A key difference would seem to be that feudal lordships expanded and contracted as a result of the fortunes of war, fortunes made more erratic by the struggles of the Great Powers for overlordship. After rather pathetic efforts by Scanderbeg's son and grandson to renew the struggle at the end of the fifteenth century and a brief Venetian rally in the sixteenth century, Ottoman Turkey in a final invading wave became and remained the only great power. Tribal boundaries then became ossified. Strict rules involving marriage were established along with the blood feud, governing what constituted a tribe. There is no evidence for restrictions on marriage or the blood feud in medieval times. Two families were involved in a fatal quarrel on the occasion of Scanderbeg's wedding, but both the murder and the marriage to a member of the great southern family of the Arianiti do not seem like a story from the pages of Durham and Hasluck. Scanderbeg casts a long shadow over Albanian history, but to understand the substance of modern Albanian life we must study the Turkish period.

7. OTTOMAN ALBANIA, 1501-1912

As indicated in the previous chapter, after a relatively stable period as part of the Byzantine Empire in the eleventh and twelfth centuries, Albania endured rather than enjoyed many different kinds of rule in the next three hundred years. Rule is perhaps hardly the right word for the various forms of suzerainty exercised by major or minor rulers over the average Albanian. Such an inhabitant of a village in the plains and even in the mountains might owe some fleeting loyalty to a minor baron who would in his turn show shifting allegiance to some major family like the Kastriots or the Thopias who would also from time to time acknowledge the overlordship of a dominant power like the Angevins or Serbia or Venice. A large section of the population for a large section of this period owed allegiance to nobody except themselves. Annual transhumance, other forms of community movement and the prevalence of brigandage, though uncomfortable features of Northern Albanian life, were useful devices for avoiding taxation and conscription.

The Ottomans changed all this. They tried to control if not eradicate lawlessness and tax evasion, and to regulate military service and the movement of population. Present in Albania during the second half of the fourteenth century they were strong enough in 1431 to make an exhaustive catalogue of their holdings in Southern and Central Albania. Scanderbeg delayed the conquest of the North until the end of the fifteenth century, but the Ottomans defeated attempts by his son and grandson to return, and mopped up the remaining Venetian possessions fairly rapidly, capturing Shkodër in 1471 and Durrës in 1514. There were other wars against Venice in the sixteenth and seventeenth centuries, and sometimes there were local uprisings in Northern Albania, which Venice encouraged, but it is a mistake to see the history of Albania in this period as a long and valiant struggle against the foreign invader. It is almost certain that as many

Albanians fought for the Ottomans as fought against them in the Venetian wars.

It should be borne in mind that some of the action in these wars took place in distant spheres like Crete and Cyprus, and that Venice usually came off second best, losing both islands and other outposts in the Eastern Mediterranean like Madon and Monemvasia. Oddly, Budva and Butrint remained in Venetian hands until the collapse of the republic in 1797, but long before this Venice had been replaced by Austro-Hungary as the main threat to the Ottomans whose power had begun to wane in the seventeenth century. Vienna had to endure a second siege in 1683, but Austrian armies got as far as Kosova in 1689, receiving some help from the tribesmen of Northern Albania who had previously revolted against the Ottomans in 1634. There was a further Austrian invasion in 1737. In both cases the army was forced to retreat, taking with them Serbian and Albanian allies. The attacks and subsequent retreats form a controversial part of Kosovan history. The Kelmendi tribe from north-west Albania played a prominent part in both Austrian campaigns. In 1638 Turkish forces had taken the field against this tribe to punish them for brigandage although it is a matter of dispute whether this campaign was successful, or how far, if at all, the Kelmendi raids were motivated by a desire for independence or by simple greed. The seventeenth century was a time of weakness for the Ottoman Empire, but the threat from foreign powers decreased in the eighteenth, when Western states were occupied in wars against each other. At the time of the Napoleonic Wars the principal danger for the Ottomans was the presence of independent governors like Ali Pasha of Tepelene and the Bushati family based in Northern Albania.

This rapid summary of three hundred years has been presented as a series of uprisings against the Ottomans, and indeed lengthier histories from Albania do use the word *kruengrite* a great deal, this being a useful blanket term to cover other more successful feats of rebellion such as the campaigns of Scanderbeg and the Partisan struggle in the Second World War. I have tried to show that resistance against the Ottomans in Northern Albania took different forms at different times and was partial at the best of times, but the exact nature of each revolt is difficult to determine owing to the incompleteness of sources. Very few of these are written in Albanian since the first writings in this language, largely theological, do not appear until the sixteenth and seventeenth centuries. Albania cannot boast of the external triumphs or artistic achievements of some other European nations, but it is still wrong to represent its history merely as a series of guerrilla campaigns against the Turkish oppressors.

History is about more than wars, and instead of enumerating minor acts of rebellion it might be better to look at four features of Albanian history which were less likely to be popular with communist historians although they did some creditable work on them. These are religion, the system of land tenure, tribal organisation and the celebrated and mysterious Kanun of Lek Dukagjin. All four belong to the antiquated world of the past, to be replaced by the new order of Enver Hoxha, and are also irrelevant for the celebration of this revolution unlike earlier acts of resistance. Ottoman *defters* are extremely informative about the number of Christian and Muslim households in various parts of the country, and these numbers, gathered for tax purposes, have been well analysed by scholars like Pulaha. They show very few Islamic households in the sixteenth century, a time of Ottoman strength, but a great change in the seventeenth, a period of weakness when Austrian armies advanced as far as Prishtina. This is unexpected. More to be expected, because of the present religious position, is the fact that the North-West held out against this trend, while the North-East and Central Albania began to be converted to Islam in the seventeenth century and became generally Muslim in the eighteenth. The *defters* do not, unfortunately, distinguish Catholics from Orthodox Christians.

Various explanations have been offered for the time and place of the conversions. It is generally acknowledged that the Ottomans did not favour forcible conversion or even feel an urgent mission to convert the nations they conquered. This might explain the low number of Muslims in Albania during the sixteenth century. As modern Evangelical Christians have found, an enthusiastic approach to conversion can be counter-productive, but the Austrian campaign in the seventeenth century may have hastened the change in favour of Islam, with diehard and defeated Christians leaving the area to be replaced by a population of newcomers who could see together with those remaining which way the wind was blowing. This seems to have been the pattern in Kosova in both the seventeenth and eighteenth centuries. The whole subject is confused because of the modern conflict in the area, but there were major movements of population in both centuries.

North-western Albania was more remote from the Austrian war than Kosova, but was also remote from the major shrines of Slav Orthodoxy like the patriachate at Peć, reestablished in 1559. Fortunately, there are now no ethnic problems in north-eastern Albania to blur the issue, although the odd Slav-speaker reminds us that the language can be a difficulty for the followers of any religious rite. North-eastern Albania had in late medieval and early modern times been a bone of contention between Catholic and Orthodox believers. In early medieval times there had been disputes between Greeks and Slavs for control of Orthodox churches, and even in the Ottoman period the Greek patriachate situated close to the seat of power in Istanbul could still supply an alternative focus of loyalty. Thus, as in Bosnia, where the third Christian player after Catholicism and Slav Orthodoxy was not Greek Orthodoxy, but the shadowy Bosnian Church, any version of Islam was helped by the confusion of conflicting claims to the truth from various divisions of Christianity.

In the North-West Orthodoxy had never been very strong, and Venetian influence persisted even after Venice had lost Shkodër. There was a heroic effort by the Franciscan order to keep the flame of Catholicism burning. Bishops continued to be appointed although not all reached their sees. It did not help matters that after the capture of Bar in 1571 all three Catholic archbishops in the area were under Ottoman rule. The other two sees were

Skopje and Durrës. In 1706 there was an extremely gloomy report from the Archbishop of Bar about low morale among Catholics in Northern Albania, but two hundred years later Edith Durham was able to show gallant Catholic priests surviving difficult times, and Catholicism has survived active persecution in the past sixty years. The inbred conservatism of the villages of the North-West helped in this remarkable story.

Further south in Mat, the central coastal plain and the mountainous districts north of the Shkumbin, Islam prevailed. Durrës had been the last Venetian possession in Albania apart from Butrint, and should have been a stronghold of Catholicism. It had also been an outpost of Greek Orthodoxy, and we can use the confusion of faiths and languages as a factor in driving the inhabitants of Central Albania into the arms of Islam. In addition, the Bektashi version of Islam was, and is, strong in this area, particularly in the east. Bektashism is a tolerant faith, allowing, for instance, the drinking of alcohol. There is also in central Albania some evidence of crypto-Christianity, of people pretending to be Muslims while retaining Christian beliefs, or of having both a Christian and a Muslim name, or at the lowest level adopting a folk religion combining Christian, Muslim and pagan practices. A veneer of Islam may have been adopted for selfish financial reasons, and this leads us to the subject of land tenure.

The rapid Ottoman advance across the Balkans had been achieved not only by military success but by an administrative system that was both efficient and effective. Tracts of land were awarded in *timars* to cavalry commanders or *spahis* in return for providing a body of armed men who fought in the usually successful Ottoman campaigns. Those who did not fight paid for the armed warriors either directly to the *timar*-holder or indirectly in taxes to central government. Initially these latter taxes were low, although higher for Christians than Muslims. Initially too, there was no religious discrimination in deciding who could become a *timar*-holder, and there are several Christian *timariots* in the *defter* of 1431 which showed Ottoman rule as far north as Kruja. Outside this rather fluid boundary the Turks as the Byzantines and Romans had done before them softened future resistance by making neighbouring areas, still self-governing, owe allegiance to their cause. Scanderbeg checked this progress, but after his death the Ottomans resumed their seemingly irresistible advance, awarding *timars* in Northern Albania. They had some difficulty in the North-West, not ideal country for extracting rents and taxes.

In the seventeenth century, when the tide began to turn against the Ottomans along the Danube frontier and against cavalrymen faced with gunpowder the *timar* system also began to collapse. Wars were no longer profitable, and it seemed senseless to exempt warriors from taxation. But taxes still had to be raised, and regrettably all over the Ottoman Empire *timars* were turned into *ciftliks*, hereditary estates, to which the poor peasantry had to contribute. There were still the taxes to be raised, taxes that had to be increased in order to pay for the new armies replacing the *spahis*, and of course troops were needed to man these armies. The taxes were paid to the central government rather than to the *timar*-holders, who were gradually becoming obsolete, and these were heavier for Christians than for Muslims. Thus the collapse of the *timar* system coincided with the growth of Islam. The *devrsirme* or levy of young Christian boys to serve at the Ottoman court as officials or in the rightly feared Janissary corps was another reason for 'turning Turk', especially as many Albanians taken into Ottoman service in this way became benefactors to their native land, thus providing a good advertisement for their forcibly adopted faith.

In the North-West life was a little different. Again we must pay tribute to the success of the Ottomans in softening up districts next to their sovereign realm by making them acknowledge a vague suzerainty before imposing direct rule. But in the mountains of Northern Albania and Montenegro direct rule met a direct check. The *timar* system never really took hold here, and well before the seventeenth century it had been abandoned in favour of a scheme whereby individual tribes fought for the Ottomans in return for paying little or nothing in the way of taxes. Such a scheme operated in other mountainous parts of the Empire, both remote and yet important for communications. In the same way certain individuals were given specialist status for guarding vital roads and passes. These individuals were given names like *armatoles* (a Greek term derived from Latin) or *voinuks* (a Slav term), but were often Albanians or Vlachs. In the Pindus Mountains there is a rich oral tradition of *armatoles* turning into *klephts* (thieves) and in Slav territories *voinuks* turned into *haiduks* (bandits), and no doubt guardians of law and order in North-Albania often became brigands. Similarly, along the major routes from Kosova to the coast and along the Drin valley tribal communities including the Mirditë clans gained some kind of tax exemption in return for occasional service or guard duty, sometimes as we have seen in the case of the Kelmendi tribe indulging in a little brigandage on the side. Further south and west, Mat and central Albania had no tax exemptions, *timars* became *ciftliks*, and the inhabitants embraced Islam.

As I have shown in Chapter 2, the tribal area of Albania only really encompasses the northern third of the country: Mirditë is tribal, Mat less so, and the area around Kruja hardly tribal at all in spite of the efforts of the British to represent King Zog and Abas Kupi as tribal chieftains in the Second World War. Most tribal leaders were in fact on the German side. This abrupt modern intrusion into an account of Ottoman Albania can be excused on the grounds that we are dealing with a very conservative area. It is thus worth mentioning that the Kelmendi and Mirditë tribes, reluctant to join the Allied cause in the Second World War, claimed exemption from taxes at the height of Ottoman power on the grounds that they had fought on the Turkish side at the Battle of Kosova.

We need not believe this claim, made harder to down because there were two battles of Kosova. A desire to economise with taxes can lead to economies with the truth. We know that before Scanderbeg direct Ottoman rule extended as far as Kruja. Further north the Turks faced a difficult terrain inhabited by a motley collection of tribes, some Albanian, some Slav, some Catholic, some Orthodox, who for three hundred years or more had owed occasional and vague allegiance to a variety of feudal overlords. The *timar* system seemed to offer an easy way of adapting this uncertain allegiance to the stricter demands of Ottoman rule, but up in the mountains with a transhumant population and a tradition of brigandage as well as a tight knit sense of family loyalty neither *timar*-holders nor the central government would find it easy to collect taxes in cash or in kind. So fairly early with admirable pragmatism the Ottoman authorities seem to have granted tribes in the North, both Montenegrin and Albanian, virtual independence in exchange for military service. This arrangement seems to have worked fairly well. At times we find tribes like the Kelmendi fighting on the wrong side as in the Austrian wars or waging war on innocent travellers or fighting other tribes as a result of blood feuds, but in general the tribal system suited the Ottomans and vice versa.

In the fourteenth century we hear of Albanian or Vlach tribes without kings invading Greece, and in the fifteenth many of Scanderbeg's fellow feudal leaders fled to Italy. Genealogies of tribes in Albania going back as far as twenty generations are recounted in the late nineteenth century. This oral evidence, sometimes combined with a story of the tribes moving from further north, is clearly not very reliable, but it suggests that the fifteenth century was the formative period of the Albanian *fis*. This is the name for a group of people, acknowledging a common ancestor and prohibited from marrying descendents related to the male line. Confusingly, there was also in Northern Albania another organisation known as a *bairak* led by a hereditary *bairaktar*. *Bairak* means a standard, and it is not difficult to see this as a military grouping created at about the same time as the Northern Albanian tribes agreed to serve the Turkish armies in return for tax exemptions.

Edith Durham confuses the issue by making the *bairaktar* the head of the *fis*. Hasluck paints him as a rather less superior character working in concert to settle local disputes with what she calls men of good family in each *fis*. Malcolm points out the essential difference between a *fis* based on lineage and a *bairak* based on location, and that sometimes a *bairak* consisted of several *fis*, while sometimes several *bairaks* made up one large tribe. This was the case with the Mirditë, and we cannot quite believe Durham's statement that most of the *bairaks* of the Mirditë could not marry with each other, as this would be a serious limitation on the bachelors of this quite large area. With smaller tribes like the Kastrati and Hoti, however, we can believe Durham's statement that men from one group chose women from the other. Such a ruling ignores the possibility of inbreeding through the female line, but women did not count for much in Northern Albania. In the very remote mountains a *bairak* might coincide with a *fis*, and this might explain Durham's mistake. The hereditary and military nature of the *bairaktar*'s post gave the structure continuity and effectiveness in war. An aristocracy of regimental sergeant majors would make a conservative if reliable organisation. Unfortunately much of the *bairaktar*'s business was concerned with violence both within the tribe and against other tribes.

Governing both *bairaktars* and the men of good family we have the mysterious Kanun of Lek Dukagjin. *Kanun* is a Greek word meaning rule which has entered Albanian via Turkish, and the unwritten customary law of Lek is usually supposed to have been formulated at the time of the Turkish conquest, there being the contemporary of Scanderbeg called Lek Dukagjin. Others with the same name lived earlier, and some have claimed that the origins of Lek's law lie in remote antiquity. Others more prosaically maintain that Dukagjin is a geographical expression for the northern section of Albania, there being a *sandjak* with this name in Turkish times. Indeed, the name is still used for the area above Mirditë and Dibër, where confusingly a hundred years ago a different Kanun, that of Scanderbeg, seemed to apply, although in a less stringent fashion. The Kanun of Lek has acquired a fearsome reputation for bloodthirstiness and backwardness with strict and fierce rules for regulating blood feuds, from which women were gracefully exempt, though disgracefully dismissed as 'sacks, made to endure'. It is somewhat surprising to find that the written version of the code, admittedly drawn up by a

Catholic priest, Father Shtjefen Ghecov, sadly murdered by the Yugoslavs in 1929, begins with the word *Kisha*, the Albanian for church. Durham and more emphatically Hasluck, neither of whom seem like sacks, do lay stress on the possibility of flexible interpretations of the Kanun and the intervention of arbitrators. The concept of *besa*, including peace and reconciliation as well as absolute honesty, is a feature of the Kanun as prominent as the absurd sense of honour which has led to a cycle of violence resulting from a trivial offence. It is interesting that the Kanun deals with such minor matters as footpaths and dogs, two aspects of life in modern England which occasionally lead to bloodshed. The Hoxha government tried to stamp out the blood feud, and probably succeeded; recent violence in places like Shkodër may involve the settling of old scores, of which there were many to be settled, but such crimes cannot be excused by invoking Lek Dukagjin and should not be used to accuse him.

Armed with the Kanun, Northern Albania seems to have virtually governed itself in the three centuries following Scanderbeg's death. The Ottoman authorities received a token offer of sovereignty, may have collected some taxes and received some armed support if they were lucky, and some refusal of taxes and armed rebellion if they were unlucky. Like the Roman Empire, the Ottoman Empire tried to administer peace and justice throughout its realms, but gets a bad press for doing so, particularly when it began to decline and fall. The Danube remained, in theory, the frontier of this empire as it had for the Byzantines in the fifth, sixth, eleventh and twelfth centuries and the Romans in the third and the fourth. Under all three empires in their period of semi-decline, groups in the North periodically established semi-independence, while oddly Albania provided a focal point for resistance by the imperial power. We have noted the importance of Dyrrachium in late Roman, early Byzantine and late Byzantine times. Durrës played a rather different role in the late Ottoman period, but it remains a fact that at the time of the final collapse of Ottoman power in the Balkans in 1912, the year of Albanian independence, the Turks supported by the Albanians still held the fortresses of Ioannina and Shkodër.

GREAT POWERS AND OTTOMAN DECLINE

This degree of collaboration between Albanians and the occupying powers runs counter to the picture of Albanians as natural rebels. The truth lies somewhere in-between. The Bushati family, based in Shkodër, a powerful point of resistance, became semi-detached from the Ottoman Empire. Their rule is often compared to that of Ali Pasha of Ioannina, but is less well known because more visitors from the West, including Byron, went to the South. Like Ali Pasha the Bushatis intrigued with the Great Powers, notably France, but at times made peace with the Ottoman central government. Like Ali the Bushatis ruled a multi-ethnic state, in their case Albanians and Slavs rather than Albanians and Greeks, and just as Ali nearly set up a Greek-Albanian state which might have changed the course of Balkan history, so the Bushatis almost succeeded in founding a strong independent realm in Northern Albania and Montenegro. Such an entity had existed in the time of the Kingdom of Zeta and under the Balšićs. A proposal for such a state was on the table after the First World War. In the case of the Bushatis the vision of such a state fell foul of the Great Powers and the rising tide of linguistic and religious nationalism which was to set Montenegrin and Albanian tribes against each other for more than a century.

The first ruler of the Bushati dynasty, Mehmet Pasha, became a governor of the *sandjak* of Shkodër, which stretched as far as western Kosova in 1757. He extended his power over the neighbouring *sandjak* of Dukagjin covering most of Northern Albania, and was thus able to draw on the loyalty of the tribal forces accustomed to fight for their Ottoman overlords. Unlike Ali Pasha, who could only rely on Albanian irregulars, and thus has a poor reputation in Greek and Vlach villages to this day, the Bushati forces were a little more indigenous, disciplined and popular. Indeed, the rule of Mehmet's son Mahmut, who succeeding in 1775 claimed to be following in the footsteps of Scanderbeg, is praised by contemporary Catholic chroniclers. Unfortunately in 1796 Mahmut was defeated and killed by the rising power of Montenegro, for a long time semi independent, supported by Russia against France, Mahmut's patron, and granted full independence in 1799.

Mahmut's brother Ibrahim was more loyal to Turkey than Mahmut, and quietly submitted to Ottoman authority when he took over the Shkodër *pashalik*. Turkey played its hand quite well in the Napoleonic Wars and in the settlement of 1815 still maintained the Danube frontier apart from Dalmatia, taken over by the Austrians and the tiny Montenegrin state. Serbia gained some kind of autonomy in 1815, Greece full independence in 1832, but Albania remained Turkish until 1912. The Bushatis continued like Byzantine generals in the twelfth century to show signs of independence in the most loyal parts of the empire, of which they were officials. Mustaf Bushati, Ibrahim's son, raised a serious revolt against the Ottomans which was suppressed with difficulty in 1831. Ali Pasha had met a violent end in 1822, and in 1830 the Ottomans had sought to suppress any movement for independence among local rulers in Southern Albania by inviting five hundred of them to a conference in Monastir and slaughtering them all.

Such a bloodthirsty solution was unthinkable in Northern Albania, home of the blood feud. In our area local chieftains remained loyal to the Ottomans as they had to the Bushati dynasty, but they found their loyalty stretched by a series of reforms, loosely known as the Tanzimat, which enlightened liberals in Istanbul tried to pass in the first quarter of the nineteenth century. These reforms, sadly unappreciated by those whom they were aiming to help, were designed to abolish the difference between Christians and Muslims, to make taxation fairer, to introduce a professional army, and to increase the role of the central government which had been challenged by Ali Pasha and the Bushatis. For obvious reasons, including the unthinking conservatism which distrusts all reform, Northern Albania disliked most features of the Tanzimat with the North-East and Kosova rejecting the moves that favoured Christians.

The Tanzimat was a lost opportunity for the Ottoman Empire, which in the nineteenth century most people in the West began to see as a lost cause. Romantic poets like Shelley and Byron, trained in the Classics, viewed the Ottomans as oppressors of liberty in the first years of the century. Later, Gladstone, also trained in the Classics, fulminated against the savagery of Turkish oppression. In the middle of the century Britain, France and the fledgling republic of Italy were actually on Turkey's side in the Crimean War, but Florence Nightingale did her bit from Scutari to impress upon Western audiences the squalor of Ottoman rule, as did the other travellers who noted brigands in charge of the routes they tried to take. Squalor could be picturesque in the same way that brigands could turn into protectors of the peace, and the baffling contradictions of Balkan history were ill met by the certainty of Evangelical Christianity which saw all Turks as Muslims and all Muslims as heathens.

Albania came out badly in this particular equation, although oddly the Albanians with their crypto-Christianity and the wise tolerance of the Bektashi sect were not the right whipping boys for anti-Muslim propaganda. Nor were they the right nation to oust and throw off the Ottoman yoke.

Britain and France, although distracted by internal troubles, were generally on the side of nations trying to achieve independence from the Turks. Russia, a Slav empire, and the heir of Byzantium, was on the same side except in the Crimean War. Italy, resurgent after this war and subsequent campaigns against the Austro-Hungarian Empire, began to stake a claim to old Venetian territories. The Hapsburgs, ruling a multi-ethnic empire like the Ottomans, became the best defenders of Albanian interests. Links between Catholic Albania and Catholic Austria go back and forward a long way. The campaigns in the seventeenth and eighteenth century, the fairly friendly reception of Austrian and German troops in both world wars and even the recent rebuilding of Catholic churches in Northern Albania by Austrian charities are all a tribute to this link which, as the last example shows, is rather touching. Less touchingly, between 1815 and 1912 the main motive for Austrian support of Albania was Austrian fear of Slav nations like Serbia and Montenegro nibbling at the southern borders of its empire. Prussia, in the shape of Bismarck who refused to countenance the existence of an Albanian nation, was less sympathetic. In the nineteenth century there was an impressive array of Teutonic scholarship interested in south-eastern Europe, whereas Britain, though strong on Greece, lagged far behind. Disraeli, a good defender of Turkey's interests, wrote a short poetic novel in which he made Scanderbeg a Greek.

Disraeli and Bismarck clashed at the Congress of Berlin in 1878, an important date in Albanian history as it not only gave territory inhabited by Albanians to the Slav states, but it also marked the first gathering of Albanian national leaders at Prizren. Before this year there had been a degree of peace in the Albanian part of the Ottoman Empire and even a degree of progress. A railway line between Salonica and Mitrovica in Kosova was opened in 1872. There was unrest near Dibër owing to the suppression of the Bektashi order, but far worse trouble further east. In 1876 the Bulgarians revolted, Russia, aided sporadically by Serbia, declared war, and Gladstone thundered in the Midlothian Campaign that the Turkish bashibazouks should be driven bag and baggage across the Bosporus.

Albania had in a way been detached from these battles fought to the east and the south of Albanian territory. But there had been an intellectual revolution in the shape of a movement known as the Rilindjë or Reawakening. A small elite produced works in poetry and prose which assumed and asserted an Albanian identity. Sometimes these were written in Albanian, although this was difficult in the absence of a standard alphabet. Sometimes writers published in Albania, although this too was difficult especially in the North, where literacy was rare. The Arberesh community in southern Italy and the Albanian diaspora in places like Istanbul were principal agents in this movement, whose best representative from Northern Albania is Pashko Vasa, confusingly also known as Wassa Effendi, and Vasa Pasha Skodrani. The latter title shows his place of birth in 1825, while the second reveals the fact that he died in 1892 as an Ottoman official governing the Lebanon. In between Vasa served as a secretary to the British Consul in Shkodër, helped the cause of the Risorgimento in Italy, wrote in

French the first Albanian novel, and in 1879 published an account of Albanian history which was subsequently translated from the French into Albanian, Arabic, English, German and Greek. He was also author of a famous poem entitled 'Oh Albania, Poor Albania', first published by a Czech in 1881. This poem contains the remark, seized upon by Enver Hoxha, that the religion of Albania is Albanianism.

Vasa did not play much of a part in the League of Prizren. A more significant figure at this gathering was Abdyl Frashëri, one of the three brothers coming from the South with an equally poyglot range of publications. Abdyl made an impression at Prizren in spite of the fact that many delegates at this congress came from the deeply conservative tribes of Northern Albania, unprepared for the intellectual Albanianism preached by the Frashëri brothers. At Prizren there was a division between Catholic and Muslim leaders. Orthodoxy was not represented, although Prizren and its neighbourhood has some impressive monuments to this faith. But much of the feeling generated at Prizren was caused by the threat of Albanians being incorporated into Montenegro.

Further south, Prenk Bib Doda, the hereditary chief of the Mirditë clans, had led an unsuccessful revolt in 1877, hoping for the recognition of an independent Mirditë state. There were divisions of opinion at Prizren between those who wanted total independence and those who wanted to preserve their ancestral rights as an integral part of the Ottoman Empire. Many of the latter group had raised armies in their native villages, had fought battles on the Turkish side and were in a way model Ottoman citizens. Others campaigned for a compromise position. Some suggested that all Albanian provinces should be united in one *vilayet*, while others advocated that Albania should be granted the same autonomous status that other Balkan states had been given before achieving full independence.

In these discussions it was universally agreed that Albania should not form part of a Slav state. The Great Powers were on Albania's side on this point, but the treaty makers who met at San Stefano near Istanbul to carve up the Ottoman possessions in the

Balkans were not very good at geography. At San Stefano Bulgaria had been awarded all of Macedonia and a small part of eastern Albania, where the presence of a few Slav-speakers in Gollobordë gave some credence to their claim. San Stefano, however, left many more Albanians near Gostivar in Bulgarian territory. All this ground was lost by Bulgaria at Berlin, but the congress here threatened to give to Montenegro certain tribal areas such as Hoti, Gruda, Guci, Plava - the repeated line in Fishta's poem. The treaty makers eventually agreed to leave all these areas in Turkey in exchange for Ulcinj, an almost entirely Albanian town which has never been part of Albania except, briefly, during the Second World War (see Appendix V).

Likewise, rather sadly, the Hoti and Gruda areas near Tuzli became part of Montenegro after 1912, while Plavë and Gusinjë in Kosova were awarded to Serbia. These changes of frontier came long after the clarion call of the League of Prizren, which had controlled Kosova and Northern Albania for about three years until the Empire struck back, sending a large and disciplined army which routed the ramshackle forces raised by the League against them. Abdyl Frashëri was captured and sentenced to death, though this sentence was commuted to exile. His brothers and other members of the Rilindjë movement continued to agitate for the recognition of the Albanian language and educational rights, but in many ways the League of Prizren seems to have proved to be something of a damp squib.

In the next twenty years the main trouble spot in the Balkans was Macedonia, contested between Greece, Bulgaria and Serbia. Albanians lived in the disputed area as they live today, but they do not seem to have had much of a role in the liberation struggle. They were minor players like the Vlachs and some Turkish-speakers, sometimes appearing on the Ottoman side, sometimes the victims of marauding bands who found it difficult to distinguish between patriotism and banditry. Kemal Ataturk, the future leader of Turkey, was born in Salonica, probably partly of Albanian stock like Mother Teresa, born in Skopje. Albania itself, though not free of violence, was a relatively tranquil place in comparison to Macedonia.

Edith Durham's *High Albania* describing journeys starting from Shkodër in March 1908 has much less about war and its aftermath than her previous book, *The Burden of the Balkans*, which dealt with travels in Macedonia and Southern Albania in 1904. By the time of the later book she had become committed to the Albanian cause, and was therefore delighted to report in August 1908 that the constitution officially granted in 1876, but quietly shelved, had been restored, that Prenk Bib Doda was returning and that Albania was rejoicing, But by the end of the year and the end of the book, joy had turned to disillusion. The Young Turk movement which had taken power in August had not lived up to its promises. They had not produced more efficient or more democratic government, but a more centralised and more Ottoman regime which did not please the independent Albanians.

When with difficulty the Albanians agreed upon alternative alphabets, the Young Turks insisted that they used the Arabic script. There were elections, and future leaders like Esad Pasha and Qemal Bey Vlora joined the parliament in Istanbul. By this time the Empire was on its last legs. In 1911 the Turks lost Libya to Italy and there was a revolt in the Northern Highlands of Albania, supposedly instigated by Prince Nicholas of Montenegro. The revolt spread to Kosova and an Albanian force marched on Skopje in August 1912. The Ottoman authorities made considerable concessions to the Albanians at this point, but unfortunately Albanian success prompted other Balkan nations to attack Turkey in October. The Serbs and Montenigrins had occupied most of Northern Albania by the time Qemal Bey Vlora declared Albanian independence in his native town on 28 November.

There is much more about war in Durham's next book, *The Struggle for Scutari*, Shkodër being one of the few places to hold out against the Slav invasions, although it fell by treachery in 1913. The events of the last years of Ottoman rule have all the crazy logic of the blood feud. Montenegro had encouraged the Albanians to revolt against the Turks; they had done so successfully, thus encouraging the Montenegrins and the Serbs to revolt in their turn, invading Albanian territory in the process, thus persuading the Albanians to take up arms with the Turks to defend themselves against the invaders. Fishta's high-minded epic reveals rather than conceals these sudden and surprising changes of tack, although the main part of *The Highland Lute* is concerned with the campaigns of 1878 and 1879 when the Albanians were fighting not only the Montenegrins but the Ottomans who were trying to hand over Albanian lands to Montenegro. The events of 1912 were not a happy omen for independence and provide a sad combination of bangs and whimpers to mark the end of nearly five centuries of Ottoman rule.

It is difficult to sum up these centuries. Graceful mosques in Tirana and Shkodër are reminders that the Ottomans were not entirely philistines, although Hoxha's campaign against religion did much damage to such monuments. He also cleared away some of the picturesque but squalid alleyways, a less salubrious souvenir of Turkish rule. Oddly enough it is at Ulcinj, almost never part of Albania, and for quite a lot of the Ottoman period ruled independently by pirates, that, in the delicate white houses rising steeply above the ravines around which the town is built, one can see the best of Ottoman Albania which the Turkish traveller Evliya Celebi so much admired in the seventeenth century. Thanks to Edward Said we are now on our guard against Orientalism, a disparaging and condescending attitude to Eastern ways. We are also on our guard against a blind belief in progress. The fact that so little changed in these five centuries and that we can use Durham's picturesque, if not wholly accurate, picture of the northern tribes to work out what happened in the seventeenth century can now be taken as a sign of the strength of traditional values rather than cultural stagnation.

Of course, one of the traditional values of the tribesmen was fighting, and Albanian society in the Ottoman period does seem a fractured one. Indeed, as the years after 1912 show, Albania was rarely united, the problem exacerbated by the presence of large numbers of Albanian-speakers in other states. We are also on our guard, thanks to Todorova, against seeing the Balkans in a bad light as a series of squabbling tribes left in an uncivilised condition by the heedless Turk, and then splitting and resplitting into different fragments as indeed has happened more recently in what was Yugoslavia. In Albanian the word Balkan has no pejorative meaning, but twentieth-century Albania with its revolutions and counter-revolutions, assassinations and civil wars does seem at times the quintessential Balkan country in the bad sense of the word, and this too can be blamed on the Turks who apart from rousing Scanderbeg to fight against them did little to promote Albanian unity.

However it is Scanderbeg's statue rather than Ethem Bey's mosque which dominates the central square of Tirana, which was a sleepy provincial town in Turkish times. Much has changed since 1912.

8. INDEPENDENT ALBANIA, 1912-1992

Accounts of Albania between 1912 and the present day are largely dominated by two men, King Zog and Enver Hoxha. This is unfortunate for a number of reasons. We can begin with the trivial matter of names. Unused to x's and z's English-speakers find both Zog and Hoxha irredeemably comic. They should not do so. Zog, originally Zogu, is the Albanian for bird, while Hoxha, pronounced to rhyme with dodger, and sometimes so rhymed, is a Muslim priest. We do not find either Priest or Bird comic as surnames, and the history of both men covers situations that were far from comic. Indeed, this is a second source of worry. Both rulers were the subject of extravagant adulation when they were in power, and extreme vilification when they or their party had lost power. We have noted the difficulties encountered by the Historical Museum in Tirana when its curators had to describe the history of Albania after both world wars. King Zog still does not get a mention in this museum except for one idealised portrait of someone looking like Enver Hoxha denouncing Zog and fascism in a protest march. For a time, during reconstruction, this was the only mention of Hoxha too.

Faced with such contradictory judgements or with a silence that refuses to take sides, modern historians have found it difficult to give an objective verdict on either figure, although on the whole verdicts have been hostile. The ruthless suppression of political rivals either by assassination or state trials was commonplace under Hoxha, or even as in the case of Mehmet Shehu, Hoxha's former right-hand man, a supposed suicide is noted. Zog did not imprison people in concentration camps, but he did less than Hoxha in improving basic communications, a process that went into reverse with the collapse of communism. Both men made strenuous efforts to drag Albania from medieval barbarism by trying to suppress the blood feud, improve education and improve the lot of women, although even today in the average Albanian household it seems to be the women who do most of the work in spite of Zog dressing his sisters in Western fashions and Hoxha and his wife writing earnest pamphlets on female emancipation. Zog began and Hoxha completed, admittedly with forced labour working in appalling conditions, the drainage of malarial swamps along the coast and inland at Lake Maliq. It was in Zog's reign that Albania began to develop the beginnings of a transport system with some major roads built under Italian tutelage. In Hoxha's time tourists in carefully guarded buses used to bowl along these roads and were asked to admire the drained and terraced landscape as well as a few carefully selected housing estates near important industrial plants. Hoxha also built a rudimentary rail system. Rather sadly, things went downhill in many respects after the collapse of communism, and it is perhaps timely to remember that Zog and Hoxha, in spite of despicable crimes and cruelty, did achieve some advances for the average Albanian, in whose cause they probably believed their sins might be forgiven.

History, as we are constantly reminded, is more than the story of great men, and in any case Zog and Hoxha, clearly flawed rulers, were not the only people to strut the Albanian stage. In the years after 28 November 1912, when Qemal Bey Vlora declared Albanian independence, raising Scanderbeg's flag on what has become a day of celebration for all Albanians, Albania suffered many rulers and endured considerable misrule. This anarchy did not really subside until Zog, who had played a part in events during the intervening years, finally took control on 24 December 1924, known as Legalitet Day, acknowledged still by the decreasing number of people in Albania who hope for the return of the Zog dynasty to rule their battered land. Until the 1990s there were also in Albania and further afield people who still pined for the rule of Enver Hoxha, whose name used to be written in stones on every mountain, and who ruled a land where apparently there was no inequality, pollution or distortion of truth. Hoxha's thousands of bunkers, now a tourist attraction, are not an advertisement for this version of history. Foreign relations between Albania and other countries were probably the main reason why Zog and Hoxha should be written down as failures in the great historical examination. Zog finally came to power in 1924 with Yugoslav help, thus abandoning any claims to Kosova. In between 1924 and 1939, though endearingly retaining trust in a British-run police force, he became increasingly dependent on Italian help to finance his bankrupt kingdom. All ended in tears when the Italians invaded in 1939, although the impressive public buildings around Scanderbeg Square are some tribute to this period of Albanian history. Hoxha's architectural legacy is less impressive. He too was first dependent on Yugoslavia, then on Russia, then on China, and then on nobody.

The result was a crumbling legacy of useless industrial plants and decaying urban housing. Because Hoxha came from the South, it was Northern Albania which particularly suffered after the Second World War. The climate here is hardly suited to the agricultural improvements which could be made along the southern coast. Even in the 1920s there were reports of starvation in the North, where conditions deteriorated further after the Second World War. So much for the common people for whom Zog and Hoxha thought they strove.

Even so, they were arguably better qualified to take this role rather than other potential leaders. In 1912, when Hoxha was still an infant and Zog a precocious seventeen-year-old, those in charge of Albania's destiny seemed to have other disadvantages. Qemal Bey Vlora, the man who raised the flag, was a southern aristocrat who had been the Turkish Governor of Libya. He came from Vienna, with Austro-Hungarian support. In January 1914 he resigned the presidency of the Provisional Government after William of Wied had been appointed king, and left for France. During 1913 Serb and Montenegrin troops had occupied most of Northern Albania, Esad Pasha had set up a rival administration, and the constitution and boundaries of the new state were in the hands of the London Conference of Ambassadors. So it was hardly a glorious presidency, although Qemal Bey seems always to have acted honourably. He returned briefly in July to take up the post of foreign minister before the government totally collapsed with the outbreak of war and the departure of King William. Qemal Bey died in Perugia on 26 January 1919.

William of Wied occupies an even less glorious role in Albanian history. A Protestant from a minor royal family in Germany, he was unlikely to appeal much to the ordinary Albanian. His appointment was announced by the Great Powers on 23 November 1913, and immediately accepted by Qemal Bey on behalf of the Albanian government. This was already in some disarray because Esad Pasha, who wanted to rule himself, had set up an alternative government. William did not hurry to grasp his crown or this particular nettle. Instead he made a leisurely tour of European capitals, having lunch with King George and Queen Mary in London ôn 18 February 1914. No European power did much to help William. His greatest ally was his eccentric aunt Queen Sylvia of Romania, and some Romanian troops did arrive in Albania after the murder of Archduke Ferdinand had left the Great Powers hopelessly divided. On 21 February 1914, William was formally offered the Albanian crown in his ancestral castle at Neuwied by a delegation led improbably by Esad Pasha. Visits to Berlin and St Petersburg followed before the new king arrived in Durrës on 2 March. He must have been a little tired. Before his arrival an insurrection had broken out in southern Albania, and in May Esad, the minister for the interior and for war, had been expelled to Italy. This led to a different revolt against the newly-appointed king who now found himself blockaded in Durrës. A motley force of Dutch policemen, German volunteers and the gallant British Colonel Phillips commanding an international force at Shkodër did their best to defend William. Albanians were rather less eager. Prenk Bib Doda, chief of the Catholic Mirdités, promised help, but it was slow in coming, and he was suspected of making common cause with the insurgents. Ahmet Zogu led an army towards Tirana, but made no attempt to engage the rebels and retreated in July to Kruja. In the same month William left Durrës briefly for Vlorë. This was seen as a sign of weakness, and though he returned to Durrës he rapidly became overwhelmed by the hopelessness of his position and on 3 September he set sail for Venice en route for Germany. He left a pathetic note for the Albanian people and equally pathetically handed over Albania to the rule of the Great Powers, who were already at war with each other.

Not surprisingly, the Great Powers were not able to do much for Albania in the first year of the war. Two years after Qemal Bey had raised the flag the country he had declared independent was under eight different kinds of ruler, more if the northern tribes in some loose confederacy of chieftains around Shkodër were counted as separate rulers. Further south, Mirditë under Prenk Bib Doda formed a distinct entity, as did Mat under Zogu who declared himself loyal to William of Wied. Esad Pasha had returned with Serbian help, declaring himself ruler of Albania, but only in control of the area around Durrës. He claimed to be on the side of the Allies. Further north around Kruja a peasant rising against landowners had turned into a revolt against Esad, and the short-lived Union of Kruja wanted a return to rule by the Ottomans. There were also Greek, Serbian and Montenegrin troops in the country. With so many rulers changing so rapidly, anarchy and brigandage flourished, as regrettably it did at various other points in the twentieth century.

The year 1915 brought about more changes. The Treaty of London, signed in April, brought Italy into the war on the Allied side. It was and is still rightly denounced by all sides in Albania, as it carved up the country without any reference to the wishes of its inhabitants, although it could be argued that these inhabitants had already carved up the country among themselves. The treaty envisaged a small rump independent Muslim state in the centre, and gave the rest of the country to Serbia and Montenegro in the North, Greece and Italy in the South. Italy, which had also been promised gains in Dalmatia, wanted a protectorate over the small Albanian state, but entered the war in any case, having already occupied its potential gains. Serbia and Montenegro, in the war from the start, now tried to claim their spoils. Troops from these countries invaded Northern Albania, propped up

Esad, sent the ephemeral Union of Kruja packing, but did not interfere with Zogu. Slav dominance did not last long. Defeated in Serbia by the Austrians and Bulgarians, the Serbian Army began to retreat across the Northern Albanian mountains in November, losing vast numbers of men to cold and starvation. This march, commemorated in a moving exhibition in Corfu where the shattered army eventually arrived, did not improve Serb-Albanian relations. There were attacks by Albanians on the retreating army, prompted in part by Austrian agents, in part by self-defence in an area where food was always in short supply.

By the end of January 1916 an Austrian army was in full occupation of Northern Albania. The Bulgarians had invaded from the east and had taken Elbasan. Esad Pasha was still in Durrës, protected by the Italians, but had been repulsed by Zogu when he tried to invade Mat. An impressive list of Albanian statesmen welcomed the Austrian invasion. They included Prenk Bib Doda, Aqif Pasha Elbasan, who had been minister of the interior in 1914, and Luigj Gurakuqi, a left-wing Catholic intellectual. Zogu joined this group, marched against Elbasan and Durrës, from which Esad was forced to flee, and tried to set up a government still loyal to William of Wied, friendly to the Austro-Hungarian cause but not forgoing neutrality. The Austrians thought otherwise, and this attempt by Zogu to seize the initiative was not a great success. At the end of the year he went to Vienna as part of an Albanian delegation, was given an Austrian decoration, but was asked to remain in Austria. By this time the French had arrived to replace the Greeks in south-eastern Albania, and for the rest of the war the country was divided between Austrian, French and Italian rule.

All three states professed respect for Albanian independence, and the Austrians and French had no wish to gain Albanian territory unlike the Serbs and Greeks whom they had replaced. Italy did have such aspirations and was the least popular of the occupying powers. Austria ruled the North fairly well, winning support by introducing Albanian schools in Kosova, by now under the same government as Northern Albania where the tribes were allowed their traditional independence.

We hear little of native Albanians in the second half of the war. Esad Pasha went with the Italians from Durrës, taken by the Austrians, to Salonica, where he ingratiated himself with the French, but he had little but his self-esteem to recommend him to any power. A sinister figure with a penchant for smart uniforms, Esad turns up at various stages in this early unhappy period of Albanian independence, claiming that he was the ruler of the country, and almost by his effrontery persuading foreign powers that he was so. In betraying Shkodër to the Montenegrins he made it clear that he would gladly sacrifice his country's interests to preserve his own. The same charge was to be levelled, less justly, against King Zog, and in saying that the two men were related when they weren't, historians have helped to blacken Zog's name.

In the latter half of 1918 French and Italian forces advanced through Albania. Elbasan was reached by the Italians on 7 October, Durrës on the 14th and Dibër taken by the French on the 15th. With the French were marching the Serbs whose army had been transferred from Corfu to Salonica. It was the Serbs who entered Shkodër first. The French general Franchet d'Espèrey made them withdraw, but allowed them to occupy a large section of North-Eastern Albania with the Drin as a rough boundary. Most of the country at the end of the war was occupied by the Italians with the Greeks and French in the South. Shkodër was held by an international garrison. On Christmas Day there was a conference of Albanian delegates at Durrës which elected a provisional government with Turhan Pasha, prime minister under King William, holding the same post. Prenk Bib Doda was appointed as his deputy. In the cabinet there were also Mehdi and Midhat Frashëri, inheritors of a famous name, from the South, and Gurakuqi from the North. The government was supposed to be representative of all districts and religions, but meeting under Italian tutelage it never achieved much authority. Prenk Bib Doda was assassinated in March 1919 as a result of a blood feud, and Turhan Pasha after presenting plans for a vastly enlarged Albania to the Paris Peace Conference virtually signed away all the powers of his government to an Italian high commissioner.

1920 was a better year for Albanian independence. The Americans expressed hostility to a revised form of the Treaty of London partitioning the country and allowing the Italians mandatory rights. Albanian nationalists organised a conference at Lushnjë in January and elected a different government. Conferences play an important part in Albanian history, and this was an important one. Zogu, with armed bands from Mat supporting him and boasting some achievements in the past, was a prominent figure at the conference and at the age of twenty-four was made minister of the interior and commander in chief of the army. There were four regents to replace the absent sovereign, and Tirana was proclaimed to be the new capital. In February the provisional government resigned. The Allied forces moved out of Shkodër. Esad Pasha, suitably clad, was still claiming to be a representative of Albania in Paris, and his agents were still creating trouble in central Albania, helped by the Yugoslavs to whom he was prepared to concede the North. His followers were less smartly dressed, and their cause collapsed in June when Esad was assassinated in Paris. In August the Italians were forced to withdraw from Vlorë. They avoided complete humiliation, but their departure, hastened by socialist agitation among their troops, contributed to the later policy of a fascist Italy determined on revenge.

The Italian exodus was followed by a massive Yugoslav invasion. Almost all of Northern Albania apart from Shkodër and parts of Mat fell into their hands. Under international pressure they withdrew in November to the D'Esperey Line along the Drin. A general election was held and a new government dominated by rich landowners took power. Zogu had no place in it. Albania was admitted to the League of Nations, where it was represented by a new character in Albanian history, Fan Noli, the Orthodox Bishop of Durrës.

Noli came originally from an Albanian village on the Bulgarian-Turkish border. He had travelled via a Greek school in Egypt to America where he had organised his own enthronement as bishop. He was more democratically inclined than most Albanian leaders and therefore received moderate respect from communist historians in spite of his religious status. This status was a little irregular, as it took some time for the patriarchate in Constantinople to recognise Albanian bishops, but Noli could be seen as a representative of the Orthodox South. In the Punch and Judy world of Albanian politics it is not difficult to cast him as the first in a line of left-wing southern leaders pitted against reactionary northerners, but this analysis is a little crude. Noli lived most of his life away from Albania, and could hardly claim to be a typical Albanian. The anecdote of the English cricketer C.B. Fry being offered the throne of Albania by a diminutive W.G. Grace - though it gives a fair description of Noli's impressive bearded appearance - scarcely makes him a very serious figure, although his literary achievements, as for instance his translation of Shakespeare, make him a sympathetic one. He worked tirelessly for Albania's interests at the League of Nations, and the eventual boundary settlement, long protracted, was not too unfavourable, although it left many Albanian-speakers in other countries.

Unfortunately for Albania, in the years between 1920 and 1924, a year in which Zogu was succeeded by Noli only to be replaced by Zogu in an armed coup, the country did not prosper. This did not help the boundary settlement. The condition of the population was poor. The departure of troops from the Great Powers had led to a decrease in foreign food supplies. Yugoslavia still occupied a swathe of territory in the North and East, periodically destroying villages. There was little help coming from this quarter. In central Albania much of the countryside was held by rich landowners in plantation-like *ciftliks* which offered no hope of prosperity for the peasants who worked them. In the tribal North, which foreign visitors occasionally reported as charming, there was still the blood feud and primitive poverty, exacerbated by war and politics. It was the rich landowners rather than the tribal chiefs who tended to dominate early governments. Rather ironically they were known as the Progressive Party.

There were six different governments during 1921, one only

lasting twenty-four hours. The Yugoslavs were a constant menace, aided by Marko Gjoni, the cousin and successor of Prenk Bib Doda, who declared an independent Mirditë republic. At the beginning of December 1921 the prime minister was Hasan Bey Prishtina and Luigj Gurakuqi was minister of the interior. Bajram Curri was commander in chief, replacing Zogu. All these men were northerners and, breaking the mould, vaguely left-wing. All three met untimely ends. This government in which Fan Noli was foreign minister did not last long. Zog, accompanied by the tribesmen of Mat and Mirditë, the latter won over from the leadership of Marko Gjoni, arrived in Tirana, and on 20 December a new set of regents and a new government, in which Zogu was minister of the interior, took over.

Hasan Bey Prishtina and Bajram Curri led an armed revolt in February 1922. They hoped to regain Kosova. Another northerner from Dibër, Elez Jusuf, marched on Tirana, but thanks to the offices of Harry Eyres, the British Ambassador, Zogu succeeded in winning over Jusuf and Bajram Curri, thus quelling the insurrection. Fan Noli resigned as foreign minister and together with Luigj Gurakuqi campaigned for a programme which would give less power and less land to the great magnates. On 2 December Zogu became prime minister and announced a list of reforms. He promised more foreign investment and discouraged irredentism against Yugoslavia and Greece. The boundary commission had started work during this year, and its work must be seen against this background of division and unrest.

Another revolt was started in January 1923 by Hasan Bey Prishtina and Bajram Curri, but this quickly fizzled out. The frontier commission worked slowly, handicapped by the murder of the Italian representative. Refugees from Yugoslavia added to the problems of the frontier region, where the harvest had twice failed. A League of Nations adviser, rather oddly and sadly called Hunger, suggested a range of administrative and financial reforms. Zogu's authoritarian style aroused opposition, but he had the support of the big landowners of central Albania and the leaders of the northern tribes. In this year, as in 1922, there was only one revolt, although there were conspiracies to assassinate Zogu.

There were yet more conspiracies and revolts in 1924, an eventful year. Elections in January were inconclusive. Zogu retained office, but wounded in an assassination attempt by Beqir Walter, a member of a socialist group, he resigned on 28 February. His place was taken by Shefqet Verlaci, a prominent landowner who was Zogu's prospective father-in-law. In April Avni Rustemi, a supporter of Fan Noli and the assassin in Paris of Esad Pasha, was shot outside the buildings of parliament, of which he was a member. (In France Rustemi had been fined one franc for the murder of Esad, but his own murder did not do much good for the cause of Albania's reputation among parliamentary democracies or for parliamentary democracy in Albania.) Noli's supporters walked out of parliament and demanded that Zogu should leave the country. Verlaci resigned in May, and he and his successor fled to Italy. Zogu escaped to Yugoslavia and three of the regents resigned. The Orthodox regent invited Noli to become prime minister on 10 June.

Noli promised a genuinely progressive slate of reforms, checking feudal despotism and introducing the rule of democratic law. Unfortunately he alienated the rich by proposing reforms and the poor by his failure to achieve them, as rather disarmingly he admitted. Gurakuqi was an able finance minister, but neither he nor Noli won any foreign help, tainted by being thought far too left-wing. Various communist parties and the Soviet Union lent moral but not financial support. Zogu had ingratiated himself with the Yugoslav government. His brother-in-law Cena Kryeziu was a prominent Kosovar. The Anglo-Persian Oil Company was prepared to give him financial support in return for future concessions. He hired some White Russian mercenaries based in Belgrade. Yugoslavia, acting covertly, lent troops as well as support by opening the frontier at Dibër on 13 December and then quickly closing it again. Another army advanced from Montenegro. The pro-Zogu forces converged in Mat where they were joined by the northern tribesmen. Some resistance was encountered near

Tirana, but Fan Noli fled to Durrës on 23 December, arriving via Vlorë in Italy. Zogu reached Tirana on Christmas Eve, and we now embark on a period of his absolute rule which lasted until the Italian invasion on Good Friday, 7 April 1939.

King of the Albanians

Ahmet Zogu became prime minister on 5 January 1925; president on 31 January; and king on 1 September 1928. He took the name of Zog on the latter occasion. He also took the title of King of the Albanians, a more provocative name, designed to upset the Yugoslavs who had helped to bring him to power, since there were so many Albanian citizens of Yugoslavia. Zog's knack of being in the right place at the right time had brought him to power. It deserted him after he prematurely left Albania for Greece following the Italian invasion, and then, financed by gold from the Albanian treasury, passed in a circuitous route from Paris to London's Ritz Hotel, to Lord Parmoor's house in Buckinghamshire and then to King Farouk's Egypt and finally the South of France - showing an uncanny knack for choosing regimes as doomed as his own. Romania, Poland, Latvia, Norway and Belgium before the Second World War seem rather unlike the Great Powers visited by William of Wied before the First. In his period of absolute power Zog seems neither the brilliant opportunist of the early years nor the doomed failure of the protracted decline. Assassination and aid seem key factors in the middle years, which have been well chronicled and will therefore receive summary treatment.

Various attempts were made on Zog's life after this episode in 1924. In 1928 there were plans to kill him in Durrës and in Korcë. In 1931 Zog went to Vienna for medical reasons, and was attacked at the opera. Some alleged that his poor health was due to poisoning. A visit to Italy in 1938 was cancelled through fear of assassination or abduction. On the other side, various opponents of Zog like Luigj Gurakuqi in 1925, Ceno Kryeziu in 1927, Gjon Marko Gjoni in 1932 and Hasan Prishtina in 1933 were murdered, and some accused Zog of being responsible. Bajram Curri was more openly hunted down in the Valbona valley during

1925. All these victims came from the North, and it is - and was - a mistake to think of Northern Albania as a stronghold of Zog supporters.

Zog soon abandoned Yugoslavia for Italy as his main protector. Italian money paid for improved roads and the impressive government buildings in central Tirana. Italian advisers arrived to help in civil and military projects, although for a time Zog retained a police force under English control, described by him in 1934 as splendid fellows. The Italians were not popular in Albania, and some support was forfeited in Albania by Zog's reliance on them. Attempts to improve the lot of the average Albanian by splitting up the large estates were not very successful as there was not enough money to implement this reform properly. It did upset some landowners like Shefqet Bey Verlaci, whose daughter Zog did not marry, preferring after a few other dalliances to marry in 1938 Geraldine Apponyi, the daughter of a Hungarian Catholic count and an American mother. Neither Hungary nor America were of much use to Zog in his hour of need when Italy invaded two days after Geraldine had given birth to a son on 5 April 1939.

Zog was a Muslim. His marriage required papal dispensation. He did make some efforts to win over the northern Catholics who revolted briefly in 1926 and were savagely repressed. He became reconciled with the Mirditë chiefs and in 1928 received the standard bearers of all the northern tribes who pledged their loyalty to him. On the other hand, Muslims were made uneasy by liberal reforms, forbidding women to wear the veil, although it was mainly in the South that such reforms led to open rebellion in 1937. The loyal pledge of 1928 followed a winter of famine in the North. In 1935 there was a minor revolt in the North led by Muharrem Bajraktari from Ljumë, followed by a much more serious insurrection around Fier.

Zog had regained power in 1924 through Yugoslav help. This help ensured that the final settlement of the frontier in 1926 was not opposed. Hasan Prishtina and Bajram Curri as well as holding left-wing views were also Kosovar irredentists, and were suppressed for both reasons. The Kryeziu family, based in Kosova, were related to Zog but also his enemies. Belatedly in the 1930s Zog tried to patch up relations with his northern neighbour. Albania did not join the Balkan Pact in 1934, but Yugoslavia supported her attempts to do so. Efforts were made to make cross-border communications easier, and the economic position of Northern Albania improved in the latter half of Zog's reign. Nevertheless he had incurred enmity in the North, as well as the South from which most members of the infant Communist Party sprang. But Ali Kelmendi, the party's most prominent member, was a northerner, as was Koçi Xoxe, who came from the Goran community in North-East Albania.

Zog was clearly an opportunist. Eventually his luck ran out when the Italians invaded. Resistance was feeble apart from a brave effort by Abas Kupi at Durrës. Zog fled almost immediately, thus ensuring perpetual exile, and a rather dubious place in Albanian history. In his youth he had been admired in various quarters. Rose Lane Wilder in her gushing way praised his masculine vigour, and presents a reasonably attractive picture of Northern Albanian society, as do the Gordons. Colonel Giles, the brusque English officer in charge of the frontier negotiations, is less complimentary about living conditions, but calls Zog a triton among minnows. Colonel Oakley-Hill in his artless account of Albania before the Second World War praises Zog's optimism and the stability he brought to Albania, which he too presents in fairly rosy terms. The colonel with typical candour says that there were only three revolts between 1924 and 1938, and that one of them was the work of 'intellectual progressivists', a nice old fashioned term of abuse. Actually there were four revolts when Zog was in total control and two when he was either prime minister or minister of the interior.

It is hard to keep a proper balance between Zog and Hoxha in writing about Albanian history before and after the Second World War. It is therefore doubly difficult to write an objective account of Albanian history during this war. In earlier chapters we were faced with too little material supplied by sources who had little experience of the country. In the few years of the war we have plenty of first-hand information, but this information does not tell the same story. Five British officers who aided the Albanian resistance published books on the subject. They form a distinguished team, but neither in the war nor after it were they on the same side. Brigadier 'Trotsky' Davies and Sir Reginald Hibbert are in the red corner, associated with the communist Partisans in the South. In spite of his sobriquet Davies was no socialist firebrand, merely a mildly radical army officer with a decisive manner, and Sir Reginald, a lieutenant in the Albanian campaign, became a pillar of the establishment, ending his career as ambassador in Paris. In the blue corner there is the equally respectable but obviously conservative Julian Amery, Peter Kemp who had fought in the Spanish Civil War on Franco's side and David Smiley, who organised resistance against the communists after the war was over. These three officers had more contact and sympathy with non-communist forces like Abas Kupi in the North. It is unfortunate that such gallant senior figures as Colonel Arthur Nicholls and Major Philip Leake, a good Anglo-Albanian name, left no memoirs, only two rather moving graves in Albania.

Historians have to come off the fence, and we have to support Davies and Hibbert. Resistance in the North was not particularly impressive. One organisation, Legalitet, supported King Zog; another, the Balli Kombëtar, opposed him but hoped for the annexation of Kosova which the Germans and Italians had largely restored to Albania. As in Yugoslavia right-wing forces were keen to preserve the status quo, and violent resistance against the occupying power did little to ensure stability. In the South and in the cities there were more intellectuals and oppressed peasants who had little to lose by revolution, whereas in the North there was more deference to tribal leaders and respect for old fashioned customs. In the South resistance was well organised, although the nationalist Balli Kombëtar threatened the stranglehold of the communists. The North had always been more divided with the difference between Muslims and Catholics complicating friction between supporters of Zog and his opponents.

Muharrem Bajraktari of Ljumë was one of the more vigorous

leaders of the non-communist resistance, but he had quarrelled with Zog. Abas Kupi, once an opponent of Zog, had valiantly fought for him in 1939, but though the British trusted him he produced little concrete support against the Germans. Amery's praise of Kupi and Kemp's enthusiasm for Bajraktari are at times persuasive, but at times both writers seem to have ignored the Balkan habit of telling gullible foreigners what they wanted to hear rather than the truth.

All British authorities in the war appear oddly gullible. We begin with the unfortunate episode of Colonel Oakley-Hill and a small band from Kosova led by the Kryeziu brothers tramping across the northern Albanian mountains, which he had visited before. This time their reception was less hospitable. It was regrettable that they were accompanied by some regular Yugoslav troops, not likely to win over support, especially as Hitler had just invaded Yugoslavia. An unpopular ally was bad enough, a defeated ally even worse.

An earlier sortie might have caused difficulties for the Italians who in early 1941 were hard pressed by the Greeks in southern Albania. But the Greek successes were another cause of embarrassment for Britain, as by supporting this gallant ally they often appeared to be neglecting Albanians interests. Zog found himself cold shouldered by the Foreign Office. He never received the same treatment as King Peter of Yugoslavia or King George of Greece, two monarchs ruling over divided countries who though defeated had definitely joined the Allied side. Those involved in coordinating Albanian resistance were an interesting collection of people, but neither Colonel Stirling, former commander of the Albanian gendarmerie, nor Mrs Hasluck was all that knowledgeable about the average Albanian. Mrs Hasluck knew a great deal about modern Albania, and her presence there during the years between the wars is testimony to the stability of Zog's reign. But just as she was wrong in making light of the communist prospects in Yugoslavia, so in Albania the communists were not taken seriously in sufficient time. By the time Special Operations Executive soldiers began arriving in the North the Germans had replaced the Italians, establishing a government that was both more efficient and more popular. The Partisans were in control of resistance in the South, and northern resistance leaders who opposed the occupation opposed the Partisans even more bitterly.

Bravely the British tried to bring the two sides together. In September 1942 a conference at Pezë, though dominated by the Partisans, had included Abas Kupi and Muharrem Bajraktari. They had set up the National Liberation Front or LNG. In August 1943 there was a meeting at Mukjë between the Balli Kombëtar and the LNG with Kupi in the latter group. A decision by the conference to reclaim Kosova was unpopular with the Partisans, and a second conference at Labinot in September denounced the Mukjë agreement. The Italian surrender on 5 September was followed by a sharp deterioration in the cooperation of Albanians with each other and the British. Kupi resigned from the LNG and there were attacks by the Germans on Partisan positions. New arrivals by parachute at Bizë found it difficult to know who their friends and enemies were. Even under pressure and perhaps because of it the Partisans seemed hostile to the Germans, while in the North there was hostility to the Partisans and a good deal of sitting on the fence. The Germans saw their opportunity and appointed four regents, three of them from the North. One was Lef Nosi from Elbasan, a very close friend of Mrs Hasluck. Davies was betrayed to the Germans at Kostenje near Bulqizë in central Albania. In the east officers like Kemp and Hare nearly succeeded in persuading local chieftains like Fiqri Dine to join their side, but he later became prime minister in a collaborationist government. Further north the British had achieved some results from a base in Tropojë with the help of Muharrem Bajraktari and the Kryeziu brothers, non-communists hostile to the Germans. They had also been hostile to Zog and were thus not natural allies of Abas Kupi and the population of Mat. The Catholic tribes of the North-West and Mirditë saw no reason to endanger their traditional autonomy, which they were shortly to lose to the Partisans.

By the summer of 1944 the pattern was clear. It was the

communists against the rest, and the communists were winning. They had the support of the British and of Tito in Yugoslavia. Against them were the embattled Germans with varying degrees of cooperation from the puppet government in Tirana, the Legalitet movement of Abas Kupi and the Balli Kombëtar. These three forces were divided on a range of issues, including how much help to give to the British. In April Fiqri Dine, Abas Kupi and the Balli Kombëtar agreed to make a move against the Germans and on 5 September there was an unsuccessful encounter with German troops at the village of Kurat. Two days later the Partisans stormed Kruja and burnt Kupi's house. In October officers like Amery who had supported non-communist forces escaped to Italy as did some of the Balli Kombëtar leaders. Abas Kupi followed with difficulty. Tirana fell on 17 November and Hoxha arrived in triumph as the acknowledged leader on the thirty-second anniversary of Albanian independence. Shkodër was captured the next day in slightly sinister circumstances with many alleged collaborators arrested.

THE NORTH UNDER HOXHA

This last sentence sets the tone for a brief account of the unhappy history of Northern Albania during the communist era. Only a purblind admirer of Hoxha would maintain that any part of Albania prospered during these years, of which his concrete bunkers erected at vast expense are a symbol, both tragic and farcical. There are reasons why the North suffered particularly badly. Most of Hoxha's government were southerners, notable exceptions being Koçi Xoxe, who was purged in 1948, and Ramiz Alia who succeeded Hoxha in 1985. Albania was governed by a closely knit *fis*, but it was not a northern *fis*. It is not surprising and indeed quite sensible - although also symptomatic of prejudice against the North - that Tosk rather than Gheg became the basis for the standard language imposed in 1972. Religion was banned in 1969, as it was argued - again not unreasonably - that it was a cause of division, but Catholic priests before this had been more vulnerable to persecution than their Orthodox or Muslim counterparts, being more obviously linked to Italy, Germany and the Western powers. Most of the North had been at best lukewarm in the resistance, and accusations of collaboration were easy to make. In addition, the feudal structure of the northern tribes with its apparatus of hereditary chiefs and standard bearers was clearly anathema to the communists and was ruthlessly broken up. The feudal system was, of course, antiquated and unfair, although not as unpleasant as the blood feud, but in abolishing these relics of the past those responsible for the new order may have taken the opportunity to pay off a few old scores, revenge being part of the Northern Albanian way of life. It was easy to find pretexts for the arrest and even execution of enemies. Friendship with the German or Italian was fatal. So too soon became friendship with the British, and it was for that reason difficult for a time to make enquiries in the North about those who helped the SOE officers, risking their lives in the process and forfeiting them in the grim aftermath. The British did not help matters by sending in Albanians to provoke Hoxha. Either through clumsiness or treachery these missions failed, although they continued until 1953.

After 1948 it was equally unfortunate to be friendly with Yugoslavia, as Koçi Xoxe found to his cost. Relations with Yugoslavia were always bound to be difficult because of Kosova, especially for those in Tropojë with family links to the Albanian population across the border. Before 1948 the party line was that Kosova belonged to Yugoslavia, Hoxha like Zog repaying the benefactor in this way. This official line did not change when Tito fell out of favour with Stalin in 1948, or when Khrushchev in 1961 made some kind of rapprochement with Tito. Hoxha could maintain, like Big Brother in Orwell's *1984*, that Kosova belonged to Yugoslavia, and that Tito and Khrushchev had deserted the Stalin legacy. Others might say that he was only intent on preserving his own power in 1948 and 1961. In both years he faced some nasty moments, but not as nasty as those who had taken the wrong side in these years, or who had continued resistance in remote parts of Albania with a tradition of armed rebellion against the central power.

Such resistance and its repression continued until the 1950s, and there is a long list of inhabitants of Northern Albania who were either executed or sent to soulless prison camps like Burrel and Spaç. It is difficult with so many painful memories to learn about the Hoxha years or to write about them. The prison camps do not look all that different from the broken down collective farms, failed industrial projects and grim housing estates which litter a beautiful countryside. Not even Hoxha could destroy the magnificent scenery of the northern mountains and in Theth we can still see the church and the watchtower where people used to retreat to avoid the consequences of a blood feud. These rare relics of the past may owe their existence to a wish, now increasingly fulfilled, to establish the northern corner of Albania as a tourist attraction. There is hope here. Oddly, Northern Albania has another tourist attraction in the shape of the vast dam that encompasses most of the Drin river. This was created for hydroelectric purposes, but provides a boat journey into the northern mountains as impressive as the coast of Norway. From the boat one can see scattered farms and villages and wonder how people survived in the past. Hoxha would have maintained that life in these village had improved. They had electricity and the boat could bring supplies. Of course, some villages and even the whole old town of Kukës were drowned by the dam. Among the villages to go was historic Dushman. Some villagers moved to small towns where apartment blocks were built, of little aesthetic charm, but perhaps slightly more comfortable and convenient than village houses - and easier for the authorities to control. The population grew, procreation being a pleasure which the government could not control, but it did not grow in rural areas.

People living in these rural areas used to talk in a baffled and bewildered way about the nightmare of the Hoxha years. They were unlikely to know much about what went before, having learnt like characters in *1984* a few lies about the bad past to be contrasted with the glorious recent past, the more glorious present and the still more glorious future. Hoxha, a former schoolteacher, was keen on education, it being like the ubiquitous television a good weapon for indoctrination, although we should not ignore achievements in eradicating illiteracy and improving standards of health. Archaeologists did valiant work in rediscovering monuments of the Albanian past, although these were interpreted in a strongly nationalist fashion. A paranoid fear of foreigners meant that in archaeology and other scientific spheres Albania fell behind, as it did also in its attempts to develop industry. Odd foreigners like the comedian Norman Wisdom and the occasional carefully watched visitor from abroad were no substitute for the massive foreign aid needed to keep the population above basic subsistence level. The novelist Ismail Kadare in carefully disguised allegories exposed the surreal horror of the Hoxha years which lasted twice as long as the reign of Zog.

Hoxha died on 10 April 1985. He had been sick for some years, as had his country. Mourning for him was widespread and genuine. People had been trained to look up to him as the apex of a pyramid, another suitable symbol for his reign, as a large, ugly and useless building in this shape went up in Tirana. Between 1985 and 1992 the metaphorical pyramid gradually crumbled. Ramiz Alia introduced a few mild reforms to placate the population but also oversaw some repressive moves such as an incident in Shkodër where four people were shot in a demonstration. In Tirana there were student marches and industrial plants began winding down, as did law and order and the infrastructure of the state. A Democratic Party was formed, and it won some seats in a kind of democratic election, though not in rural areas. In 1992, after a winter of discontent, there were more elections, and we end, or almost end, where the Historical Museum ends or almost ends with the triumph of Sali Berisha on 23 March 1992.

9. 1992 AND THE FUTURE

Bliss was it in that dawn to be alive,
But to be young was very heaven!

Wordsworth's words about the French Revolution must have applied to the many young people who flocked into Tirana's Scanderbeg Square and other town centres to hear the 1992 election results. Albania was a young country, and students had played a large part in overthrowing the communist regime. But disillusion came more swiftly in Albania than it came to the young Wordsworth. At first everything went well. The Socialist Party leaders handed over power to Sali Berisha and wished him luck. After the elections of 2005 a similar cast played the same roles in a rather different way with the Socialists being distinctly reluctant to leave office. This change is, rather strangely, a change for the better. In 1992 their compliance in transferring government was probably due to the fact that Albania was virtually ungovernable. Nothing and nobody was working. There was little law and less order. The communists had ensured that people were kept alive, but in 1992 the government relied upon foreign aid to perform this task. This aid, though generous, was distributed in a haphazard fashion. Cauliflower seeds and useless garments were unsuitable gifts. Some gifts fell into the wrong hands. Northern villages saw little of consignments delivered at Durrës and Vlorë. Industrial and agricultural projects had already faltered, and were not going to start making progress of their own accord. Foreign governments were not all that sympathetic. Greece and Italy had to cope with large numbers of illegal immigrants mainly from the South. In the North there was less opportunity and even less encouragement to migrate to Yugoslavia, which was already beginning to fall apart. The troubles in Yugoslavia gave the Balkans a bad name. Albanians were not welcome as legal immigrants, and illegal immigrants often turned to crime, thus further worsening the reputation of Albania. The healthy and active continued to leave the country for the towns and the towns for abroad, thus making the viability of small villages even more precarious.

Naturally and unfairly, Berisha was blamed for these misfortunes. He tried to act firmly, and his firmness caused offence. In 1992 prominent politicians were expelled from the Democratic Party, and others left to form splinter groups after disastrous local elections which saw a considerable fall in the party's vote. Strikes at Bulqizë and Kukës were forcibly broken by the army. Outbreaks of crime were savagely suppressed, in one case at Fier by public executions. Nevertheless there were thirteen cases of vengeance killings at Shkodër during 1993, and it seemed as if the blood feud had returned. Neither the crimes nor their punishment did much good for Albania's image abroad. The persecutions of Hoxha's widow and various communist leaders created a good impression in certain quarters, but sending the Socialist Party leader Fatos Nano to prison on corruption charges in 1994 was probably a mistake. Kosova was another problem. Berisha saw that Albania was in no position to offer anything but sympathy to the Albanian movement in that country, and that even this sympathy might alienate Western allies, still desperately trying to avoid the dismemberment of Yugoslavia. He managed with difficulty to make the right noises on this issue, which was later to return in a more tragic fashion to offer some kind of redemption for Albania.

Berisha's dictatorial methods seemed to some more like those of Enver Hoxha than those of Napoleon. But Hoxha by protecting in a paranoid fashion his citizens from any knowledge of the West was able to persuade at any rate some of the population that they were living in prosperity. Berisha, by allowing Western television and encouraging other contacts with the rest of the world, showed Albanians the possibility of unheard of luxuries, but offered no way of affording them. Such a way seemed to be offered by unscrupulous banking organisations which gave high rates of interest paid by attracting further investments. The bubble of this capitalism without capital eventually burst after the elections of 1996, which Berisha won, although his opponents protested that the polls were rigged. Berisha was blamed for allowing the so-called pyramid schemes to exist, and some blamed him for profiting from the banks. In 1997 resentment broke out into armed rebellion, spreading from the South. There was widespread looting ironically of museum, hotels and aid depots, all designed to help Albania's future. There were also raids on army stores, and soon almost everybody carried a gun.

The West intervened and imposed new elections. Fatos Nano, released from prison with some rather less desirable criminals by the revolutionaries, won these, although Berisha retained some support in the North. Albania's reputation among potential foreign donors was at an all time low. Salvation came from an unexpected quarter after another bad year in 1998 when it seemed likely that there would be another popular uprising in the North to restore power to Berisha. Slobodan Milosevic started expelling Albanians from Kosova. Some arrived in Macedonia, where the government prompted by the West provided some support. Some arrived in Kukës, where the Albanians prompted by nobody responded magnificently. Food and clothing arriving in Durrës was rushed by inadequate roads to Kukës, where individual Albanians in spite of their own poverty were helping the unfortunate refugees. There were, of course, family ties between the Albanians of Kosova and those of Tropojë, but there had also been jealousy of the Kosovars for their higher standard of living. The destitute Kosovars who crossed the border were clearly more like Cinderella than the ugly sisters, and Albania by acting as a rather impoverished Prince Charming was rewarded by various fairy godmothers in the West.

The Kosova issue succeeded in uniting, although in rather a fragile fashion, left and right in Albania and supporters of Albania abroad. There were other more tangible results of the horrible Kosova conflict in Northern Albania. New border crossings were opened, and life became easier for remote villages at last able to visit market towns like Gjakova and Prizren. International officers crossed the border in the other direction, and spent their money in Albania. Kukës now has a number of small smart new hotels to replace the Hoxha-period hotel, looted in 1997, used to house refugees in 1999, and by 2003 a battered shell. Looking in vain for a bookshop in Kukës I counted twenty-six bars and three billiard parlours. There is some prosperity here, possibly derived in a slightly less honourable fashion from the Kosovan conflict. Many people in the Tropojë district were able to pass themselves off as Kosovar refugees seeking political asylum. This provided an easy route to the West from which, voluntarily or involuntarily, they returned with money to boost the local economy.

This new money kept the Albanians after 1998 from starving, although old cars and new cafés did little to improve the appearance of town or countryside. Roads and housing continued to deteriorate. It did not help matters that local government was often at variance with central government, one supporting Nano, the other Berisha, and neither supporting the electors. There was not enough money to maintain schools, hospitals and roads in the countryside, and the population drifted into inadequate housing in the towns, leaving the villages even more derelict and destitute. Tourism in the remote villages of the North seemed and seems a possible solution, but without roads it was impossible to attract the tourists or the materials to provide them with accommodation. There was not enough money to build new roads, and foreign aid seemed largely devoted to feasibility studies and the production of glossy brochures, promising but not delivering idyllic vacations in a mythical Albania.

I wrote these rather bitter words in the remote north-eastern village of Theth over which Edith Durham lavished lyrical praise. Gallant efforts have since been made to bring this area to the attention of the world. There was at some distance from the main village a small, simple but extremely pleasant hotel built in the shadow of a Hoxha holiday home for workers. By a rather unlucky stroke of fortune the owner of this hotel had just been awarded by lottery the chance to migrate to America. Efforts have been made to record the history of the village and to break down previous barriers preventing links between Albania, Kosova and Montenegro. The even more remote village of Vermosh is more easily reached from Montenegro, although the road cutting the distance between Western and Eastern Montenegro has not been completed. Such a road with Vermosh on it will do much to make up for the errors of frontier makers after the First World War. In Theth roads still present a problem. There is a road via Boga from Shkodër which takes three hours, but it is closed by snow for six months. There is a longer, worse road down the Shala valley which is closed for two months.

Theth is a collection of small hamlets, some off the main road, as are others further south across the Shala river with only footbridges giving access. The mountain path to Montenegro which Edith Durham tried and failed to complete still exists, but it would take a brave planner to build a road on this route. Not surprisingly only eighteen families spend the winter in Theth, many emigrating to Vraka, conveniently vacated by Slav-speakers going to Montenegro. There is a lot of courage and kindness to foreigners in Theth, but one rather fears that the Shala valley will soon become uninhabited as it appears to have become in the Dark Ages.

There has been a great deal of history and political commentary concerning Albania over the past twenty year. Events have proved much of this commentary to be misplaced. In 1997 there were some surprising defenders of President Berisha and some more predictable prophets of doom. There is more caution today. Kosova, of course, attracted special attention. But it is impossible to write the history of the future of Northern Albania. Writing about the past is hard enough. Berisha was successful in parliamentary elections in 2005 and just won again in 2009. In 2013 the Socialists, this time under the leadership of Edi Rana, took over and won elections again in 2017. The political system is still dominated by the two main parties, Socialists and the centre-right Democratic Party, and democracy of some sort seems to prevail. In 2019 the Economist Intelligence Unit considered Albania to be ruled by 'a hybrid regime' and concluded that 'some sort of democratic government' was in place.

There have been many false dawns in Albanian history. Opportunities were missed in 1992, 1945 and 1914, when the

West was at fault for offering insufficient support to a new and struggling country. Further back, in the time of the nineteenth-century Ottoman Tanzimat or Scanderbeg or even the Fourth Crusade, it is also possible to blame ignorance, greed and cowardice as the main obstacles to Albanian prosperity. But these sins are the sins of leaders, foreign or Albanian, and ordinary people outside and inside the country cannot be held to account for not knowing what happened in the past nor what to do in the future.

APPENDIX I
USCANA

In 170 BC the Romans occupied several places in the territory of the Illyrian Penestae tribe including Uscana, where Perseus had installed some Cretan mercenaries. In the winter of this year Perseus starting from Styberra re-took Uscana and attacked several other towns including Oaeneum on the River Arathus and Draudacum on his way to the kingdom of Gentius in Northern Albania. This campaign was successful in the short run as Gentius declared war on the Romans but was easily defeated, as was Perseus himself. Both defeats took place a long way from Uscana and the campaign of 170 may not seem very important in history, making it less important to know its exact location. But it would be useful to know the site of Uscana as it was clearly in a kind of no-man's-land between Roman and Macedonian spheres of power, technically under the control of the independent Penestae.

We know that the Penestae lived along the high mountain ranges that form the border between Albania and Macedonia. The English scholars Walbank and Hammond place Uscana at Kičevo well inside the Macedonian state, although they do mention Dibër as an alternative. Albanian historians have generally been prepared to accept the identification of Uscana with Kičevo, thus placing the Illyrian Penestae firmly in the part of Macedonia that is inhabited by Albanian-speakers, although this is largely coincidental. The Barrington Atlas cautiously only marks Styberra at Prilep where there is epigraphical evidence for this site, but it marks the Arathus as a tributary of the Drin not the Vardar. In contrast, the *Tabula Imperii Romani* places Uscana at Kičevo and Oaeneum and Draudacum at the well-known Macedonian centres, Albanian-speaking, of Gostivar and Tetovo in the Vardar valley.

One argument against identifying Uscana with anywhere near Dibër, particularly the important large strategic site of Grazdhan, is that it is a very long way from Prilep, and Perseus is said to have made the journey during winter in less than three days. From Prilep to Kičevo it is 68 kilometres by modern roads, from Kičevo to Dibër a further 50 with a few more on to Grazdhan. But as Philip had shown in the second Macedonian War in his long march along the Drino, Macedonian armies moved swiftly. Perseus himself made a rapid long winter march across the Pindus Mountains in the campaign of 169. Speed was of the essence and it may only have been the cavalry who took two days.

There are some arguments against identifying Kičevo with Uscana. Kičevo is a long way east for the Romans to establish a forward garrison, particularly as under the treaty of 197 the area of Lyncestis west of Kičevo was left in the hands of Pleuratus. The same arguments apply to making Gostivar and Tetovo Oaeneum and Draudacum. Oaeneum is said to be on the River Arathus and near Mount Sarda. This mountain is usually assumed to be the Sar Planina, the massive mountain range which separates Macedonia from Kosova. Under its shadow lie Gostivar and Tetovo. But the Sar Planina near these two towns is almost impenetrable. Further south, where the range forms the boundary of Macedonia and Albania, there are still high peaks like Mount Korab at 2753 metres but also an obvious way through at Dibër. A site in the Dibër area for all these locations is obviously on the way to Gentius, whereas marching to Gostivar and Tetovo would seem to be marching backwards on the way to nowhere.

Some Albanian historians, notably Kristo Frashëri and the local historian of the Dibër area, Iljaz Kaca, who reproduces Frashëri's map, have bravely retreated into Albania for the site of the three towns, placing Uscana at Grazdhan, Draudacum at a site west of Peshkopi (Ushtelencë) on the eastern side of the Drin, and Oaenum at Çidhnë, which provides, as Kaca shows, a beginning to a rough medieval road to the Adriatic. There are some ancient remains at Çidhnë.

If Uscana was to be found at Grazdhan we would expect some remains of Illyrian and Roman occupation to be found at this site. There are as yet, no such remains, although this site has been excavated in such a way as to show a medieval church nearby and a wall bisecting the site to make it more defensible. The church suggests a Bulgarian presence, very probably around the year 1000 AD, and the wall suggests the kind of rebuilding that Justinian prepared five centuries earlier. A site like Grazdhan is clearly of strategic importance. It is just possible that a trace of the ancient names lurks in Usiana, a place mentioned by Procopius as being refortified by Justinian. Over the Drin in Epirus Nova, Procopius' Aoion - like Oaeneum - has plenty of vowels but the site of Çidhnë has been linked to Procopius' Cithinas, and in any case speculating about place names is the province of armchair historians and it really needs archaeologists to establish these sites for certain. Livy, himself an armchair historian used as the apologist for imperial Rome, is hardly the ideal subject for Albanian archaeologists, but in recent years in spite of difficult conditions local scholars have made and will continue to make many discoveries about this period.

APPENDIX II
THE LISSUS-NAISSUS
ROUTE

This route is clearly marked in the Peutinger Table, but not in the Antonine itineraries. The Peutinger Table is usually dated to the early fourth century, the age of Diocletian, who came from Dalmatia, and Constantine, who came from Naissus, but there is no particular reason to date the building of the road in question to this late period in Roman history. The network of roads from Salona on the Adriatic coast across difficult terrain in the former Yugoslavia to the Danube frontier was built after the Illyrian revolt of 6-9 AD. Further south the Via Egnatia was constructed in the second century BC. The Lissus-Naissus route can probably be dated in between these periods.

Place is almost as hard as time to determine. We can be fairly certain about the Naissus end of the route where stations like Ulpiana, near modern Lipljan, can be found and other points on the Peutinger Table moved to fit accordingly. But further west there is doubt about the location of Crevenium and Gabuleo and indeed about where the road went. Modern Albanian scholarship has come up with the ingenious suggestion that there were alternative routes in Roman times as there are now from north-eastern Albania to Kosova. This situation deals with difficulties about the distances shown in the Peutinger Table and fits in with two lines of forts in Albania, one along the White Drin leading to Prizren and the other through Has leading to Gjakova. The latter route does not follow the same lines as the modern road, but can be seen from it. Modern scholars place Crevenium at Vau Spasi and Gabuleo at Kukës both sites being inconveniently submerged under the Orin Lake. If we follow the Peutinger Table and the Barrington Atlas in giving but a single line for the road, Gabuleo is near Prizren and there are then difficulties with fitting in stations like Theranda up the line to Naissus.

From Vau Spasi, where there was presumably a bridge, we start off promisingly westwards with an obvious Roman site at Shëmri which is near the modern motor road via Pukë to Shkodër. The Roman road would not have followed this route, which in two places crosses passes that are closed in winter, but would have struck more directly further north through Iballë to join the Drin where the present artificial lake begins and then proceed in a south-westerly direction past the great castle of Sarda to a point equidistant between Shkodër and Lezhë, overlooked by the equally impressive site of Vig with its echoes of Vigilia, a watchtower. Such a route bypasses Pukë, often regarded as the modern equivalent of Ad Picaria in the Peutinger Table, Pacue in Procopius and derived from Via Publica, a public highway, but as we have shown, this identification and derivation may be suspect.

There are arguments against this route. Though strongly linked to ancient sites near the coast and near Kosova it is lacking them in the central part of Northern Albania where the landscape is very rugged. Apollon Baçe marks a fortress at Iballë and puts Pacue on his map, but the latter seems wishful thinking, and I have seen no report of the former. Edith Durham whose efforts to reach Gjakova form a recurring leitmotif in *High Albania* did eventually cross near Vau Spasi but had great difficulties in the earlier parts of her journey. It is perhaps worth considering the alternative route north of the Drin first put forward by Arthur Evans whose archaeological reports on the Balkans have recently been helpfully reprinted. ·

Before he gained first fame and then discredit for his discoveries in Crete, Evans did valuable archeeological work in the Western Balkans. The young Evans is a rather attractive figure fulminating in favour of Slav independence, reading *Jane Eyre* in his cell when imprisoned by the Austrians in Dubrovnik, and in the intervals between doing valuable work on Roman roads and inscriptions in Illyricum. The older archaeologist of Knossos is less admirable. Like many academics he thought he was always right and was often wrong. In Illyricum he was wrong about Justinian's birthplace, now almost universally agreed to be at Caričin Grad in southern Serbia rather than near Skopje in Macedonia where Evans placed it, using among other evidence the dangerous testimony of modern place names.

Evans comments on the savage and inaccessible nature of Northern Albania and declares that the route of the road across it must remain a matter of pure conjecture. Wilkes writing in 1976 states that matters have not advanced since that time. Evans' account of Roman roads crossing the mountains from Salona north of Split has never been disputed, and he is on strong though less acknowledged ground in suggesting that a powerful Roman presence in the western Balkans may explain the presence of today's Vlachs. His views on the Lissus-Naissus road should therefore at least get an airing. They are best illustrated by his map of Dardania and Southern Dalmatia in which he shows a route starting from the coast north of Lezhë and proceeding south of the Drin, which it crosses near Dushman, up the Shala valley as far as Nlkaj, then turning east near Abat to join a straight road through Krasnich tribal territory to Gjakova. By nineteenth-century standards Evans' map is not a bad one, although the rivers run like Roman roads in suspiciously straight lines. The Shala river does run in a north-south direction, but the Drin and the Valbona are portrayed in such a way that it looks as if rivers could only flow either from north to south or from east to west whereas both rivers exhibit graceful curves.

The map shows Evans claiming that he had travelled along both the Shala and Valbona rivers, but unfortunately he has left no direct account of his journey. For this we have to turn to Edith Durham, who started north of the Drin and had an extremely uncomfortable journey crossing the river where the Shala joins it and then crossing back at a place called Apripa Gurit (a good Latin name), proceeding northwards through Nikaj-Mërtur, which she found very savage, before coming to an impressively straight piece of road leading to Abat. This would seem to be the central part of Evans' road. Further east there is a fairly straight modern road from Nikaj-Mërtur to Gjakova, although when Durham did eventually reach Gjakova she went via Shemrii and

Vau Spasi keeping south of the Drin all the time on the route that is generally taken to be the Lissus-Naissus road. This route actually goes through more difficult country and is less straight.

From Abat Durham proceeded up the Shala valley to Theth and then returned by a circuitous road to Theth and then via Boga to Shkodër like the modern traveller who is brave enough to visit these remote regions. On a previous occasion Durham had returned from the Shala valley to Shkodër by what she calls a fairly good route via Kir and from which there is a very straight modern road to Shkodër. The combination of this straight road and the track east of Abat suggests a modification of Evans' route keeping north of the Drin all the way to Kosova passing near important Roman sites like Rosunjë in its latter stages. Of course the mountains on this straight line are more formidable than the Cotswolds, which the straight Fosse way takes in its stride, but are perhaps less difficult than the ranges east of Salona, and some enterprising archaeologist should be scouring the countryside east of Abat for Roman remains.

Of course, there are advantages in a southern route. Vig and Sarda are south of the Drin, perhaps guarding the road along the coast from Lissus rather than the road into the interior. We also have the impressive line of fortresses north of the Vau Spasi and east of Kukës along the alternative routes suggested at the beginning of this appendix. It is possible that the route we have provisionally outlined as what the Peutinger Table depicted is itself one of a whole series of routes crossing Albania from east to west. People must have lived in places other than on the Lissus-Naissus road and the Via Egnatia. The Peutinger Table gives no indication of a route along the Drin from Kukës to Ohrid and yet along this part of the Drin there is a line of forts of late Roman construction. This was an important road in medieval times, and in the time of Scanderbeg there are plenty of well attested roads from Dibër to the Adriatic passing south of the Drin and north of the Via Egnatia.

Goths, under first Alaric and then Theoderic, invaded Albania at the end of the fourth and fifth centuries. The Romans would no longer have controlled the Lissus-Naissus road, and the absence of Praevalitana north of the Drin in Procopius' *De Aedificiis* suggests that they took some time to regain it. Hierocles writing in Justinian's reign does mention Praevalitana, but this may be wishful thinking. Hierocles also mentions the towns in Epirus Nova, namely Alistron and Skepton, of which the former may appear as Procopius' Alistrus. Kurti has identified these with Lis and Shkopet in northern Mat, curiously both on an alternative modern road from Peshkopi to Lezhë although not one traceable in medieval times. Such a route, and indeed the usually accepted route south of the Drin, may well have been alternative ways of getting from Lissus to Naissus in Gothic times.

APPENDIX III
PROCOPIUS' *BUILDINGS*

It is very frustrating to be handed a map only to find that it bears little relation to the area it is meant to be describing. Procopius does not actually draw a map in his treatise *De Aedificiis* or *Buildings*, but he does give us a list of places allegedly fortified or refortified by Justinian. This might give us an indication of the nature and extent of Byzantine power in the Balkans and it could be used to show how Albanian-, Greek- and Vlach-speakers survived the Slav onslaught. It is clear from archaeological evidence, place names and a few melancholy chronicles that this invasion was fairly catastrophic. The presence of Albanian-speakers in Kosova and Greek- and Vlach-speakers in South Albania is a matter of controversy and we cannot be certain when these speakers arrived in these areas. But they must have arrived from somewhere and the obvious place from which they would have arrived is from Justinian's forts, first manned by Latin-, Greek- and Illyrian-speaking soldiers and then used as places of refuge by Latin, Greek and Illyrian communities, the last group being the largest thus securing the dominance of Albanian. Near the coast such refugees would flee to Dalmatian islands or even Italy and Sicily. We have evidence of the Bishop of Lissus seeking such an escape route. But inland forts were far from the Adriatic and if only we knew where such forts were we could suggest a pattern whereby when the forts became unmannable or unmanageable the inhabitants fled from them to the recesses of the mountains or valleys in these mountains to emerge four or five centuries later as Albanians, Vlachs or Greeks.

This is where Procopius should come to our aid. Tantalisingly, as if to show that we are at any rate in the same continent, he gives us some names like Dyrrachium and Scampa (Elbasan), both rather badly spelt, in the province of New Epirus. The city of Skydreon, probably Shkodër, spelt even worse, is placed in the same province, although we would expect it to be in the northern province of Praevalitana. Tantalisingly, too, we have evidence of restoration in the time of Justinian at sites like Byllis and Butrint. In the case of Byllis there is even an inscription about such restoration work. But Byllis and Butrint do not appear in Procopius' list. Instead we have a long list of unidentifiable names. They do not include Grazdhan, clearly a Slavonic name, but a major fortress with an inner wall of a later date. The Albanian climate and the fortunes of war have not been kind to Justinian's fortresses. They have survived much better in the Atlas Mountains and in eastern Turkey. Ironically, the inscription about Byllis boasting of the eternal qualities of the restoration of Justinian's envoy Victorinus was found in nearby Ballsh.

All these factors make our map unreliable and for other reasons it is tempting to throw it away. A list of proper names is difficult to copy correctly. We have noted the misspelling of major centres. Procopius or his copyists fail to put the word new in front of Epirus when moving from the south to the centre of Albania and we have shown the omission of Praevalitana, although there may be a reason for this. Dardanian forts are helpfully listed, but after Dardania Procopius strays widely and wildly all over the Balkan Peninsula before getting, away from lists to a coherent and useful discussion of the defence of the Danube frontier. In addition, Procopius' fawning adulation of Justinian's achievements in *Buildings* is flagrantly contradicted by his vituperative condemnation of the same emperor in *The Secret History*.

Procopius has his limitations, but so have we. Byllis and Butrint may be in the list lurking under other names. Praevalitana may not be included because after the Gothic invasions and occupation it had never really been recovered by the Byzantine Empire apart from the coastal district. In this case Procopius is up to date, and it is Hierocles writing in the early years of Justinian with an account of the two Epirus provinces Praevalitana and Dardania and their cities who is out of date. It is odd that Procopius does not refer to some of the few cities mentioned by Hierocles like Lissus, but this may be because no building took place at Lissus.

This excuse does not work for Byllis. Sarda is oddly omitted by Hierocles and Procopius. The loss of Praevalitana suggests a slight weakness in Byzantine power and supports the thesis of *The Secret History*, although this is exaggerated in the same way as *Buildings* exaggerates Justinian's achievements. Some think that the two works cannot be from the same hand, but in a way they tell the same true story. Justinian did do a lot of building, but he did overstrain the resources of the Empire.

This defence of Procopius does not help with the identification of place names. However accurate a map it is of no use if it cannot be read. Places' names are bound to change with various foreign invaders. The names in Procopius' list have been interpreted in various ways. From Albania Frashëri says there few Greek and Latin names, some Illyrian-Albanian and some of unknown origin. This seems unfair. Besiliev and Skok perhaps exaggerate the Latin element although not unduly. It is hard to define a Greek or Roman name but certain names like Piscinae, Therma or Thesaurus seem to ring classical bells. We also have the splendidly bilingual Gynaecomites (girlfriends) and on a loftier Tolstoyan note, Martis and Eirene, War in Latin and Peace in Greek. Some of these names suggest not towns but stations, Victoria and Waterloo, not London. In Dardania we do actually find Victorias and Victoriana. Some may even be the names of taverns, as Beseliev has pointed out, and we could in Greek, Latin and Albanian be looking at the equivalent of the Dog and Duck, not actually a very popular pub sign. Ptocheion and Ptocheiou occur; Ptocheion means poorhouse in Greek.

In September 2004 I visited the impressive late site of Grazdhan accompanied by Professors Adam Bungari and Luan Përzhita for whose help I am deeply grateful. The site is an enormous one covering thirty-four acres. Further excavation will reveal more of the history of this fort built in the time of Constantine and rebuilt with a reduced wall in the time of Justinian. It may have been Uscana in Illyrian times (see Appendix I). Professor Përzhita thought it might be Deuphracus in Procopius, a name reasonably like Dibër, confusingly the name of an Albanian district and

Macedonian town. Both ancient and modern names could refer to the fact that Grazdhan is an important crossroads where the north-south route along the Black Drin valley is bisected by the road from the Adriatic to Dibër. There is no evidence in the ancient itineraries of either of these roads but plenty of evidence for their existence in the Middle Ages, and in the case of the Drin valley route plenty of evidence of late Roman forts. Further west rough country and the creation of artificial lakes are handicaps to the discovery of forts, but we do have a long list of sites to fit Procopius' long list of names and can even begin to match some up with the other.

The small town of Peshkopi, twenty kilometres north of Grazdhan, has an excellent museum with useful maps of archaeological sites and a local historian, Iljaz Kaca, who gave me a copy of his book. This identifies Peshkopi with the Stephanakion of Procopius, which most authors place in the west of the country. We know that there was a Bishop of Stephanakion in the Middle Ages and Peshkopi has a suitably episcopal name. Peshkopi is famous for its hot springs now transformed into homely baths into which I plunged after scrambling along Grazdhan's precipitous fortifications. Therma and Piscinae spring to mind. Peshkopi cannot be all three, but the nearly fort at Bellovë may consist of a Slavonic version of good waters. Kaca prints a map based on the work of Frashëri in which he identifies Çidhnë with Kithinas, Lurë with Illyrin, Tartaj with Tithyra, which he in delightfully Virgilian fashion calls Tityra, and just over the Macedonian border Papradnik with Paretion.

More archaeological work is needed to make certain of these identifications. There are dangers in using modern place names as evidence of ancient sites. Resemblances can be misleading. Sir Arthur Evans thought he had located Justiniana at Skopje on the grounds that near Skopje there were two names similar to villages near where Justinian was born. But as I have shown in previous appendices, there is much in Albanian geography that suggests this is, to use a favourite term of Evans, pure conjecture. Such conjecture is fascinating. It can be seen how modern Albanian has mangled Latin words like Oraculum into Mbrakull. It may be that Procopius' forts are concealed rather than revealed by an Albanian name.

With the scanty amount of definitely identified forts at our disposal it is hard to see the plan or purpose of Justinian building them. With more information on the Danube frontier we can see a strategy of defence in depth with inner lines behind the frontier. Perhaps there was some plan like this in Albania and the appendix on the Lissus-Naissus road may suggest such a plan. It is odd that there are so many forts along the Drin valley as this seems not like a frontier but an invasion route. Standing on the northern walls of Grazdhan I was reminded of Hadrian's Wall, imagining myself as a Roman soldier anxiously awaiting the enemy from the North. On Hadrian's Wall it was fairly easy when Picts and Scots crossed the barrier to send for reinforcements along the wall to pin the marauders against it on their way back. No such pattern can be seen in the forts strung along the Drin although Grazdhan has some good fortifications on its southern side in which Slav invaders could be caught in a murderous cross fire if they decided to attack the fort on the way back. Perhaps they simply bypassed it, leaving the defenders of the fort stranded. For Justinian was no Hadrian. His fortifications did not last three hundred years, but barely thirty. *The Secret History* is more accurate than *Buildings*.

APPENDIX IV
THE PRIEST OF DIOCLEA

The Chronicle of the Priest of Dioclea is an important source for medieval Albanian history, even though it never mentions Albanians. With the notable exception of Paul Stephenson who has translated passages in his books on the Balkans, Western scholars have been sceptical about the value of the chronicle. Fine is dismissive although he uses the Priest, and Ferluga points out inconsistencies and defects. Elsie does not include the *Chronicle* in his long bibliography of books by and about Albanians, presumably because the Priest and his *Chronicle* do not fit into either category. Among earlier scholars Runciman in his history of Bulgaria retells the tales of the Priest as if they were fairy stories, clearly believing that they are. Even a more recent guidebook to Montenegro, clearly proud to recognise the Priest of Dioclea as a famous early citizen of that country, says rather condescendingly that his chronicle should be counted as literature rather than history. In England we are not so dismissive in relegating Bede and The *Anglo-Saxon Chronicle*, written about roughly same period in roughly the same way, to being early novels.

The history of the text is obscure. There is a long version, thought to be originally written in Slavonic, translated between the twelfth and sixteenth centuries into Latin. Orbini in 1601 translated not very accurately *The Chronicle* into Italian. There is also a shorter Slavonic text. The Croatian scholar F. Sisič produced in 1928 a critical edition of all three texts and Orbini's translation. This is adequate as are more recent editions in Serbo-Croatian such as that by V. Mošin in 1968. Stephenson has announced on the internet a full translation into English with historical notes.

It has to be said that for the beginner in Dioclean studies even Sisič's edition is hard to find. It does not help matters that Dioclea is spelt in many different ways, that presbyter or even pop sometimes replaces priest, and that the full title of the work varies. We sometimes hear of it as *Letopis* or *Ljetopis Papa Dukljanina*, a title with confusing and coincidental resemblances to the Albanian family of the Dukagjins. The full Latin title is *De Regno Slavorum et Gothorum*, and though there is not much about Goths in the *Chronicle* this is a useful reminder of the Gothic presence in Albania. The work is sometimes known as *The Bar Genealogy*, and this name too is not misleading, since there are many family trees in the text, one of whose aims is to establish the primacy of Bar as an ecclesiastical see. The British Library catalogue lists the *Chronicle* under Slavs, a helpful tip for those combing indices under P, D, L or Lj, or the useful acronym LPD.

Oddly the text's reliability is often supported by other dubious authorities on the Balkans in the period. Thus the essential geography of the Dalmatian region is confirmed by the Emperor Constantine Porphyrogenitus even though he had a different agenda, namely to prove a longstanding Byzantine claim to the western Adriatic coast. Similarly the Byzantine chronicler Skylitzes reinforces the Priest of Dioclea's account of the year around 1000 AD, although offering at times what appears to be an alternative version. Constantine and Skylitzes have obviously a pro-Greek bias just as the Priest is clearly hostile to Greek rule, as when he says that Bulgaria nearly brought Byzantium to its knees as late as 1017, and that Greek rule over the Balkans was terrible in the years before the revolt in 1043. Thus the degree of agreement between the Priest and Byzantine sources reflects credit on both parties. ·

Clearly the Priest should not be taken as gospel truth, although differences between the four gospels have not dissuaded most churchmen from believing in their essential truth. Like Byzantine chroniclers and for that matter nineteenth- and twentieth-century ecclesiastics the Priest of Dioclea seems obsessed with Church protocol at a time when important and distressing historical events were occurring, but he is not alone in this respect, and apart from the rather boring question about the precedence of Bar he is fairly reticent about religious matters. In a way that is a pity. He was writing in and about times that were important for the divisions between Greek and Slavonic Orthodoxy, and between Orthodoxy and Catholicism. It has to be said that he is not very useful in describing either division.

Appendix IV The Priest of Dioclea

The best known passages in the chronicle concern John Vladimir, the ruler of Dioclea, captured by Samuel the Bulgarian emperor, marrying his daughter, appointed to rule Northern Albania, but falling a victim to his wife's cousin, confusingly called John Vladislav. John Vladimir is an important figure in Albanian history. There is a shrine to his memory at Elbasan, and it was in Dyrrachium that he appeared in a vision to confound his wife's cousin, who was also his successor and murderer. He ruled Northern Albania at the beginning of the eleventh century, and appears to have been killed in the part of Macedonia that is Albanian-speaking, and originally buried in the part of Montenegro that is Albanian-speaking near to the appropriately named village of Vladimir. We have shown how Runciman's romantic account of Vladimir's love affair with Samuel's daughter is more fact than fiction, and this lends credence to the Priest's account of eleventh-century history.

In previous centuries something has gone wrong with the chronology, and it is not totally surprising to find that even a defender of the Priest like Stephenson dismisses this portion of his narrative as mythical. Vladimir died presumably as a relatively young man in 1015 or 1016. We may be uncertain of the year, but the exact day is given as 22 May. Saints and shrines are suspicious sources, but given the circumstances of the Bulgarian Empire after Samuel's death we can work back to the romance with Kosara being in the last decade of the tenth century, and John Vladimir's birth occurring around 970. He cannot therefore possibly be the great great grandson of Prodimir, the contemporary of John Tzimiskes, who died in 976. This has led most to dismiss Prodimir and his predecessors as fictional figures, and indeed much of the earlier part of the narrative has stock folklore elements like good kings, bad kings, seven brothers, the prince returning from abroad and so on.

Interspersed among these legendary elements are historical figures. Totila the Goth is mentioned by Procopius, and we have no particular reason to disbelieve in the existence of his brother Ostroylus, mentioned by the Priest but no other source. There are some interesting but hardly informative mentions of Praevalitana. The statement that the original inhabitants of Illyricum retreated into the mountains gives an insight into the history of the Vlachs and the survival of Albania. Odd mentions of links with Italy, including a warlike Latin character called Bello, suggest ways in which along the Dalmatian coast Illyricum preserved a connection with Catholicism and the Latin language. Ciaslav, the great great uncle of Prodimir according to the *Chronicle*, is a historical figure in Serbian history. Earlier we find good king Svatopluk, recognisable as the King of Moravia who received the gospel from Cyril and Methodius, and is in an odd way responsible for Catholicism in parts of East Europe and the Cyrillic alphabet in others.

Rather sadly, Albania receives little mention in either the allegedly legendary parts of the narrative or the historical section about Vladimir and his successors. Dyrrachium is referred to under the odd name of Balibona. Claims that Northern Albania were under Dioclean, i.e. Slavonic, control must be taken with a certain amount of scepticism in view of the Priest's anti-Greek prejudice. The comparison with Bede and *The Anglo-Saxon Chronicle* is clearly not an exact one, but is perhaps useful in showing the Priest's mistakes. Like *The Anglo-Saxon Chronicle* he reports genealogies of various kingdoms, but unfortunately blends them into one family tree. Like Bede he is interested in ecclesiastical history, but Bede does not distort his sources for ecclesiastical purposes as the Priest does by making all monarchs Dioclean in order to boost Bar. But in spite of their merits neither *The Anglo-Saxon Chronicle* nor Bede contains much information about the Welsh, and the failure to mention Albanians should not be held against the Priest. Instead he should be consulted to try and find out what happened in the Dark Ages of Albanian history.

APPENDIX V
THE ALBANIAN-
YUGOSLAV BORDER

In writing a history of Southern Albania I spent some time in the main body of the text explaining the intricacies of the Greek-Albanian border, provisionally outlined in 1913 by the Protocol of Florence and finally settled again at Florence in 1926. In the years between, Greece had always claimed, had frequently occupied, and sometimes seemed to be awarded a large area of Southern Albania which they called Northern Epirus, and in which most of the population were Orthodox in religion and some spoke Greek. Eventually the frontier suggested in 1913 was adopted in 1926 with a few small rectifications.

Paradoxically the largest of these was in the area round Lake Prespa, originally Greek, given to Albania, but inhabited by Slav-speakers. Along the Grammos Mountains the frontier had not been properly delineated, but this was of minor significance in an area largely uninhabited except for the odd roaming Vlach who had little regard for boundaries. This arrangement left a considerable body of Greek-speakers in the south-west of Albania still present today, and a considerable body of Albanian-speakers in Greece, largely assimilated or expelled to Albania after the Second World War. In drawing and preserving the 1913 Greek-Albanian frontier which has survived almost intact until today statesmen faced difficult problems with an ethnic jigsaw, where the pieces did not fit, where bilingualism and a common religion were complicating factors, and where strategic factors like commanding heights, and economic factors like communicating roads, had to be taken into consideration. Needless to say the frontier did not please either side, nor did my account of it.

In relegating my discussion of the frontier between Albania and the former Yugoslavia to an appendix I am not trying to avoid disapproval or to court it. The northern and eastern boundaries

Albania and its Borders

MONTENEGRO

Vermosh
Podgorica
Theth
Tuzi
Vraka
Drisht
Shkodër
Pukë
Lezhë
Mat
Burrel
Mt. Dajte
Shijak
TIRANA
Durrës

Bajram
Curri
Gjakova

White Drin

KOSOVÁ

Prizren

Drin
Kukës
Zapod
Shistavec

Mt. Korab

Peshkopi
Bllatë
Dibër
Bulqizë
Bizë
Ostren
Lukova

Tetovo

Gostivar

Kičevo

MACEDONIA

Struga

Lake Ohrid

Ulcinj
Bunë

Elbasan
Shkumbin
Lushnjë

Seman
Fier
Berat
Devoll

Sveti Naum
Gollomboc

Lake Prespa

GREECE

Vlorë
Vjosë
Osum

Korcë

N

Gjirokastër

Adriatic Sea

Sarandë

CORFU

0   20
km

Areas of Albanian
spoken in former
Yugoslavia

© S.Ballard (2020)

of Albania are longer than the southern, and the story of their demarcation is even more complex. The results were different. The 1913 frontier was altered more drastically in 1926, but has more or less held until today. This frontier has left, unlike in the South, few non-Albanian-speakers in Northern Albania, but many Albanian-speakers in Montenegro, Macedonia and of course Kosova. Oddly the 1926 rearrangements increased rather than decreased the unfairness to Albania.

In the Second World War most of the Albanian-speaking areas of the former Yugoslavia were briefly united with Albania under Italian and German tutelage, thus repeating the situation in the latter half of the First World War when the Austro-Hungarian Army occupied both Serbia and Northern Albania. Again it was different in the South, although the Italians briefly and disastrously occupied the Albanian-speaking part of Greece between 1941 and 1943. In the First World War various boots were on various other feet in both South and North. Ethnic rectitude, difficult like most forms of rectitude to establish, is one of the many casualties of war. Serbia and Montenegro were victorious in two Balkan wars, and were on the winning side in the First World War, although at one stage heavily and tragically defeated. In contrast, the Greeks had played a slightly less glorious role. Their arrival in the Balkan wars at Ioannina and Salonica was tardy, but enabled them as in Southern Albania to stake their claim. But in the First World War they were even tardier in joining the Allied side, and during this war Southern Albania was occupied by the French and Italians, also on the winning side almost from the start. In the North the defeated Austrians, who did want some kind of firm government, were not contenders in post-war boundary settlements, whereas the Kingdom of the Serbs, Croats and Slovenes was clearly in the ascendant. Greece had been divided by rivalry between royalists and republicans and aspirations in Asia Minor, tragically thwarted in 1923. Between 1913 and 1926 the Serbs, now artificially united with the Croats and Slovenes, had won many friends, and the Greeks in spite of Pericles had lost a few.

Albania never had many friends, although Aubrey Herbert and Edith Durham performed yeoman service in protecting its interests against the rapacity of Serbs and Greeks. Albania had been neutral in the war, but most of it had been dominated by the Austrians. It did not help matters that the nominal King of Albania had served as a German officer in the war, during which some Albanian leaders had asked for him to be replaced by a member of the Turkish royal house, hardly in favour with the allied powers. The future King Zog had been made a colonel in the Austrian Army. Other leaders like Esad Pasha were more inclined to favour the victorious side, but at the expense of Albania's interests. Even if these competing rivals had all been on the right side, their competition had produced such a state of anarchy that it was difficult to award territory to a country where there was no stable government. Interestingly, the final settlement only occurred in 1926 when Ahmet Zogu had finally established his rule, although even he would seem to have sold out.to the Yugoslavs who had helped him regain power.

Maps of Albania in the period between 1912 and 1926 show a variety of frontiers. We are principally concerned with what was notionally awarded in 1913 and finally established in 1926. We may note in passing the maximum claims of the Albanians in 1919 at the Paris Peace Conference and the minimal Albanian state outlined by the secret Treaty of London in 1915. The former roughly corresponds to the area of Albanian speech, the latter to the rather more brutal demands of realpolitik, as the treaty was designed to entice Italy into the war. Unfortunately the peace treaties after the war usually resulted in a rather unhappy compromise between idealistic notions of self-determination and the more ignoble promptings of a Vae Victis policy.

We can demonstrate the unfairness of what happened in 1913 and 1926 by looking at the map and by looking at the documents relating to the boundary settlement admirably collected by Bejtullah Destani. Unfortunately maps depicting both frontiers are very inaccurate at key points. This is true of the one in Destani's volume and in other books by authoritative writers, like Swire and

Appendix V The Albanian-Yugoslav Border

Malcolm. The maps in Magocsi's *Atlas of Central Europe* differ both from those of Malcolm and Swire and from each other. The same is true of large atlases produced by reputable map makers like Bartholemew and Philips during the war years or immediately after them, and of the official Admiralty map used in the war. There are reasons for this inaccuracy. The physical geography of Albania had not been properly established. The 1913 frontier was only marked out in broad outline at the Conference of Ambassadors in London. They sent out some commissioners to provide details, but the work of these commissioners was interrupted by the outbreak of war. In 1921 a meeting of ambassadors from the victors in the First World War agreed to send out more commissioners, and an Italian, French and British group set to work in 1922, finishing their labours in 1924. We learn all this from Destani who gives in full the dispatches of Colonel Frank Giles, the British delegate. Educated at Marlborough and Woolwich with a gallant war record, Giles displays the strengths and weaknesses of his class. He complains bitterly about his fellow commissioners, the weather, the roads and his boils. His exasperation with the French delegate for being old, fat and nepotistic erupts more than once rather like the boils. The Albanians on the spot are usually dismissed as feeble, while some of the Yugoslavs are praised for being reasonably efficient about practical matters. Albania was not helped by being in a state of anarchy, and its representatives on the boundary commission, including distinguished people like Mehdi Bey Frashëri, are dismissed by Giles as being not interested in boundary areas, far from their own particular patch and affairs. Giles is, however, a fair-minded reporter and is shrewd enough to detect and deplore a pattern, discernible in the wars of the 1990s, whereby the Yugoslavs would appear to agree to a concession in theory, only to renege upon it in fact.

In *The Geographical Journal* of 1930 Giles gives a brief account of the settlement of the Yugoslav-Albanian frontier and indeed of the Yugoslav-Bulgarian frontier in which he was also involved. There is a technical explanation of trigonometrical points and boundary posts. Giles liked straight lines and clear orders, and he wanted quick action. He finished the eastern section of the Albanian frontier long before the French, handicapped by the laziness of Commandant Perret, had finished the north, and before the Italians, handicapped by the murder of General Tellini, had finished the southern border. It was in the east that the greatest concessions were made to the Yugoslavs.

We cannot blame all Albania's woes on Colonel Giles' brisk love of straight lines. He did speak up for Albania's interests in the north-west and preserved Vermosh from being taken over in order that the Yugoslavs could build a railway through it. During the war and after it Yugoslavia had occupied all the land up to the River Drin and had devastated Albanian villages. This river had become the de facto frontier making the notional 1913 frontier redundant. The trouble about the 1913 frontier is that those who drew it had without Colonel Giles' trigonometrical points only given rough indications of where it should lie. Those indications were a mixture of important places like towns, strategic lines like mountain ranges, and occasionally and rather vaguely former demarcations like tribal and administrative divisions.

In 1913 it had been decided that Ulcinj, Gusinjë, Gjakova, Prizren and Dibër should all fall outside the borders of Albania, which was considered lucky to have kept Shkodër. The 1913 border is shown coming very close to all these towns. In 1913 and 1914 we have, collected by Destani, the reports of a Colonel Gramet trying to draw the frontier near Dibër. Like Colonel Giles, Gramet did not get on well with his French counterpart Fournier, who together with the Russian delegate, General Potapoff, favoured the Serbs against the wishes of the Italian, British, German and Austrian delegates who wanted to give more territory near Dibër to Albania. War brought an end to these deliberations, leaving the commissioners to take different sides amid considerable confusion as to exactly where the frontier lay.

After the war, towns like Dibër attracted the attention of statesmen like Lord Curzon. He stated in a memorandum that the frontier should be a strong one, and it is clear that in the discussions among the Allied ambassadors in Paris considerations like strategic points and commercial viability were to play a major part in setting up the frontiers. Lip service to more idealistic issues was paid by the sending out of three commissioners from the League of Nations to Albania to investigate the complaints of minorities, but they do not seem to have got in the way of the mission of Colonel Giles, although like him they suffered from ill health. Giles is vaguely interested in ethnic issues, but these had already been ignored in 1913 by awarding towns like Dibër to Serbia. The Curzon policy was keen on strategy and commerce, and Giles like many another good soldier was only obeying orders in putting yet more Albanian-speakers under Yugoslav rule.

In the extreme south-east of Albania, Yugoslavia was eventually awarded the monastery of Sveti Naum, although a whole range of bodies had previously decided that this should belong to Albania. On sentimental grounds this final decision, conceded by Ahmet Zogu as a gesture of thanks for Yugoslav help, seems a sensible one. Naum was a Slav. On the other side of the lake Albania had made a gain at Lin, a Slav-speaking village with an impressive church, and again this decision, though owing little to sentimentality, seemed sensible, as it enabled Albania to keep control of the road and future railway link between Durrës and Pogradec.

So far so good. On the shores of Lake Ohrid boundaries are fairly easy to set, the water providing a convenient cutting off point, and the land behind being not too high. Northwards from Lin the Jablanica Mountains provide an obvious strategic boundary, and Colonel Giles would seem to have followed strategy rather than straight lines in awarding parts of this barren tract to Albania in the settlement of 1926. Further north the Albanians lost ground. The village of Lukova on the western side of the River Drin is clearly marked as Albanian territory in pre-1926 maps. It and a triangular area south of Dibër were awarded to Yugoslavia in the settlement of 1926. Colonel Giles gives us the reason for this decision. The main road from Dibër to Struga on the western side of the Drin passed through this territory. Therefore Yugoslavia had to control both sides of the Drin, south of Dibër. *Quod est*

Demonstrandum, except for the unfortunate fact that there was and is an alternative route from Dibër to Struga which would not have involved this particular set of frontier negotiations. There are, oddly, the Slav-speakers of Gollobordë whom Giles notes as Bulgarian living on the Albanian side of the new frontier ,which did however leave a few more Albanian-speakers in Yugoslavia. In 1987, 41.8 per cent of inhabitants of the commune of Struga considered themselves Albanian, and in Dibër the figure was 45.2 per cent.

North of Dibër is an area about eight kilometres square which some maps give as Albanian territory in 1913 surrendered to Yugoslavia in 1926, while others record exactly the reverse decision. The territory north of a village called Bllatë is now Albanian, Bllatë being the present frontier post. The muddle appears to have arisen because of the dispute between the six commissioners in 1913. If the French and Russian commissioners had had their way, this area would have gone to Serbia, and thus this would have been, like Lin, an Albanian gain, awarded for the same reason namely that the main road to Peshkopi from the west passes through this small area. In fact, as Monsieur Fournier and General Potapoff did not prevail, Albania was only really reclaiming its own, and this area should not be claimed as an Albanian gain except in the sense that as the Serbs had made the Drin their de facto frontier any land to the east of the river could be counted as territory regained.

The frontier around Dibër is very unsatisfactory.Taking the road from Tirana to Peshkopi one can clearly see the minarets of Dibër nestling in a little plain. The town is therefore not very easy to defend, as various forces found in the Second World War. At the same time the view is an awkward reminder to Albanians in nearby villages of the tribal centre and commercial link that they had lost. Perhaps these considerations influenced Giles in what appears to be his greatest injustice to Albania, the removal of quite a large area of territory near Prizren and Gjakova, apparently awarded to Albania in 1913, but given to Yugoslavia in 1926. Here most modern atlases are in agreement. There are two large lobes of territory, one extending between Prizren and Gjakova covering some quite fertile land stretching to a bend in the White Drin. Further south the larger but less prosperous salient stretched as far as the Sar Planina mountain range between Kosova and Macedonia, forming a line very close to the present boundary between these two states. The present frontier between Albania and Kosova follows a slightly less high ridge to the west. The two frontiers eventually converge at Mount Korab, but at its widest this particular loss to Albania measures more than thirty kilometres. The extent of the southern lobe is obscured by the British maps of the Balkans which appeared during the war. The 1:400,000 map of Serbia, Montenegro and Albania has a frontier which actually contrives to give Gorani villages like Zapod to Serbia because it gets the physical geography of this area entirely wrong.

Again one can see the reasons for this decision. After deciding to give Prizren and Gjakova to the Serbs in 1913 it would seem to make sense to give them villages in their hinterland. Giles does talk about the Gora (sic) tribe all going to Yugoslavia, but ethnology is not his strong point, and he fails to notice that the revised frontier as well as leaving thousands of Albanians in Yugoslavia actually included a few Slav-speaking Gorani in Albania. Another complicating factor is that one of the principal elements in the population of the southern lobe is not Slav or Albanian but Turkish.

From Gjakova to the northernmost point of Albania Giles made no changes to the obvious frontier, the high points of a range of mountains known as the Prokletijë or Accursed Mountains, and not really a bone of contention. Controversy and confusion only really enter when we come to Vermosh, an isolated village in the extreme north of Albania. Our sources report that Vermosh and Sveti Naum were the last points to be settled in Yugoslavia's favour. But Vermosh, unlike Sveti Naum, remains Albanian, and some atlases actually mark a small area north of the Vermosh river as a gain for Albania. Others show some rectifications in the area, difficult to decipher on a small-scale map. Giles shows what happened. In 1913 the London conference decided that the Klemendi tribe should remain in Albania - unlike the unfortunate Hoti and Gruda tribes which were given to Montenegro for strategic reasons. The Klemendi tribal lands did not extend quite as far as the present frontier in the north, but they had some lands to the east which threatened Gusinjë. Giles suggested an exchange and his suggestion eventually seems to have been followed. The Yugoslavs had they gained Vermosh would have been able to build a road and greatly shorten communications between Podgorica and Gusinjë. Life might have been rather less bleak for the inhabitants of Vermosh, long hours away from any major centre of population. But in this instance the frontier settlement did keep some Albanian-speakers in Albania.

Elsewhere it did not. We have shown how Giles fought hard to keep the boundary in the north-west intact, although some atlases mark rectifications against Albania even here. There seems some confusion between the old pre-Balkan War frontier dividing Turkey and Montenegro and the new line settled provisionally in 1913. On first visiting Northern Albania I was treated to a pompous lecture at the frontier station in Han i Hotit to the effect that we were now entering the Orient, as this spot had once marked the Turkish frontier. In fact the original frontier was a few miles back in Yugoslav territory, and a better lecture would have been on the injustice of a frontier which left so many Albanian-speakers from the Hoti and Gruda tribes outside Albania. Montenegro with only 6.5 per cent of its population in 1987 Albanian-speaking does not have problems like Macedonia (19.8 per cent) or of course Kosova (77 per cent according to this same out of date Yugoslav atlas), but the decision of Montenegro to become independent revealed some disturbing trends with Tuzi, the main centre of Albanians after Ulcinj, not being given commune status.

If 1987 seems a long time ago, 1926 is even longer. At one stage Giles reckons that his boundary changes had affected about fifty thousand people. Not all these 50,000 were Albanian-speakers, and of those who were some may have preferred the relative stability of Yugoslavia in the same country as their market town to the anarchy of life in Albania governed or misgoverned from Tirana. And Giles with his fellow commissioners had their hands firmly tied by the 1913 settlement, prepared in some haste and with considerable ignorance. Nevertheless we cannot help feeling that the 1926 settlement should have been better managed. There is something strange nowadays about the assumption that towns like Prizren and Dibër must be Serbian, and something rather pathetic about the Albanian delegates in 1923 faced with the loss of a large tract of land near Prizren, to say nothing of never having had any claim for Kosova, making a muted and unsuccessful challenge to retain two small villages, Gorozub and Ubnica, right on the frontier through which refugees were to pour three generations later.

In the twenty-first century such concerns about Balkan borders might seem only of interest to academic historians, but the processes arising from the disintegration of Yugoslavia have resulted in eleven countries in the Balkan peninsula (depending on how the Balkans are defined) when at the end of the Cold War in 1990 there were only five: Greece, Romania, Bulgaria, Albania and Yugoslavia. Although in theory borders were meant to disappear in a uniting Europe, in reality many of them are as sensitive and heavily policed as ever, particularly since the illegal migration crisis that began in 2014 and continues today, So the deliberations of Giles and others are still worth study, both in the library and on the ground by the traveller, and the basic human geography determined by mountains, lakes and rivers remains unchanging.

The fifty thousand people who Giles thought had been affected by border changes in the 1920s has risen after the ex-Yugoslav conflicts to maybe ten million, and some states like Bosnia-Herzegovina have ostensibly fixed borders but deep internal fissures in society that may result in future territorial and border demarcations. The dilemmas of the post-First World War period boundary commissioners have not disappeared, but, like Marx's revolutionary mole, have gone underground for a while only to resurface in new forms. Northern Albanian borders are the meeting place of newly-independent Kosova, in 2008, newly-independent Montenegro, from 2006, and the newly renamed Macedonia, in 2018. Albania's own borders are porous and in many places on such inaccessible terrain as to defy all security controls, however technologically advanced. In that sense, Northern Albania remains 'Nobody's Kingdom', a place of movement and transition between different peoples, religions and identities, but with a traditional and abiding way of life with centuries-old Illyrian roots.

NOTES

NOTES TO CHAPTER 1

In my previous book *Badlands-Borderlands*, pp. 171-2, there is a list of bibliographies and general histories of Albania, none of which is very satisfactory. Elsie (2004) is a great improvement on the previous historical dictionary of Albania compiled by Hutchings, although it has a literary bias. A. & C. Black produced a number of books on Albania, especially by Pettifer (2001). Gloyer was revised and enlarged two years after its original publication in 2004. We note later a rash of books about Albania after the collapse of communism, but there is less coverage of the twenty-first century. Pettifer and Vickers wrote the standard account of the immediate post-communist period, *Albania: From Anarchy to Balkan Identity* (1999). Myftiu is disappointing except on religion. The Anglo-Albanian Society continues to produce a useful newsletter, but most other such publications in English on Albanian matters have fallen by the wayside.

In Albania the four scholarly periodicals *Iliria*, *Monumentet*, *Studia Albanica* and *Studime Historike* provide invaluable insights into ancient, medieval and modern history and into the communist interpretation of it. After 1992 there were clearly difficulties for all four publications, and I have been unable to find copies of *Studia Albanica* after 1992. This periodical was written mainly in French, while the others, which seem to have survived better, have summaries in French or even occasionally in English. Many articles appear rather confusingly for reference purposes in more than one periodical, and the sense of déjà vu is increased when one reads the same author giving the same view in different publications or different authors giving the same view in the same publication. Thus the Albanians are Illyrians, and they fought a gallant fight against Romans, Byzantines, Ottomans, Italians, Germans and the world. Scanderbeg is good news, King Zog, the Catholic Church, imperialism, foreign powers including the

Anglo-Americans are bad news. Enver Hoxha and even Ramiz Alia were contributors to these volumes, in which up until 1991 the former receives fulsome praise. The change in 1991 clearly caused more than a hiccough in editorial policy. After these cruel criticisms we have to acknowledge the invaluable work done on archaeology and ancient history by *Monumentet* and *Iliria* and the contributions to medieval studies by such scholars as Anamali and Pulaha in the other two periodicals. Other names appear in the notes to other chapters and the bibliography. Without the help of these articles this book could not have been written.

As will be shown in the notes to each chapter, there is a dearth of Albanian scholarship translated into English and a dearth of English scholarship on Albanian matters. In the Second World War British participants in the struggle like Davies, Amery, Hibbert and Kemp wrote very different accounts, but are cruelly lumped together in articles by Plasari, Daçi and Pollo (1974) and cruelly misspelt as Emmery and Camp. Hibbert, the most reliable source for the period apart from Fischer, wrote a war diary recently published for the first time. Tomes supplements Fischer for the Zog years, airbrushed out of periodlcals in the same way he is a non-person in the Historical Museum. Allcock and Young supply information about Hasluck, Wilder and Durham, although more work could be done on these heroic figures. The Bodleian Library and Taylorian Institute in Oxford have unpublished letters and notebooks of Hasluck. Destani (2001) collects Durham articles from obscure sources, Hasluck published less than Durham but was a better scholar, as Hodgson, Clark and Bailey (2004) show. Both were shrewder and wiser than other travellers to Albania, later and earlier, male and female.

For Albania in Ottoman times there is a shortage of material in English. Stadtmuller shows the superiority of continental scholarship. Jezernik reveals the prejudices of Western travellers against the Balkans in general and Albania in particular. Von Hahn mentions Albanian men with tails, an unlikely tale repeated by Thornton as late as 1939. In the nineteenth century Brown and Knight do not do for Northern Albania what Byron and

Hobhouse did in the South. Some insights into eighteenth- and nineteenth-century Albania are provided by Degrand writing at the beginning of the twentieth century, but his genealogies of leading families are not very reliable and, some would say, not very important. Albanian scholars like Zamputi and Pulaha have collected valuable source material with a slight bias towards showing Albanians as competing against rather than collaborating with their Ottoman overlords. Celebi, translated into English by Elsie and Dankoff, is not as helpful about Northern Albania as he is about the South though he is useful in giving some balance in favour of the Ottomans. In suggesting that Shkodër in 1662 was an entirely Muslim town, Celebi almost certainly underestimates the numbers of what he calls the infidel.

Frashëri (2002) provides a thorough investigation of Scanderbeg. His bibliography shows a shameful lack of books on this subject in English. Venetian, Neapolitan and Ragusan documents are available, the former now collected in a 25-volume series by Valentini, unfortunately ending in 1463. Ducellier (1981) has done much to disentangle this evidence. He is of course an invaluable source for most of the medieval period pointing out the weaknesses of the earlier collection *Acta Albaniae* recently reprinted. Byzantine chroniclers are now beginning to be translated, although of those interested in Albanian affairs only Anna Comnena and Procopius are easily available. For Skylitzes, the Priest of Dioclea and a host of minor authors the reader ideally needs Greek and Latin.

There are of course Loeb and Penguin editions for the classics of Greek and Roman history, although of major texts dealing with Albanian history only Polybius (Walbank 1957-9) has received the benefit of a scholarly edition. Similar work on the later books of Livy would be desirable. Albanian archaeologists have paid more attention recently to the remains of imperial invaders hitherto considered as less important than Illyrian sites. There is slight chauvinist bias in some articles on these sites in *Iliria* and *Monumentet,* and at odds with this, a slight bias in favour of monuments in the South, less Illyrian and more prone to Greek and Latin influence. This is well shown by Ceka (2002) full of pictures of Dyrrachium, Apollonia and Buthrotum, famous sites in Albanian archaeology, but hardly Illyrian sites.

The *Times* leader said by Pettifer (2007), presumably ironically, to be Olympian, is dated 23 January 1997. A.A. Gill called Albania a Ruritania of brigands and vendettas and pantomime royalty in *The Sunday Times* of 23 July 2006. This statement is rather unfair to Rudolf Rassendyl and indeed to King Zog and C.B. Fry, the only monarchs or potential monarchs mentioned, although Gill has some fun with Norman Wisdom and Enver Hoxha. Alpion, p. 34, mentions St Paul, Alexander the Great, Napoleon and Ataturk as Albanians, but has some doubts about Mother Teresa.

NOTES TO CHAPTER 2

Maps of Albania - like books on Albania - have a nasty habit of mounting error upon error. Reasonable modern maps are printed by Bartholomew (1:400,000), Freytag and Berndt (1:400,000), Geocenter (1:300,000) and World Mapping Centre (1:200,000). In all cases the marking of roads, like the roads themselves, should be treated with extreme caution. Earlier maps, frequently reprinted, are an Albanian version, originally compiled in 1951 (1:275,000) and an Austrian version made by H. Louis in 1926 (1:200,000). These are occasionally useful for place names, sometimes mangled, and contour lines, sometimes difficult to distinguish from mountain streams and paths. Large-scale maps made by the Italians between 1928 and 1939, and reprinted by their allies and adversaries during the Second World War, ought to be invaluable, but are not so. The Italian maps are difficult to read, even though Hasluck in the Bodleian Library copies has carefully and helpfully overprinted the names of certain key points. The large scale (1:50,000) is not very useful in locating roads and routes. In the First World War when aerial reconnaissance was not possible maps were even more inaccurate. The Admiralty maps of the Balkans (1:400,000) are good on North-Western Albania, but woefully weak on the North-East. Destani (1999) includes this map, which is discussed in Appendix V. The Admiralty probably relied in part on an Austrian series compiled in difficult circumstances between 1902 and 1918. I have only studied the sections of these maps which show the coast with its vast lagoons and marshes, subsequently drained by the usually vilified Zog and Hoxha. Durham (1987, p. 303) is not very complimentary to the Austrians as she struggled along the Drin, and their faults in this area may have contributed to the failure of the 1916 Admiralty map, and to the difficulties of drawing the frontier between Albania and Yugoslavia. The Second World War Admiralty guide gives a rather different picture of the cartography of the previous conflict and reproduces some of its errors.

Earlier maps of Albania under the Ottoman Empire are colourful but make no claim to accuracy. The coast is fairly well delineated, but inland there is total chaos with the Prespa lakes and Lake Ohrid sometimes all amalgamated, advancing up the Drin to be part of Northern Albania. Von Hahn writing in the middle of the nineteenth century separates the lakes not very accurately, and pulls them south a little. Magocsi and Berxholi supply examples of such maps, and are useful in delineating administrative divisions in Ottoman and modern times, Berxholi providing essential information on the not very exciting subject of *rrethe* and *qarke*. An Albanian school atlas, produced by Mjete-Mësimore Culturore e Sportive, gives an accurate account of Albania's physical geography and some useful maps of climatic conditions. Cold and wet in the winter, Northern Albania is a difficult place to visit and the climate has left archaeological remains in a poor state of preservation. There are local guides to Pukë, Shkodër, Kukës (Perzhita 2004) and Klemendi (Progni) which have English summaries, although the English is optimistic, as are accounts of travelling conditions and the possibility of seeing archaeological.sites. Perzhita is good on archaeology in the Kukës area, and Progni is valuable on recent history in North-Western Albania. Pounds and the Admiralty Guides produced in both World Wars supply general geographical information, honestly acknowledging the difficulty of their task. Guides like those of Murray, which went through several editions, show routes which could be taken by intrepid travellers on horseback in the most improbable places.

For ethnology Andoni is neutral, up to date and interesting, giving information on Slav minorities in Gollobordë and the Goran district, not reckoned as national minorities because the language spoken in thes areas is not the same as the official language of any national state. Thus these Slav-speakers are relegated to a minor division of minorities, known as ethnic minorities like the Roma and the Vlachs with a status inferior to that enjoyed by the Greeks in the South, the Montenegrins of Vraka and the Macedonians near Lake Prespa. Members of this minor league find emigration to another state much harder than, for exaniple the Greeks, and their numbers are likely to have held up, but exact numbers are hard to calculate. Official figures must be treated with extreme caution. They rapidly become out of date. Berxholi is handicapped by using 1960 figures, by considering each district separately and by only considering national minorities. In neighbouring Greece, hostile to minorities, and in Yugoslavia up to 1991, officially giving free rein to minority rights, but in fact encouraging rather optimistically its citizens to think of themselves as Yugoslavs, statistics for minorities were clearly unreliable, but at least we know this. In Albania, even under the harsh communist regime, the government did acknowledge the existence of minorities, although there was clearly pressure on people to think of themselves as Albanians. This pressure led to the relegation of ethnic minorities. The relegation is explained well by Memusaj, who also gives a variety of rough and ready figures almost certainly too low for Slav-speakers. Schukalla writing at a time when communism had just collapsed is not very informative. In contrast, Bartl writing in the same volume as Schukalla has useful information on religious affiliations difficult to ascertain owing to the institution of an official policy of atheism in 1964. Myftiu gives a good history of Albanian religion past and present. Emigration from the South, and extensive rebuilding of the Catholic and Bektashi faiths in the North and East would make the figures of 7 per cent Bektashi, 10 per cent Catholic, 20 per cent Orthodox and 63 per cent Sunni

Muslims suspect. Berxholi, though using 1960 figures, is useful for showing the- main areas of religious strength and also the pattern of emigration. The struggle for Kosova was not good for Orthodoxy, and there was also some migration from the North-East by Albanian Muslims passing themselves off as political refugees. Religion is no longer a taboo subject, and it should be possible to collect reliable statistics, although it is always difficult to evaluate and interpret such statistics. Clayton is probably the most reliable authority on this difficult subject.

Durham (pp. 353-4) gives a rough map of Albanian tribes possibly more accurate than the Admiralty guide (1945, p. 173), which is presumably based on the Admiralty map reproduced in Destani (1999). The long excursus on tribes in this guide is taken from the First World War guide. It may have been the part of the guide to which Hasluck referred when with typical tactlessness she wrote to Sir John Myres (Myres Collection, Bodleian Library) complaining that the Admiralty guide was useless. Courteously Myres replied that he was the author, although it is not clear whether this reply indicates his responsibility as general editor in the Second World War or actual author in the First. For names of districts I have relied heavily on the Freytag Berndt map. This does not name Dushman as a place or district, and I assume like some premature obituarist that both have vanished in the process of turning the Drin into a lake. Procopius' Dusmani may be a coincidence. They are (*Buildings* IV, 4) placed either in Dardania or possibly even further to the east.

NOTES TO CHAPTER 3

Wilkes (1991) is invaluable on Illyrians, and I have relied heavily on him, even borrowing his allusion to *Twelfth Night*. From Yugoslvia Garasanin and Papazoglou are useful, like Wilkes making extensive use of the work of Albanian archaeologists, although like Wilkes including a good deal of material concerned with areas to the north and east of Northern Albania. We have already noted that, though Northern Albania is more Illyrian than the South, Albanian archaeologists have done more work in the South with more accessible and better preserved sites. There may also be a political motive for this preference. The volumes of Korkuti (1971), Strazimiri and .Eggebrecht supply handsome photographs, and their maps show the extent of Albanian archaeological discoveries after the Second World War.

There are general articles on Albanian archaeology by Ceka, H., Islami (1972a), Karaiskaj (1977), Korkuti (1982), Prendi (1975) and (1976). Work on particular northern sites has been done by Andrea (Nezir), lslami (1970, Xibri), (1972b, 1975, Zgerdesh), Jubani (1972, Gajtan) and (1982, Kruma), Jubani and Ceka (Rosunjë), Karaiskaj (Marshej), Kurti (1971, 1976, Lezhë), Perzhita (1986, Bushati), (1993, Bardhoc), (1995, D omaj), Prendi and Zheku (Lezhe). Without literary evidence it is often hard to distinguish which of these sites were isolated fortresses and which were urban centres, and in the absence of numismatic and epigraphic centres it is hard to identify the date atwhich proper cities were established. Paradoxically at Shkodër, where we do have written and numismatic evidence of a city in late Illyrian times, proper excavation of the Rozafat site has been impossible because of the continuous occupation of this site since those times.

The major classical texts.dealing with Illyrians are Herodotus I, 196, IV, 49, VIII, 137, IX, 42; Thucydides I, 21,26, IV, 124-5; Scylax I, 15-44; Theopompus F 39-40, 182; Diodorus Siculus XIV, 22, XV, 2, XVI, 2, XIX, 67, 74, 78; Polybius I, 196-237, II, 2-12, III, 16, 18-19, V, 109-10; XXXII, 34; Livy XXIX, 12, XXXI, 28, 35, XL, 42, XLII, 26, 48, XLIII, 18, 19, XLIV, 30-32, XLV, 26; Strabo VII, 5; Pliny III, 32-3, Appian, *Illyrike*; Polyaenus IV,12, VII, 42; and Justin VII, 5, VII, 6. This is a list in chronological order, not in order of merit. Of these authors only Herodotus, Thucydides and Polybius have been properly edited, and their interest in Illyria and Illyrians is limited. Herodotus' geography is vague, but he does clearly see the Illyrians as occupying most of the former Yugoslavia and Northern ·Albania. Thucydides is mainly concerned with incursions to the south and east, while Polybius deals with the wars against Rome. Hammond (1966, 1968, 1972, 1982, 1989) and Wilkes (1991) have good comments on the other sources, but Wilkes is too kind to Appian writing long after the events he describes, and Hammond too kind to Strabo writing a long way away from Illyria. Both are like Livy quintessential armchair historians although Strabo may be borrowing material from the much earlier and better travelled Hecataeus. This is in itself a source of confusion for the location of Illyrian tribes, whose authority waxed and waned over five hundred years. Pliny is our main source for the *Illyrii proprie dicti*. Diodorus Siculus provides the main evidence for the invasion of Dionysius of Syracuse and indeed for the period of Illyrian strength in the wars against Macedonia, but his chronology is suspect, he is not really interested in our area, and his universal history is universally abused as well as used.

For affinities between the Illyrians and Albanians, Cabej (1958, 1971, 1976) supplies the official line. Anamali (1976), Gjinari, Domi and Mansaku more technical explanations. Matters are not helped by the fact that in equating Illyrians withAlbanians we have to acknowledge that one half of the equation is almost blank. Names of people are suspect for the reasons named, while names of places survive from one dominant race to another without proving any link between one race and the other. We can see this from Celtic toponyms in the

Celtically named Britain. Cultural and archaeological links (bibliography in Wilkes, p. 278) are even more suspect, as shown in Chapter 5. Buda (1986) gives in English a representative account of the standard Albanian view. Some opposition to this view is provided by Popović, Katičič, Georgiev and Schramm. Crosland, Malcolm · (1998) and Fine (1983) are reasonably balanced.

Maps of Illyrian tribes can be found in Ceka, N. (2002, p. 42), Garasanin (p. 171, Wilkes (1991, p. xxi), Hammond (1972, p. 614), the Barrington Atlas (p. 49) and the *Tabula Imperii Romani* (K.34). Ceka and Garasanin give fairly rudimentary maps with many omissions. Hammond has many maps in his many publications and is the main contributor to this section of the Barrington Atlas, but he is principally interested in Southern Albania. Wilkes is an admirable informant on tribes, but his map is handicapped by a small scale in spite of which.there seems a large gap between the Shkumbi and the Drin where the Parthini and Taulantini seem to rule the roost. Horizontal and vertical notation is confusing. In his text Wilkes shows the difficulty about the Atintani and the Encheledae both found sometimes with slightly different names, in different areas. The Barrington Atlas copes quite well with the problem of different tribes being dominant at different times by using different fonts to delineate early, middle and late Illyrian times, but even so it has many gaps, one of which it boldly fills in with a tribe called Albanoi. This goes back to Ptolemy who marked the town of Albanopolis, otherwise not referred to, Ptolemy's map like my map, compiled in less difficult circumstances, demonstrates the difficulty of making maps.

Notes to Chapter 4

The narratives of Polybius and Livy dovetail fairly neatly with each other to provide a full account of the three Macedonian and three Illyrian wars. Walbank's commentary on Polybius is excellent, and it is sad that Briscoe never got beyond the fourth decade in doing similar work for Livy. Briscoe like Livy is something of an armchair historian, refusing to travel to Greece under its right-wing regime, and presumably not a frequent visitor to Albania with its different politics. There are some good pioneer articles by Beaumont, Dill (1977), Hammond (1968), May and Walbank (1976) and Hammond, who is not an armchair historian, supplies excellent background material in his histories of Epirus and Macedonia (Hammond (1967, 1972, Hammond and Griffith, Hammond and Walbank). In this period, as in the time of the Crusades and later of Scanderbeg, Northern Albania found itself caught in the middle of opposing forces, Romans and Macedonians, Normans and Byzantines, Venetians and Turks. Oddly, compared with Anna Comnena and Barlettius, Polybius and Livy writing in a more remote era are models of impartial objectivity and geographical knowledge, although not perfect in either respect.

Sadly there are no such historians ancient or modern for the next period of Roman rule where Livy only exists in epitome and the Roman frontier had moved northwards. Wilkes (1969) does his best with the piecemeal acquisition of the Dalmatian coast. The main source are Livy, Ep LVI, LXII and Eutropius VII, 4. Appian in spite of his interest in Illyrian matters does not say much about them in his general history of Roman affairs, nor is there much in the relevant volume of the Cambridge Ancient History (Lintott, pp. 31-3). The campaign between Caesar and Pompey near Durrës is treated in depth by Rice Holmes III, pp. 330-81, but though there is plenty of information about Roman armies here and in Caesar's own words, *De Bello Civili*, I II, 11-79, there is little about Albania or its inhabitants. For Shkodër as the dividing line between Antony and Octavian and for the revolting Parthini, see Appian, Civil Wars, V, 65 and 75. The revolt may have been due to the fact that the Parthini had supported Brutus in the Philippi campaign, but neither Appian nor Plutarch is very informative about the part played by Albania in any of the civil wars fought in or near Albanian territory. Tiberius' campaign against the Illyrian rebels almost certainly took place a long way away from Albania, although the Historical Museum proudly quotes the not very reliable Velleius Paterculus II, 99-112, to show what a formidable opponent the Illyrians were. In the next two centuries they did not prove very formidable, although the difficulties of the terrain prevented much Roman settlement.

The harsh terrain also makes archaeology difficult. It so happens that Scodra, Dyrrachium and Lissus are all the sites of modern towns whose familiar names reveal continuous occupation but prevent detailed excavation. For the region north of Shkodër, see Cameron and Pettifer (2008). Foreign archaeologists (useful article by Gilkes) have done little work in the North. Evans and Ugolini did some pioneer work, using primitive methods. Ugolini provides interesting photographs of the Drin before it was turned into a lake. Baçe (1986), though sensible, is rather short, Anamali (1986) is longer but more general, Prendi and Zheku write about Lissus, and Mirdita (1976 and 1983) writes about Dardania, but these articles are exceptional. There is much more about late antiquity in Albanian periodicals, anxious to establish links between Illyrians and Albanians, and even the essays in Garasanin's collection which do not have this aim do not have much to say about the period of maximum Roman power.

NOTES ON CHAPTER 5

Historians of this period suffer from a shortage of primary material. There are, of course, plenty of sources for the story of the Roman Empire in the third, fourth and fifth centuries. Disaster attracts more commentary than prosperity. The divisions and subdivisions of the Empire under Diocletian and Constantine are well attested, as are the attitudes of both these powerful emperors towards Christianity. Ammianius is almost as good as a stylist and a historian as Tacitus, and Matthews supplies an admirable commentary on his account of most of the fourth century. The period between the Battle of Adrianople and the succession of Justinian is less well served. Marcellinus Comes is brief, Priscus survives only in fragments, and Claudian and Jordanes are unreliable sources for Goths. Procopius is a better source of information for the next century but is tantalising and elusive when it comes to the Balkans. He only has one dubious mention of Praevalitana (Praekalis in Gothic Wars 1.15), also mentioned in similarly imperfect fashion by Hierocles (Prevalis, 656, 3). We rely on the *Notitia Dignitatum* (1, 123, v, 3) for the proper name.

When Byzantine authority collapsed in the Balkans chroniclers like Zosimus, Theophanes and his continuator, Theophylact Simocatta, and others have little to say about Albania. In the seventh and eighth centuries the Empire was often nearly at the end of its tether, and Albania was just beyond this tether. Skylitzes, beginning where Theophanes left off in 811 AD, is better informed particularly towards the end of this period, but even for the wars against Samuel of Bulgaria we are partly dependent on improbable authors like the Armenian historian Asoghic and our first Slav source, the Priest of Dioclea. There are, of course, no Albanian chroniclers, and the paucity of information from the West can be demonstrated by the fact that of the 835 entries in

Acta Albaniae taking us from 334 to 1343 AD only 57 cover the period from the fourth to the tenth century.

Secondary sources are rather better. Jones is an invaluable authority for the later Roman Empire, including, a full account of the *Notitia Dignitatum*. Sakellariou and Kountora are quite good on bishops, although the exact boundaries of civil and ecclesiastical provinces, marked boldly by Jones on his maps, are hard to determine. Even the boundary between the Eastern and Western Roman Empires is curiously hazy. We could do worse than consult on this point Hodgkin writing at a time when the Balkans were still divided between the Ottoman and Austro-Hungarian Empires, and we could do better than Roberts writing just after Montenegro became independent again. She is very good on the Ottoman and modern periods, but appears to have difficulty with the points of the compass in the Byzantine era.

There have been some interesting more recent studies of the collapse of the Roman Empire by Smith, Ward-Perkins and Heather (2005). These are general accounts, although Heather (1991) is good on Balkan Goths. Ward-Perkins takes a rather more savage view of the horror of the Gothic invasions than the other authors, although he has an interesting account of Severinus in Noricum clinging onto the remnants of Roman authority. Magdearu does the same for life in Scythia Minor, the Danube delta. Arguments by analogy from these provinces including the preservation of languages, religion and urban life are clearly imperfect. In Western Europe Roman subjects had generally abandoned their languages for Latin before the barbarian invasions, and generally persuaded the invaders to adopt this adapted tongue, but the ancestors of the Slavs, Albanians and modern Greeks did not behave in the same fashion, leaving the Vlachs and the Romanians at the margin to adopt the West European norm.

This fact slightly colours the accounts by Slav, Greek and Albanian scholars of the early Byzanine period. Nevertheless there have been excellent articles by historians from all three parties on these dark ages. There are scholarly papers by Frashëri

(1998) and Saradi, as well as by Ducellier (1998) in the symposium organised by the Byzantine Institute in Athens. Garasanin from Yugoslavia cites Albanian articles extensively and reproduces the excellent map in Baçe (1976). Baçe as well as Kaka and Shtylle gives interesting information about roads and forts, where British scholarship has not done much since the days of Evans (Destani, 2006). We have shown in notes to the previous chapter that much of Albanian scholarship is devoted to general statements of the link between Illyrians and Albanians. There are also a number of articles designed to demonstrate this link established by aspects of the Komani-Kruja culture, e.g. Anamali (1966). Here British scholarship (Wilkes 1992, Bowden) acts as a corrective.

NOTES TO CHAPTER 6

This period in contrast to the previous one has almost too much source material. There are many entries in the *Acta Aibaniae* and in the even longer collection of Venetian documents made by Valentini. The copious footnotes in Ducellier (1981) referring also to Neapolitan and Ragusan records show the complexity of an era when Albania was being fought over by various nationalities, and he is only really dealing with the coast. Buda (1983) is useful for the last century of this period. There are a few Slav documents dealing with the Nemanjid dynasty, controversial when it comes to discussing ethnicity, as Buda giving an Albanian view reveals. The main Byzantine historians (Acropolites, Anna Comnena, Attaleiates, Nicetas Choniates, Psellus, Skylitzes) are fairly easily available, and some of them have been translated. The Cambridge Medieval History V, VI and VIII has some good articles on the Balkans, but apart from Ducellier (1999) there is not much about Albania in them, and the same is true of general histories of Byzantium in particular periods like Angold and Nicol. Fine (1987), much longer than Fine (1983) has some difficulty with the disparate nature of his subject and the controversies it has engendered.

Thus the references to Albanians by Attaleiates (p. 9.9, p. 18.18 and p. 297.21) and by Anna Comnena (1, 168, 11, 60 and 111, 104) have been the subject of a prolonged and at times acrimonious discussion between Ducellier and Vranousis. Ducellier (1998) gives his last word on the subject. In the Yugoslav corner Ferančić is fairly balanced. For Arianites, see Skylitzes 11, 454, 459, 596, and Attaleiates 34, 596. Ducellier raises the question of Albanians in Western sources, mentioning the brilliant observations of Grégoire about the appearance of d'Albeigne and other Albanian names in the *Chanson de Roland*. This suggests that Albania was known in the West at the time of the Crusades; but also how unreliable these source are on geography, since clearly Albania is not in the Pyrenees. Ducellier is more convincing than Vranousis about the number of references to Albanians in the eleventh century, since though some of them can refer to inhabitants of Italy or even (a long shot) to Scottish members of the Varangian Guard they are unlikely all to do so. The apparent subservience of the Albanians to the Byzantine cause is best explained by the fact that, contrary to Albanian historical orthodoxy, the Albanians were subservient.

Ducellier (1981) retreats slightly from this idea of subservience in tracing the rather brief rise and fall of the dynasty of Progon seized upon by Albanian historians (Shuteriqi, 1967b) as evidenoe of a national state. Ducellier (1998) veers in the other direction. The primary evidence in *Acta Albaniae* 1,134 and 140 is hardly conclusive. In the anarchy following the Fourth Crusade loyalty to the Byzantine Empire is likely to have been strained, but by 1252 in the time of Golem Byzantine power was slowly recovering. In later times Albanians proved surprisingly loyal to the Ottoman Empire, and there were probably similar vestiges of support for various Greek states as late as the fourteenth century. The Angevin dynasty attracted less loyalty, although it supplied copious documents and made extravagant claims. It is a pity that we have no equivalent for Albania of the old-fashioned, but still valuable, account by Miller of the Latins in Greece showing how the feudal system both worked and did not work with various underlords and overlords competing with shifting loyalties for small patches of land. The allocation by Philip of Taranto, the grandson of Charles of Anjou, of fiefs to various feudal lords in Albania (*Acta*

Albaniae 1, 563) is useful for naming the lands, but Philip was granting land he did not have to give to people who had already claimed or in some cases lost it. The boast of Charles Thopia, great grandson of Philip, to be ruler of Albania towards the end of the fourteenth century is equally baseless.

Not surprisingly, modern Albanian historians have steered clear of the feudal and genealogical niceties of the fourteenth and fifteenth centuries with only the Kastriot family (Biçoku 1973) and the Arianites (Shuteriqi 1965, 1967a) into which Scanderbeg married receiving much attention. There is a good account of the Balsičs in Rozman, who is a little kind to them, and in Roberts, who stresses their dubious ethnic origins. There were undoubtedly Vlach, Slav and Albanian people in the Balsič realm. The two battles of Kosovo have caused equal confusion, which Emmert has tried to dispel. Pulaha and Buda supply essays and documents for the fifteenth century with a clear but fair bias towards showing the ethnic composition of Kosova as Albanian. A Serbian counterbalance as supplied by Roberts is strangely silent on Albanian affairs, introducing Scanderbeg (p. 93) correctly but oddly as an Ottoman general.

Scanderbeg naturally occupies a large amount of space in Albanian historical writing. Frashëri (2002) has good maps and a full bibliography, but one needs Albanian to read it, as one does for contributions to Pulaha (1989). Of the articles translated or summarised into French Biçoku (1970. 1973), Pulaha (1970) and Xhufi (1982) are the best. For those with English only, Hodgkinson and Noli are pleasant but lightweight biographies. Inevitably all these authorities give glowing accounts of their hero. Gibbon 3, 175 goes too far in the other direction. The primary evidence is hard to find but unsatisfactory. Gibbon is rightly contemptuous of Barlettius, a work much cited but not easily available. The Latin version is like its translation from Latin into French a quaint period piece with antique printing and woodcuts. In the original Latin the many speeches are, like Livy's speeches, works of fiction. Gegaj tried to find an alternative contemporary source in an anonymous writer from Antivari, but Orly and Babinger followed by Ducellier (1981) dismiss this as a forgery by the eighteenth-century writer Biemni. Serbian sources discussed by Cirković and even Greek historians of the early Ottoman Empire like Chalcondylas, Critobulus and Ducas do little to enhance the reputation of Albania's mightiest hero, seen as a small irritant in the way of the inevitable Turkish advance. There were other forces fighting the Turks like the Venetians with whom Scanderbeg's relations were often strained and sometimes hostile, and the great Hungarian hero Hunyadi, with whom Scanderbeg mysteriously seemed unable to coordinate. Of course Scanderbeg united the Albanians, won many battles and may have saved the West.

NOTES TO CHAPTER 7

General studies of the Ottoman Empire (Babinger, Inalcik, Shaw) tend to pay more attention to the conqueror than the conquered, while general studies of the Balkans (Jelavich, Stavriarios, Glenny) tend to concentrate on the prolonged struggles for liberation in the nineteenth century. Albania, conquered rather than conquering, and a late starter in the liberation stakes, gets a short shrift on both accounts, and with Obbini finishing his history in 1601 we are also short of primary material, although there are good collections of sources, translated into Albanian by Buda (1957), Zamputi (1989) and Zamputi and Pulaha (1990). Albanian historians have also written articles on this period, albeit with a predictable nationalistic stance. Wars between the Ottoman Empire and Venice and Austria almost certainly had Albanians fighting on both sides, but this hardly fits in with the idea of a gallant native resistance against a foreign foe. The Bushati family, with their semi-independence and wars against the Montenegrins are better role models, in spite of their lack of democratic qualifications. These criticisms should be borne in mind when studying the articles of Mile (1964, 1965), Zamputi (1964, 1966), Pulaha (1967, 1968, 1976,1982). Pulaha (1976) is particularly good on the near-independence of the Northern tribes.

For the tribal structure and the primitive moral code which supported it, Hasluck is better than Durham, and there is a surprising amount of information in Malcolm's book on Kosova and Roberts' history of Montenegro. Roberts is particularly good in explaining how the warlike Montenegrins with their brotherhoods and tribes developed in a fashion different from, but parallel to, the tribes and fratries of Northern Albania. In the time of the Balsićs it would have been hard to distinguish the two, whereas under the Bushatis and in subsequent struggles during the nineteenth century the two races were clearly at odds with each other. In the sixteenth century the Ottomans occupied Montenegro, and a member of the leading family the Crnojevićs turned Turk and following the example set by George Castriot took the name of Scanderbeg (Roberts, pp. 96, 105-6). But unlike the Albanian Scanderbeg, Stanisa Crnojević remained loyal to the Ottomans, whereas his people unlike the Albanians and the Bosnians (Malcolm 1994) remained loyal to Christianity. The lead in Montenegrin affairs was taken by the Petrović family, one of whom became bishop, a hereditary title passed from uncle to nephew. The Montenegrin tribes united behind their bishops, and as a result Montenegro became fiercely anti-Ottoman, with different tribes joined by a common religion and purpose. Catholic, Muslim and Orthodox tribes in Northern Albania were less fortunate, although the movements of population in both areas, and the religious and ethnic affiliations of this population are still a matter of dispute.

Celebi, well translated by Elsie and Dankoff, tends to look at Montenegro, Kosova and Albania as principally Muslim, refers contemptuously to the infidel, and is perhaps rather disappointing as a source of information for the seventeenth century. Thengelli (2002) supplies material on Islamization. There is little information about the eighteenth century, although careful Ottoman records faithfully collected by Pulaha show this as a period of religious change. At the end of this century we find the first stirrings of nationalistic movements in the Balkans, but Albania seemed slow to stir, whereas Montenegro aided by Orthodox Russia was virtually independent. Elsie (1995) is good on the first books in Albanian, but these are uninformative about history. Western travellers did not start to arrive in the Balkans until after the Napoleonic Wars, which had made life difficult. Life in Northern Albania was always difficult.

Elsie (1995) supplies plenty of information about the Rilindjë with good potted biographies of the Frashëri brothers and Pashko Vasa, and there is an excellent objective account of late nineteenth-and early twentieth-century history in Skendi (1967). It is perhaps regrettable that the League of Prizren fell slightly flat and more than regrettable that Prizren is in Kosova. The site of the meeting of Albanian leaders was destroyed by Serbs in the Milosevic era, and has been lovingly restored since. Events leading to independence and the difficulties of the Balkan wars are well covered by Pearson (2004). Cary and Durham (1914) supply interesting insights from opposing sides into the struggle for Shkodër. Alia takes a nationalistic line on the League of Prizren, suitable for Hoxha's successor, and under Hoxha the Kanun of Lek Dukagjin is not very sympathetically treated by Pupovci (1968, 1971) and Elezi.

NOTES TO CHAPTER 8

Pearson (2004, 2005 and 2006) is an admirable source for the period from 1908 to 1998, and I have drawn heavily upon it. The selections tend to dry up in the period after Zog's death, and this is disappointing. Quite a lot happened between 1961 and 1998, but nearly forty eventful years are crammed into the last fifty pages of the third volume whereas five hundred pages of the second volume are devoted to the years between 1940 and 1945. In the third volume Zog receives as many references as Hoxha, who died in 1985, and in the second volume four times as much space, although he had fled the country in 1939 and Hoxha emerged victorious in 1944. This arithmetic might seem to indicate a right-wing bias, but Pearson was just collecting what was in the news, and it must be remembered that during the war and the period after it Zog had not lost and Hoxha had not gained newsworthy status. It is possible to cavil at Pearson's assumption that Philby betrayed the resistance to Hoxha, this assumption leading to anchronistic entries from books published in 1968 and 1984 to describe events in 1950 (Pearson, 2006, pp, 396, 412).

Zog is the object of lengthy studies by Swire, Tomes and the more scholarly Fischer. Swire, although eventually expelled during Zog's reign from Albania, is too favourable to the monarch. Some unpublished correspondence from and to him has just been discovered. Tomes is good on his origins and early years, Albanian periodicals from the Hoxha years (Belegu) less so although quite useful on Fan Noli's brief period in Albania (Pollo and Behiku, Puto 1992). For Hoxha we have in English the lightweight work of Halliday and the lengthy collected works, lengthier in the original Albanian. Clearly Hoxha was on shaky ground at the time of the break with first Yugoslavia and then the USSR, but the official history of the Party of Labour in Albania papers over the cracks. There is only a short biography of Noli, an important figure. He lasted longer than Qemal Bey Vlora or William of Wied, treated sympathetically by Falaschi and Heaton-Armstrong. The ordinary people of Albania do not figure very prominently in the lives of these supposedly great men, and regrettably the same has to be said of twentieth-century travellers who wrote about these people sympathetically but with little understanding of recent or not so recent history. These remarks apply to Edmonds, Heseltine, Newman, Matthews, the Gordons, and even to Durham's many works. Hasluck is in a different category, although her notebooks in the Taylorian Library, Oxford, are dry and disappointing. The official communist history of Albania before the Second World War is, as might be expected, a story of gallant uprisings against foreigners and fascists.

In describing the war years Amery, Kemp and Smiley slug it out with Hibbert and Davies in defending or attacking the policy of supporting the communists whose own accounts of the war years take a predictable line. There are some not very interesting accounts of particular campaigns by Plasari and Doçi. Pollo and Puto give a rather dull account of this war, which is treated however in their work and in that of others in a great deal more depth than the First World War, where the Albanians did not behave in a particularly glorious fashion, particularly in their treatment of the retreating Serbs (Petrović).

It is odd that in Yugoslavia and Greece, where there was a right-wing and a left-wing resistance, opinions about the rights and wrongs of the conflict in the Second World War were much less diivided with most people supporting, like Fitzroy Maclean, the victorious left in Yugoslavia, and most people, like Monty Woodhouse, supporting the victorious right in Greece. In Albania the Germans come out in a better light than they did in either of these neighbouring countries, and Fischer shows this in an objective light. The Italians (Cervi in fact, Kadare, 1990, in fiction) appear as less satisfactory. Bailey has published an account of SOE's involvement in Albania, rejecting any suggestion that there was a left-wing conspiracy to ensure communist success. Oakley-Hill was before, during and after the war in his dealings with different kinds of Albanians a witness to the fact that muddle rather than malice was a key factor in Brtish policy. Nevertheless Bethell, no friend to the communists in Yugoslavia, and Sulzberger are convinced that Kim Philby was behind the surprising failure to overthrow the Hoxha regime after the war. For a good account of the betrayal of some of the agents sent in by the British, see Bardha, whose narrative blames Philby indirectly, but also has some harsh words for clumsy English officers and Albanians secretly working for the government.

For obvious reasons it was difficult for Albanians or foreigners to write about the country objectively between 1945 and 1990. People from abroad were allowed in rarely and controlled carefully when they entered Albania. Accounts of such visits by Bland and Ash seem more sycophantlc than sympathetic. Albanians followed the party line. Kadare's criticisms of.the party line had to be veiled, so veiled that only with hindsight we can detect them (Kadare 1971, 1993). Some writers, mainly from the South, were penalised for making too obvious attacks on the regime, while others including Kadare found themselves ostracised after communism had collapsed for making their attacks too obscure (Elsie 1995, pp. 515-614).

Even now it is still difficult for foreigners or Albanians to write with candour about the twentieth century. In *Badlands* I drew attention to a school textbook by Myzin tactfully taking refuge in Mother Teresa and Kosova as safe subjects, although both are controversial. It is difficult to wash dirty linen in public, and bloody linen is even harder. A foreigner has to be unusually thick skinned if he or she wishes to probe old wounds. Current politics complicate matters still further as many publications and intellectuals were for a long time associated in some way with the old regime, and/or linked in some way with the divisive politics of today. Edi Rama and Fatos Lubonja are fairly exceptional. Learned periodicals print little about recent history, although Fishta has been rehabilitated (biography in Elsie and Mathie-Heck) and religion can be discussed (Biçoku 2002, Frashëri 2000, Prifti 2000). Sometimes articles take a pro-Partisan line in desribing the Second World War and its immediate aftermath. Dyrmishi is unusual in giving an account of resistance to the communists after the war, but guidebooks such as the Nagel guide published in1990 and the Albanian handbook prepared by the magazine *New Albania* in 1984 still gave a standard view of the Hoxha years.

NOTES TO CHAPTER 9

The collapse of the communist regime produced a spate of books and articles, most of them overtaken by the rapid march of events in Albania. Thus Hall is a good geographical account, but was too optimistic about Albania's economic and political recovery. Weedon, one of many moved by the poverty of Albania's population, wrote about humanitarian relief which events in 1997 quickly flattened, while events after 1997 seemed to make such aid irrelevant. Biberaj is good on the pyramid scandal. Pettifer and Vickers (1996) were prescient in hinting at impending disaster, although the title of the book *From Anarchy to a Balkan Identity* is both ironic in view of the collapse into anarchy in 1997 and ambiguous in view of the identification of the Balkans with anarchy. The lawless reputation of the Albanian part of the

Balkans was increased by events in Kosova, the subject of many books. Malcolm is the best along with Vickers (1998), although until Pettifer and Vickers (2007) such books did not say much about the rather delicate subject of Albania's involvement in Kosovan affairs. Pettifer and Vickers fill this gap and are good on other Albanian minorities outside Albania, just as their previous work supplies information on non-Albanian minorities in the country. They give a detailed account of the critical period of the 1997 uprising against the Berisha government and the links to the war in Kosova. See also Vickers (2020) for a discussion of politics and minorities in post-Cold War Albania.

NOTES TO APPENDIX I

The key passages for the location of Uscana are Polybius 8, 14 and Livy 43, 18 and 19. Walbank's commentary is fair. He quotes in favour of Uscana being near Dibër like previous scholars such as Sadiku and Kromayer, although the former makes Grazdhan Draudacum. Meloni places Uscana near Dibër, but Draudacum and Oeaneum much further west with the Fan as the Arathus. For more recent Albanian scholarship, see Kaka and Frashëri. Islami generally follows Hammond who is probably the main force behind the compilation of the two atlases. Hammond (1966) is quite persuasive about the location of Styberra, but not entirely so. Perseus did arrive *tertio die* and there were 2000 lightly armed troops. A great walker, Hammond did convincing work on previous long journeys by Macedonian monarchs (Hammond and Walbank, p. 325 for Philip and p. 525 for Perseus crossing the Pindus Mountains). The mountains between Macedonia and Kosova are a formidable barrier. Irregular troops did make this journey in both directions during the troubled last years of the twentieth century, but regular armies in the second century BC would have found it hard going.

NOTES TO APPENDIX II

Muller is indispensable for the Roman roads across the Balkans, but too precise. For the Albanian theory of alternative routes, see Perzhita. Destani (2006) discusses Evans'travels and Durham records her own. Kaka and Shtylle have little in the way of translation, but some good maps. Baçe provides information on forts in late antiquity and roads in medieval times. Kurti (1998) is interesting for routes in the time of Hierocles. The Italians built the present road from Shkodër to Kukës and the communists turned the Drin into an artificial lake. These two routes rendered all previous tracks superfluous, and they have virtually vanished, although archaeological discoveries m ay still be unearthed.

NOTES TO APPENDIX III

Procopius wrote about more interesting subjects than buildings, and general books about him like Cameron's pay less attention to this part of his work. Justinian's campaigns of reconquest did not take place in the Balkans, and there are few mentions of Illyricum, Epirus and most importantly Praevalitana, possibly lurking under Praekalis in the more frequently discussed.wars. Not unnaturally Procopius' *De Aedificiis* has received little attention in English. Dewing's edition has a good index, but his location of place names is crass. Besevliev is much better, but unfortunately concentrates on the Danube frontier. Albanian scholars have made some inspired guesses at some of Procopius' names, perhaps handicapped by a reluctance, not evident in Besevliev or Skok, to see a Latin origin for many of them.

NOTES TO APPENDIX IV

To Šišić and Mošin we must add Iwachniuk, which appears to offer a translation and is published in Ottawa. Unfortunately the translation is into Ukrainian. There are some useful maps. Fine (1991, pp. 193-4 and Roberts, p. 50, who calls the Priest lively but often unreliable, are in agreement with Radovinović, pp. 67-7 even in talking of Vladimir's story. Stephenson (2000, pp. 118-20) is less hostile with regard to this story and earlier events. Totila, Ostroylus and Praevalitana are mentioned in Chapter 2, the Morovlachi or Nigri Latini and people retreating to mountain tops in Chapters 5 and 6, Svatopluk, Poletum and Balibona in Chapter 9, and the Vladimir story begins in Chapter 3.

NOTES TO APPENDIX V

Most of the documents dealing with the long drawn out settlement can be found in Destani (1999). He also provides a number of maps which reveal but do not solve our difficulty. Giles (1930) is a useful supplement to the peppery correspondence preserved by Destani. In blaming map makers for getting things wrong I am aware how easy error is in difficult country with the additional handicaps of working to a small scale with frontiers that were hotly disputed even before they were settled - settled being rather a euphemistic name for the pre-war arrangements. Swire (p. 280) is rather surprisingly the best authority, though working with rather rough and ready maps in black and white. Such a classic text as Malcolm (1998, p. xxiv) is incorrect in suggesting that Albania lost ground all along its eastern frontier while gaining a little in the north-west. Magocsi, working with colour, deals with the frontier on three different maps: 44a shows larger gains for Albania in the north-west, the major loss near Prizren, a slight loss near Dibër, and appears to give Sveti Naum to Albania and Lin to Yugoslavia; 47b gets Lin and Sveti Naum right, but makes Albania lose territory both north and south of Dibër. This map only really deals with Macedonia. Map 47a dealing with Albania shows no gains in the north-west other than the fact that the 1913 frontier appears inside the later boundary, appears to minimise the loss near Prizren and to repeat the pattern of 47b with Lin and Sveti Naum. Philips and Bartholemew show Albania's frontiers expanded in the north-west near Shkodër, almost reaching Podgorica.

If mapping frontiers is difficult, the morality of frontiers is even harder. We have tried to show how Giles and his masters like Curzon were influenced by factors like communications and strategy. Nevertheless, as Malcolm and Magresi make clear as they drew fairly accurately the area occupied by Albanian-speakers - Magresi perhaps underestimating the size of this area in Kosova,

Macedonia and. Montenegro - the 1913 frontiers were unfair to Albanians and the 1926 frontiers made the position even less fair. It is true that some Slav-speakers were still left in Albania, as Wilkinson points out. But Northern Albania and its immediate vicinity is not an ethnic mosaic In the Banat, oddly enough never a place of ethnic tension, Romania and Yugoslavia, both on the winning side, inherited a mixed population of Serbs, Slovaks, Romanians, Hungarians, Germans and gypsies from the defeated Austro-Hungarian Empire, and the Great Powers divided the land between them. In Northern Albania Colonel Giles and his colleagues divided a land almost entirely Albanian between Albania and Yugoslavia, and this cannot have been right.

In 1947 there was a cold winter in England, and the Cold War had just started. To cheer me up my geography teacher told me an old joke about a man living on the Russian-Polish border who was asked on which side of the frontier he would like his farm to be. He said he would prefer Poland to avoid the Russian winter. He is unlikely to have been given the choice any more than Albanians after the First World War, although in 1926 many Albanian-speakers might have preferred a resurgent Yugoslavia to a chaotic Albania just as in 1998 many people would have made and did make a different choice. Borders are cruel dividers and in ending this appendix on this apparently frivolous note, I would like to stress the evils of nationalist divisions, which have turned a beautiful land into an unhappy one.

SELECT BIBLIOGRAPHY

A. PRIMARY SOURCES

Loeb editions have been used whenever possible for Classical activities. They were generally published in New York or Cambridge, Mass, as well as London, and have been frequently reprinted. The dates of publication and the universal London in the following bibliography are an inadequate tribute to a magnificent series. For Byzantine texts translations are mentioned when available. Individual editions when mentioned in the notes can be found under modern authors.

Acropolites, George, ed. A. Heisenberg, Leipzig, 1903.

Ammianus Marcellinus, ed. and trans. J.Rolfe, London, 1935-9.

Appian, ed. and trans. H.White, London, 1912.

Arrian, ed. and trans. P. Brunt, London, 1976.

Attaleiates, Michael, ed. I. Bekker, Bonn, 1853.

Caesar, ed. and trans. A. Peskett, London, 1924.

Chalcocondylas, Laontcus, ed. E. Darko, Budapest, 1922-3.

Choerosphactes, Leo, ed. and trans. G. Kolias, Athens, 1939.

Chomatinus, Demetrius, ed. G. Prinzing, Münster, 1980.

Choniates, Nicetas, ed. J. van Dieten, Berlin and New York, 1975.

Cicero, Letters, ed. and trans. D.R. Shackleton Bailey, London, 1999-2000.

Claudian, ed. and trans. M. Plalnauer, London, 1922.

Comnena, Anna, ed. B. Leib, Paris, 1937-45.
    trans. E. Sewter, Harmondsworth, 1969.

Constantine Porphyrygenitus, ed. G.Moravczik, trans. R. Jenkins, Budapest, 1949.

Critobulus, Michael, ed. R. Reinsch, Berlin, 1983.

Diodorus, ed. and trans. C. Oldfather, C. Sherman, R. Geer, C. Welles and F. Walton, London, 1933-58.

Ducas, Michael, ed. I. Bekker, Bonn, 1845.

Eutropius, trans. A. Bird, Liverpool, 1993.

Herodotus, ed. and trans. A. Godley, London, 1920-4.

Hierocles, ed. A. Buckhardt, Leipzig, 1893.

Homer, ed. and trans. A.Murray, London, 1919-25.

Jordanes, ed. T.Mommsen, Berlin, 1882.

Justin, ed. O. Seel, Leipzig, 1935.

Livy, ed. and trans. B. Foster, F. Moore, E. Sage and A. Schlesinger, London, 1919-52.

Lucan, ed. and trans. J. Duff, London, 1967.

Lupus Protospatharius, ed. G. Pertz, Hanover 1830.

Malchus, ed. G. Niebuhr, Bonn, 1829.

Marcellinus Comes, ed. T. Mommsen, Hanover, 1828.

Notitia Dignitatum, ed. O.Seeck, Berlin, 1876.

Pliny, ed. and trans. H. Rackham, W. Jones and E. Eicholz, London, 1938-71.

Polyaenus, ed. and trans. J. Melber, Stuttgart, 1970.

Polybius, ed. and trans. W. Paton, London, 1922-7.

Procopius, ed. and trans. H. Dewing, London, 1914-50.

The Secret History, trans. G. Williamson, Harmondsworth, 1966.

Psellus. Michael, ed. E. Renauld, Paris, 1967.
     trans. E. Sewter, Harmondsworth, 1966.

Scymnus and Scylax in Geographi Graeci Minores, ed. C. Muller, Paris, 1855.

Skylitzes. John, ed. H. Thum, Graz, 1983.

Strabo, ed. and trans. H. Jones, London, 1917-32.

Theopompus, ed. R. Eyss, Bonn, 1827.

Thucydides, ed. and trans. C. Smith, London, 1919.

Velleius Paterculus, ed. and trans. F. Shipley, London, 1924.

B.   SECONDARY SOURCES

Acta Albaniae (1913-18), ed. L. Thalloczy, K. Jiricek and M. Sufflay, 2 vols, Vienna.

Admiralty, The (1920), *A Handbook of Serbia, Montenegro, Albania and Adjacent Parts of Greece*, London.

     (1945), *Albania*, Geographical Handbook Series, London.

Alia, R. (1975), 'La ligue albanaise de Prizren - page brilliante de notre histoire que notre peuple a écrit de son sang,' *Studia Albanica*, 1, 23-46.

Allcock, J. and A. Young, ed. (2000), *Black Lambs and Grey Falcons*, New

York and London.

Alpion, G. (2007), *Mother Teresa, Saint or Celebrity*, London.

Amery, J. (1948), *Sons of the Eagle: A Study in Guerilla Warfare*, London.

Anamali, S. (1966), Le problème de la civilisation haute-mediévale albanaise à la lumière des nouvelles découvertes archéologiques', *Studia Albanica*, 3, 1, 199-211.

(1970) 'Basse antiquité et Haut Moyen Age dans les recherches Albanaises', *Iliria*, 9, 5-22.

(1976), 'Des Illyriens aux Albanais (les anciens Albanais)', *Iliria*, 5, 23-40.

(1986), 'Processus de transformation dans la région meridionale illyrienne aux Ier-IIVe siecles', *Iliria*, 16, 1, 15-41. ·

Andoni, B. (2003), *Minorities: The Present and the Future*, Tirana.

Andrea, S. (1985), A propos de la genèse et de la continuité de la culture de Mat à l'époque du Bronze', *Iliria*, 15, 2, 163-74.

Angold, M. (1997), *The Byzantine Empire, 1025-1204: A Political History*. London and New York. ·

Antoljak, S. (1985), *Samuel and his State*, Skopje.

Ash, W. (1974), *Pickaxe and Rifle*, London.

Babinger, F. (1976), *Mehmed the Conqueror*, Princeton.

Baçe, A. (1976), 'Fortifications de la basse antiquité en Albania', *Monumentet*, 1, 45-74.

(1979), 'Aperçu sur l'architecture des fortifications antiques dans nos pays', *Monumentet*, 17, 5-45.

(1986), 'La structure urbaine des villes de l'Illyrie dans les années 168 av. n ère - 212 de n. ère', *Iliria*, 16, 11, 215-21.

Bailey, R. (2001), 'Smoke without Fire: Albania, SOE and the Communist "Conspiracy Theory"' in Schwander-Sievers, 143-54.

(2004), 'Margaret Hasluck and the Special Operations Executive (SOE), 1942-44', in Shankland, 1, 151-82.

(2008), *The Wildest Province: SOE in the Land of the Eagle*, London.

Baldacci, A. (1912, 1917), *Itinerari Albanesi*, 2 vols, Rome.

Barbarich, E. (1903), *L'Albanie*, Rome.

Bardha, E. (2003), *Far and Yet Near Albania*, Tirana.

Barletius, M. (1506-08), *Historia de Vita et Gestis Scanderbegi Epirotarum Principis*, Rome.

(1596), *The Historie of George Castriot, surnamed Scanderbeg, Newly Translated into English by Z.I.Gentleman*, London.

Beaumont, R. (1936), 'Greek influence in the Adriatic before the fourth century BC', *Journal of Hellenic Studies*, 61, 159-204.

Bartl, P. (1968), *Die albanien Muslime zur Zeit der nationalen Unabhangigkeitsbewegung* (1878-1912), Wiesbaden.

ed. (1975-9), *Quellen und Materialen zur albanischen Geschichte im 17 und 18 Jahrhundert*, Munich.

(1997), 'Religiongemeinschaften und Kirchen', in Grothusen, 511-614.

Baxhaku, F. and K. Kaser (1996), *Die Stammesgesellschaften Nordalbaniens: Berichte und Forschungen osterreichischer Konsuln und Gelehrter (1861-1917)*, Vienna.

Belegu, M. (1971), 'L'insurrection de Dukagjin en 1926', *Studime Historike*, 8, 1, 59-84.

Bërxholi, A. (2003), *Demographic Atlas of Albania*, Tirana.

Besevliev, V. (1970), *Zur Deutung der Kastellnamen in Prokop's Werk 'De Aedificiis'*, Amsterdam.

Bethell, N. (1984), *The Great Betrayal: The Untold Story of Kim Philby's Biggest Coup*. London.

Biberaj, E. (1998), *Albania in Transition*, Westview.

Bicoku, J. (1993), 'The. Albanian Spirit of the Christian Church; and the Assembly of the Arberi', *Studime Historike*. 39, 3, 17-29.

Bičoku, K. (1970), 'Quelques problèmes liés à la vie et l'oeuvre de Georges Castrioti Scanderbeg avant l'année 1443', *Studime Historike*, 7, 2, 139-65.

(1973), La situation administrative et politique dans la region de Misja et son importance dans l'oeuvre de Georges Castrioti Scanderbeg durant les années 30 de xve siècle', *Studime Historike*, 10, 2, 29-62.

Biemni, G.M. (1742), *Historia di Giorgio Castrioto detto Scander-beigh*, Brescia.

Bland, W. (1981), *A Short Guide to the People's Socialist Republic of Albania*, London.

Bodinaku, N. (1975), Pazhok ('fouilles archeologiques', 1973), *Iliria*, 3, 407-14.

Bowden, W. (2003), 'The Construction of Identities in Post-Roman Albania' in Lavan and Bowden, 56-78.

Brown, H. (1888), *A Winter in Albania*, London.

Briscoe, J. (1973), *A Commentary on Livy Books XXXI-XXXIII*, Oxford.

(1981), *A Commentary on Livy Books XXXIV-XXXVII*, Oxford.

Buda, A. (1976), 'Les Illyriens du sud: un problème de l'historiographie', *Iliria*, 4, 39-53.

(1982), L'ethnogenèse du peuple albanais à la lumiere de l'histoire', *Studime Historike*, 19, 3, 168-89.

(1985), *The Albanians and Their Territories*, Tirana.

(1987), *Dokumente per Historië e Shqiperisë te Shekë XV*, Tirana.

Buda, A., ed., (1977), *La Conférence Nationale des Etudes Ethnographiques*, Tirana.

(1984), *Problems of the Formation of the Albanian People, their Language and Culture*, Tirana.

Cabanes, P. (1988), *Les Illyriens de Bardylis à Genthios IV-II siècles avant J-C*, Paris.

Cabej, E. (1958), 'Le problème de l'autochtonie des Albanais à la lumière des noms de lieux', *Bulletin of the State University*, Tirana, 2, 54-66.

(1971), 'L'Illyrien et l'Albanais', in Korbuti *et al*, 41-52.

(1976), 'Le problème du territoire de la formation de la langue albanaise', *Iliria*, 5, 7-22.

Cambridge Ancient History, vol. III, 1, *The Prehistory of the Balkans and the Middle East and the Aegean World, Tenth to Eighth Centuries BC*, ed. J. Boardman, I. Edwards, N. Hammond and E. Sollberger (1982).

Cambridge Ancient History, vol. III, 3, *The Expansion of the Greek World, Eighth to Sixth Centuries BC*, ed. J. Boardman and N. Hammond (1982).

Cambridge Ancient History, vol. VIII, *Rome and the Mediterranean to 133 BC*, ed. A. Astin, F. Walbank, M. Frederiksen and R. Ogilvie (1989).

Cambridge Ancient History, vol. IX, (1994), *The Last Age of the Roman Republic*, ed. J. Cook, A. Lintott and A.Rawson.

Cambridge Medieval History, vol. III, *c.900-c.1024*, ed. T. Reuter (1999).

Cambridge Medieval History, vol. IV, *The Byzantine Empire*, ed. J. Hussey (1966).

Cambridge Medieval History, vol.V, *c.1198-c.1300*, ed. D. Abulafia (1999).

Cambridge Medieval History, vol. VI, *c.1300-c.1415*, ed. M. Jones (2000).

Cambridge Medieval History, vol.VII, *c.1415-c.1500*, ed. C. Allmand (1998).

Cameron, A. (1985), *Procopius and the Sixth Century*, London.

Cameron A. and J. Pettifer (2008), *The Enigma of Montenigrin History: The Example of Svac*, Tirana.

Carver, R. (1998), *The Accursed Mountains: Journeys in Albania*, London.

Cary, J. (1965), *Memoir of the Bobotes*, London.

Ceka, H. (1976), 'A propos de certaines questions de l'histoire des Illyriens à la lumière des données numismatiques', *Iliria*, 4, 289-93.

Ceka, N. (1983), 'La naissance de la vie urbaine chez les Illyriens de Sud', *Iliria*, 13, 2,135-92.

(1985a), 'La civilisation protourbaine illyrienne', *Iliria*, 15, 1, 111-50.

(1985b), 'Aperçu sur le développement de la vie urbaine chez les Illyriens du Sud', *Iliria*, 15, 2, 137-61.

(2002), *lliret*, Tirana.

Celebi, Evliya (2000), Sebayatname: English Selections, ed. with Translation, Commentary and Introduction by Robert Dankoff and Robert Elsie, Leiden.

Cervi, M. (1971), *The Hollow Legions: Mussolini's Blunder in Greece*, Garden City.

Cirkovic, S. (1998), 'Tradition interchanged. Albanians in the serbian, Serbs in the albanian late medieval texts', in Gasparis, 177-94.

Clark, M. (2000), 'Margaret Masson Hasluck', in Allcock and Young, 128-54.

Clayer, N. (2003) 'God in the Land of the Mercedes: The Religious Communities in Albania since 1990', in Jordan, 227-314.

Crossland, R. (1982), 'Linguistic Problems of the Balkans Area in the Late Prehistoric and Early Classical Periods', in *Cambridge Ancient History*. III, 3, 934-49.

Daçi, S. (1989), 'Les réenforcements des familles féodales et leur possessions dans la région de Lezhë aux XIII-XIV siècles, *Studia Albanica*, 26, 2, 67-74.

Daniel, O. (1985), *Albanie: une bibliographie historique*, Paris.

Davies, E. (1952), *Illyrian Venture: The Story of the British Military Mission in Enemy-Occupied Albania*. London.

De Waal, C. (2005), *Albania Today*, London.

Degrand, J. (1901), *Souvenirs de la Haute-Albania*, Paris.

Dell, H. (1967), 'The origin and nature of Illyrian piracy', *Historia* 16, 30-8.

(1977), 'Macedonia and Rome: the Illyrian question in the early second century BC', *Ancient Macedonia* 2, 305-15.

Derrow, P. (1989), 'Rome, the Fall of Macedon and the Sack of Corinth', in *Cambridge Ancient History*, VIII, 290-323.

Destani, B., ed. (1999), *Albania and Kosovo: Political and Ethnic Boundaries, 1867-1946*, London.

(2006), *Ancient Illyria: an Archaeological Exploration by Arthur Evans*, London.

Doçi, M. (1970), 'La Lutte pour la libération à la Mirditë (août-octobre 1944)', *Studime Historike*, 7, 3, 13-45.

Domi, M. (1983), 'Problèmes de l'histoire de la formation de la langue albanaise, résultats et tâches', *Iliria*, 13, 1, 3-38.

Ducellier, A. (1981), *La Façade maritime de l'Albanie au moyen age: Durazzo et Valona du Xième au XVième siècle*, Salonica.

(1987), *L'Albanie entre Byzance et Venise, X-XVe siècles*, London.

(1998), 'L'Albanais dans l'empire byzantin', in Gasparis, 17-45.

(1999), 'Albania, Serbia and Bulgaria', in *Cambridge Medieval History*, V, 779-95.

Durham, E. (1905), *The Burden of the Balkans*, London.

(1914), *The Struggle for Scutari*, London.

(1920), *Twenty Years of Balkan Tangle*, London.

(1987), *High Albania*, London.

(2000), *Albania and the Albanians: Selected Articles and Letters.1903-1944*, ed. B. Destani, London.

Dyrmishi, D. (1999), 'The Mobilization of the Political Adversaries in the Postriba Uprising', *Studime Historike*, 36, 1, 107-25.

Edmonds, P. (1927), *To the Land of the Eagle: Travels in Montenegro and Albania*, London.

Eggebrecht, A., ed. (1988), *Albanien: Schatze aus dem Land der Skiptaren*, Mainz.

Elezi, I. (1974), 'La lutte contre les survivances du droit coutoumier en Albania', *Studia Albanica*, 12, 2, 33-46.

Elsie, R. (1995), *A History of Albanian Literature*, 2 vols, Columbia.

(2004), *Historical Dictionary of Albania*, Maryland.

Elsie, R. and J. Mathie-Heck (2005), *Gjergj Fishta, The Highland Lute*, London.

Emmert, T. (1990), *Serbian Golgotha: Kosovo, 1389*, New York.

Errington, R. (1989), 'Rome and Greece to 205 BC'; 'Rome against Philip and Antiochus', in *Cambridge Ancient History*, VIII, 81-106, 244-89.

Falaschi, N. (1978), *Ismail Kemal Bey Vlora: Memoire*, Rome.

Ferancic, B. (1988), 'Les Albanais dans les sources byzantines', in Garašanin, 303-22.

Ferluga, J. (1976), *Byzantium on the Balkans*, Amsterdam.

Fine, J. (1983), *The Early Medieval Balkans: A Critical Survey from the Sixth to the Late Twelfth Century*, Ann Arbor.

(1987), *The Late Medieval Balkans: A Critical Survey from the Late Twelfth Century to the Ottoman Conquest*, Ann Arbor.

Fischer, B. (1984), *King Zog and the Struggle for Stability in Albania*, Boulder.

(1999), *Albania at War, 1939-1945*, London.

Frashëri, K. (1992), 'Les Albanais et Byzance aux vie- xie siècles', in Gasparis, 47-57.

(2000), 'The Beginnings of Christianity in the Albanian lands', *Studime Historike*, 37, 1, 5-19.

(2002), *Gjergj Kastrioti Skenderbeu*, Tirana.

Gashi, S. (1983), 'The Presence of the Albanian Ethnos in Kosova during the 13th-14 th Centuries in the Light of the Serbian Church Sources', in Buda 1985, 247-86.

Gasparis, C., ed. (1998), *The Medieval Albanians*, Athens.

Garašanin, M., ed. (1988), *Les Illyriens et les Albanais*, Belgrade.

Gawyrch, G. (2006), *The Crescent and the Eagle*, London.

Gegaj, A. (1937), *L'Albanie et l'invasion turque au XV siècle*, Paris.

Georgiev, V. (1966), 'The Genesis of the Balkan Peoples', *Slavonic and East European Review*, 44, 285-97.

Gibbon, E. (1896), *The History of the Decline and Fall of the Roman Empire*, London.

Giles, F. (1930), 'Boundary Work in the Balkans', *Geographical Journal*, 75, 300-12.

Gilkes, O. (2003), 'The Rivals. Luigi Ugolini, Leon Rey and their predecessors', *Iliria* 37, 47-66.

Gjeçovi, S. (2002), *Kanuni i Lekë Dukagjinit*, Shkodër.

Gjinari, J. (1971), De la continuation de l'illyrien en albanais', in Korkuti *et al*, 173-81.

Glenny, M. (1999), *The Balkans, 1804-1999: Nationalism, War and the Great Powers*, London.

Gloyer, G. (2006), *Albania. The Bradt Travel Guide*, London.

Gordon, J. and C. (1927), *Two Vagabonds in Albania*, London.

Grégoire, H. (1939), 'La chanson de Roland de l'an 1085', *Buletin de la Classe des Lettres et des Sciences Morales et Politiques*, 25, 245-318.

Grothusen, K.-D. (1992), *Sudöst Europa Handbuch, Band VII. Albanien*, Göttingen.

Hall, D. (1994), *Albania and the Albanians*, London.

Halliday, J. (1966), *The Artful Albanian*. London.

Hammond, N. (1966), 'The Kingdoms in Illyria circa 400-167 BC', *British School at Athens*, 61, 259-83.

(1967), *Epirus*, Oxford.

(1968), 'lllyria, Rome and Macedonia in 229-205 BC', *Journal of Roman Studies*, 58,1-21.

(1972), *A History of Macedonia*, vol.I, Oxford.

and Griffith, G. (1979), *A History of Macedonia*, vol.II, Oxford.

(1982a), 'Illyris, Epirus and Macedonia in the Early Iron Age', in *Cambridge Ancient History*, III, 1, 619-56.

(1982b), Illyris, Epirus and Macedonia', in *Cambridge Ancient History*, III, 3,261-85.

and Walbank, F. (1988), *A History ofMacedonia*, vol. III, Oxford.

(1989), *Alexander the Great*, Bristol.

Hasluck, M. (1954), *The Unwritten Law in Albania*, Cambridge.

Hahn, J. von. (1853), *Albanesische Studien*, Vienna.

Heather, P. (1991), *Goths and Romans, 332-489*, Oxford.

(2005), *The Fall of the Roman Empire: A New History*. London.

Heaton-Armstrong, W. (2003), *Albania, 1914: The Six Months Kingdom*, London.

Heseltine, N. (1938), *Scarred Background: A Journey through Albania*, London.

Hibbert, R. (1991), *Albania's National Liberation Struggle: The Bitter Victory*, London.

Hodgkin, T. (1880), *The Visigothic Invasion*, Oxford.

Hodgkinson, H. (1999), *Scanderbeg*, London.

Hodgson, J. (2000), 'Edith Durham: Traveller and Publicist', in Allcock and Young, 9-31.

Hopf, C. (1873), *Chroniques gréco-romanes inédites ou peu connues, publiées avec notes et tables*, Berlin.

Hoti, M. and G. Alia (2004), *Puka: Veshtrim gjeografiko-turistik*, Shkodër.

Hoxha, E. (1974-87), *Selected Works of Enver Hoxha*, 6 vols, Tirana.

Huta, P. (1990), *Fshati në Sanxhakun e Shkodres ne shekujt xv-xvi*, Tirana.

Hutchings, R. (1996), *Historical Dictionary of Albania*, Maryland.

Inalcik, H. (1973), *The Ottoman Empire: The Classical Age, 1300-1600*, London.

and Quataert, D. (1994), *An Economic and Social History of the Ottoman Empire, 1300-1914*, Cambridge.

Islami, S. (1972a), 'Naissance et développement de la vie urbaine en Illyrie', *Iliria*, 2, 7-23.

(1972b), La ville illyrienne à Zgërdhesh de Krujë', *Iliria*, 2, 217-37.

(1972c), 'Le monnayage de Skodra, Lissos et Genthios', *Iliria*, 2, 379-408.

(1974), 'L'etat illyrien et ses guerres contre Rome, (231-168 avant notre ère)', *Iliria*, 3, 5-48.

(1975), 'Zgërdhesh (fouilles archéologiques 1973)', *Iliria*, 3, 425-32.

(1976), 'L'état illyrien, sa place et son rôle dans le monde méditerranéen', *Iliria* 2, 71-87.

Iwachniuk, H. (1986), *Chronicle of the Priest of Dioclea*, Ottawa.

Jacques, E. (1995), *The Albanians: An Ethnic History from Prehistoric Times to the Present Day*, London.

Jelavich, B. (1983), *History of the Balkans*, 2 vols, Cambridge.

Jezemik, K. (2004), *Wild Europe: The Balkans in the Gaze of Western Travellers*, London.

Jenkins, R. (1966), *Byzantium: The Imperial Centuries*, London.

Jiriček, K. (1903), *Albanien in der Vergangenheit*, Vienna.

Jones, A. (1973), *The Later Roman Empire*, Oxford.

Jones, L. (2000), *Biografi*, London.

Jordan, P. *et al.* (2003), *Albanien-Geographie-Historische-Geschichte- Kultur-Postcommuniste Transformation*, Vienna.

Jubani, B. (1972), 'La céramique illyrienne de la cité de Gajtan', *Iliria* 2, 409-50.

   (1982), 'Les tumulus de Kruma', *Iliria*, 12, 2, 147-95.

Jubani, B. and N. Ceka. (1971), 'Fouilles dans la cité illyrienne de Rosunjë', *Iliria*, 1, 66-79.

Kaca, I. (2003), *Rrugët e Vjetra të Dibrës*, Tirana.

Kadare, I. (1991), *The General of the Dead Army*, Translated from the French by D. Coltman, New York.

   (1992), *La Pyramide*, Paris.

Karaiskaj, G. (1976), 'Les fortifications préhistoriques en Albanie', *Monumentet*, 14, 19-40.

   (1970), 'La nécropole des IIIe et IVe siècles dans la ville illyrienne de Zgërdhesh', *Iliria*, 7, 201-16.

Katičić, R. (1976), *Ancient Languages of the Balkans*, The Hague.

Kemp, P. (1958), *No Colours or Crest*, London.

Knight, E. (1889), *Albania: A Narrative of Recent Travel*, London.

Kolsto, P., ed. (2005), *Myths and Boundaries in South Eastern Europe*, London.

Komata, D. (1990), 'Forteresses haute-mediévales albanaises', *Iliria*, 20, 2, 181-283.

Korkuti, M. (1982), 'A propos de l'ethnogenèse des Illyriens', *Iliria*, 12, 1, 157-90.

Korkuti, M. *et al* (1971), *Shqipëria Arkeologjikë*, Tirana.

   (1973), 'Les agglomérations fortifiées de la première période du fer en Albanie', *Studime Historike* 10, 3, 107-31.

Kountoura, E. (1998), 'The presence of the province of Epirus Nova in the so-called Notitia Dignitatum', in Gasparis, 169-170.

Kostallari, A. *et al.* (1970), *Deuxième conférence des Etudes albanologiques*, Tirana.

Kromayer, J. and G. Veith (1903-31), *Antike Schlachtfelder*, Berlin.

Kurti, D. (1971a), 'Vestiges de civilisation illyrienne dans la vallée de Mat', in Korkuti, 147-69.

   (1971b), 'Traces de la civilisation haute-mediévale à Mati', *Iliria*, 1, 267-71.

   (1976a), 'Nouveaux éléments sur la civilisation illyrienne des tumuli de Mati', *Iliria*, 4, 237-48.

(1976b), 'La civilisation de la Basse Antiquité a Mati: chaînon intermédiaire entre la civilisation illyrienne et la civilisation albanaise', *Iliria*, 5, 309-15.

(1978), 'Forteresses et citadelles inconnues dans le district de Mat', *Monumentet*, 18, 77- 92.

(1983), 'Les tumulus illyriens de Burreli', *Iliria*, 13, 1, 85-108.

Lampe, J., and M. Jackson (1982), *Balkan Economic History, 1550-1950*, Bloomington.

Lane, R. Wilder (1923), *Peaks of Shala*, New York.

Lampe, J. (2006), *Balkans into Southeastern Europe*, London.

Lavan, L and W. Bowden. (2003), *Theory and Practice in Late Antique Archeaology*. Leiden.

Leake, W. (1835), *Travels in Northern Greece*, London.

Lintott, A. (1994), 'The Roman Empire and its Problems in the Late Second Century', in *Cambridge Ancient History*, IX, 16-39.

Logoreci, A. (1997), *The Albanians: Europe's Forgotten Survivors*, London.

Luka, K. (1983), *Chansonnier épique albanais*, Tirana.

Magdeanu, A. (2001), 'The End of Town Life in Scythia Minor', *Oxford Journal of Archaaeology*, 20, 207-12.

Magocsi, P. (2002), *Historical Atlas of Central Europe*, London.

Malcolm, N. (1994), *Bosnia: A Short History*, London.

(1998), *Kosovo: A Short History*, London.

Mansaku, S. (1987), 'Onomastique et histoire de la langue albanaise', *Studia Albanica*, 24, 1, 85-96.

Marmellaku, R. (1976), *Albania and the Albanians*, London.

May, J. (1946), 'Macedonia and lllyria 217-167 BC', *Journal of Roman Studies*, 36, 48-57.

Matthews, J. (1989), *The Roman Empire of Ammianus*, London.

Matthews, R. (1937), *Sons of the Eagle*, London.

Mazower, M. (2000), *The Balkans*, London.

McGowan, B. (1981), *Economic Life in Ottoman Europe*, Cambridge.

Meloni, P. (1953), *Perseo e la fine della monarchie Macedoine*, Rome.

Memusaj, R. (2002), *The Albanian Legislation on Linguistic Rights of Minorities*, Tirana.

Mile, L. (1964), 'De l'activité politique et militaire de Kara-Mahmud Shkodra en 1782-1797'. *Studime Historike*, 1, 1, 179-206.

(1965), 'Sur le mouvement albanais de libération nationale durant le domination Ottomane', *Studime Historike*, 2, 1, 81-121.

Miller, K. (1916), *Itineraria Romana*, Stuttgart.

Miller, W. (1908), *The Latins in the Levant: A History of Frankish Greece*, London.

Mirdita, Z. (1972), 'La base illyrienne de l'ethnie albanaise: aspects de la question', *Studia Albanica*, 9, 1, 41-8.

(1976), 'A propos de la romanisation des Dardaniens', *Iliria* 5, 143-50.

(1983), 'On the Problem of the Romanisation of the Dardanians', in Buda 1985, 179-94.

Mosin, V. (1950), *Ljetopis Popa Dukljanin*, Zagreb.

Murray, G. (1856), *A Handbook of Turkey and Surrounding Territories*, London.

Murphy, D. (2002), *Through the Embers of Chaos*, London.

Musaj, F. (1987), *Isa Boletini*, Tirana

Myziri, H. (1994), *Historia e Popullit Shqiptar*, Tirana

Najbor, P. (2002), *La Dynaste du Zogu*, Sezan.

Newman, B. (1938), *Albanian Journey*, London.

Nicol, D. (1972), *The Last Centuries of Byzantium*, London.

Njegoš, P. (1930), *The Mountain Wreath of P.P. Nyegosh, Prince Bishop of Montenegro, translated by James Wiles*, London.

Noli, F. (1947), *George Castrioti Scanderbeg*, New York.

Nopsca, F. (1910), *Aus Šala und Klementi, Albanische Wanderungen*, Sarajevo.

Oakley-Hill, D. (2002), *An Englishman in Albania*, London.

Orbini, M. (1601), *Il Rebno di gi Slavi Hoggi correctamente detti Schiavoni*, Pesaro.

Papazoglou, F. (1965), 'Les Origines et la destinée de l'état illyrien', *Historia*, 14, 143-70.

(1988), 'Les Royaumes d'Illyrie et Dardanie', in Garašanin, 173-200.

Parucca, A. (2005), *Shkodra: Bastion i Qytetërimit Shqiptar*, Tirana.

Patsch, C. (1896-1912), *Archaeologische Epigraphische Untersuchen der Geschichte der Römischen Provinz Dalmatien*, Vienna.

Pavlowitch, S. (1999), *A History of the Balkans, 1804-1945*, London and New York,

Pearson, O. (2004-6), *Albania in the Twentieth Century*, 3 vols, London.

Perzhita, L. (1986), 'La forteresse de Bushati', *Iliria*, 16, 2,187-205.

(1993), 'Gradishta de Bardhoc', *Iliria*, 23, 219-40.

(1995), 'La forteresse de Domaj à Ujmisht', *Iliria*, 25, 267-78.

(2004), *Kukësi, Veshtrim Arkeologiik*, Tirana.

Perzhita, L. and G. Hoxha (2003), *Fortifikime te Shekujve në Dardaninë Perendimore*, Tirana.

Petrovic, N.-J. (1920), *Agonie et résurrection: récit de la prise de Belgrade, de la retraite en Albanie et d'un séjour au lazaret de Corfu*, Courbevoie.

Peters, M. (2003), *Geschichte der Katolischen Kirche in Albanien, 1919-1993*, Wiesbaden.

Pettifer, J. (2001), *Albania and Kosovo: The Blue Guide*, London and New York.

Pettifer, J. and M. Vickers (2007), *The Albanian Question: Reshaping the Balkans*, London.

Pipa, A. (1989), *The Politics of Language in Socialist Albania*, Boulder.

Pollo, S. (1974), 'Aperçu critique sur les mémoires d'étrangers relatifs à la lutte antifaciste de libération nationale en Albanie', *Studia Albanica*, 11, 1, 157-64.

Pollo, S. and K. Bihoku (1982), 'Fan S Noli, éminente figure du mouvement patriotique et democratique et de la culture albanaise', *Studia Albanica*, 19, 1, 63-84.

Pollo, S. and A. Puto (1981), *The History of Albania from its Origins to the Present Day*, London.

Polome, E. (1982), 'Balkan Languages', in *Cambridge Ancient History*, III, 1, 187-237.

Popović, V. (1988), 'L'Albanie pendant la basse antiquité', in Garašanin, 250-84.

Poulton, H. and Pettifer, J. (1994), *The Southern Balkans: Minority Rights Group Publication*, London. Pounds, N. (1964), Eastern Europe, London.

Prendi, F. (1975), 'Un aperçu sur la civilisation de la première periode du fer en Albanie', *Iliria*, 3,109-38.

(1976), 'L'urbanisation de l'Illyrie du sud a la lumière des données archéologiques', *Iliria*, 4, 89-100.

(1982), 'The Prehistory of Albania', in *Cambridge Ancient History*, III, 1, 187-237.

Prendi, F. and Zheku, K. (1986), 'Considération sur le développement urbain de Lissus', *Iliria*, 16, 1, 57-66.

Prifti, K. (2001), 'The Religious Diversity and Ethnic Unity of the Albanians', *Studime Historike*, 38, 1, 25-42.

Progni, K. (2000), *Malësia e Kelmendit*, Shkodër.

Pulaha, S. (1971), 'Les contrées occidentales et centrales du sandjak de Shkodër à la fin du XVe siècle', *Studime Historike*, 9, 1, 63-102.

(1976), 'Formation des régions de self government dans les Malëssies du Sandjak deShkodër aux XV-XVIIe siècles', *Studia Albanica*, 13, 2, 173-81.

(1982), 'La résistance armée du peuple Albanais contre la domination Ottomane à la lumière de nouvelles données', *Studia Albanica*, 19, 1, 31-62.

(1983), *Populissia Shqiptarë e Kosoves Gjatë Shek XV-XVI*, Tirana.

(1983), 'Les Albanais et la bataille de la plaine de Kosovo de l'an 1389', *Studia Albanica*, 27, 1, 27-50.

Pupovci, S. (1971), 'Sources à étudier du coutoumier de Lek', *Studime Historike*, 8, 1, 75-98.

(1972), 'Les origines et le nom du coutoumier de Lek Dukagjine', *Studime Historike*, 8, 1, 75-98.

Puto, A. (1982), 'Noli à la tête du gouvemement démocratique en 1924', *Studia Albanica*, 19, 1,85-94.

Radovinovic, R. (2004), *Montenegro: Tourist Guide*, Zagreb.

Rexhepi, F., ed. (1998), *Isa Boletini dhe Koha e Tij*, Pristina.

Rice Holmes, T. (1923), *The Roman Republic*, vol. III, Oxford.

Roberts, E. (2007), *Realm of the Black Mountain: A History of Montenegro*, London.

Rollyson, C. (1995), *Rebecca West: A Saga of the Century*, London.

Rozman, A. (1998), 'Sources concerning the conflict between Balsha and Venice', in Gasparis, 261-7.

Runciman, S. (1930), *A History of the First Bulgarian Empire*, London.

Sakellariou, M. ed., (1997), *Epirus: Four Thousand Years of Greek History*, Athens.

Saradi, H. (1998), 'Aspects of early Byzantine urbanism in Albania', in Gasparis, 81-130.

Schramm, G. (1994), *Anfang des Albanischen Christentums*, Freiburg.

Schwander-Sievers, S. and B. Fischer, ed. (2001), *Albanian Identities*, London.

Schukalla, K. (1992), 'Nationale Minderheiten in Albanien und Albaner in Ausland', in Grothusen, 505-28.

Shankland, D. (2004), *Archaeology, Anthropology and Heritage in the Balkans*, 2 vols, Istanbul.

Shaw, S. (1976), *History of the Ottoman Empire and Modern Turkey*, Cambridge.

Shepard, J. (1989), 'Byzantium in Equilibrium'; 'Bulgaria: The Other Balkan Empire'; 'Byzantium Expanding'; 'Byzantium', in *Cambridge Medieval History*, III, 553-623.

Shkodra, K. (1988), *La ville albanaise au cours de la renaissance nationale*, Tirana.

Shtylla, W. (1997), *Rrugët dhe urat e vjetra në Shqipëri*, Tirana.

Shuteriqi, D. (1965), 'Les Arianite - leur nom et leur généalogie', *Studime*

Historike, 2, 4, 3-38.

(1967a), 'Les Arianite - leurs domaines', *Studime Historike*, 4, 1, 57-84.

(1967b), 'Une inscription de la principauté Albanaise de 1190-1216 et d'autres inscriptions trouvées dans la Mirditë, *Studime Historike*, 4, 3, 131-58.

Šišić, F. (1928), *Letopis Popa Dukljanin*, Belgrade.

Skendi, S. (1967), *The Albanian National Awakening*, Princeton.

Smiley, D. (1984), *Albanian Assignment*, London.

Smith, J. (2005), *Europe after Rome*, Oxford.

Spahiu, H. (1980), 'Monnaies byzantins des Ve-VIIIe siècles découvertes sur le territoire de l'Albanie', *Iliria*, 10, 353-422.

(1985), 'Nouvelles bagues à l'inscription découvertes à Koman', *Iliria*, 15, 1, 29-46.

(1986), 'Eléments de la tradition antique dans la culture des nécropoles du Haut Moyen Age albanais', *Iliria*, 16, 1, 263-71

(1990), 'La ville haute-mediévale albanais de Shurdah (Sarda)', *Iliria*, 20, 2, 151-71.

Stadtmüller, G. (1964), *Albanesische Forschungen*, Munich.

Stavrianos, L. (1958), *The Balkans since 1453*, New York.

Stephenson, P. (2000), *Byzantium's Balkan Frontier: A Political Study of the Northern Balkans, 900-1204*, Cambridge.

(2003), *The Legend of Basil the Bulgar-Slayer*, Cambridge.

Strazimiri, B. *et al.* (1973), *Monumente të Arkitetkurës në Shqiperi*, Tirana.

Sufflay, M. (1925), *Srbi i Arbanasi*, Belgrade.

Sugar, P. (1977), *South Eastern Europe under Ottoman Rule*, Seattle.

Sulzberger, C. (1969), *A Long Row of Candles*, London.

Swire, J. (1929), *Albania: The Rise of a Kingdom*, London.

Tabula Imperii Romani, K 34 (1976), ed. J. Sašel, Llubljana.

Thëngjilli, P. (1999), *Historia e Popullit Shqiptar, 395-1875*, Tirana.

(2002), 'Aspects of lslamization in North Albania .in the XVIIth century', *Studime Historike*, 39, 1, 20-49.

Thornton, P. (1939), *Ikons and Oxen*, London.

Todorova, M. (1997), *Imagining the Balkans*, Oxford.

Tomes, J. (1993), *King Zog: Self-Made Monarch of Albania*, London.

Toynbee, A. (1975), *Constantine Porphyrogentus and His World*, Oxford.

Ugolini, L. (1927), *Albania Antica*, Rome.

Valentini, J. ed. (1967-93), *Acta Albania Veneta*, 26 vols, Paris and Munich.

Van Weenen, J. (1998), *Task Force Albania: An Odyssey*, Luton.

Vickers, M. (1994), *A Concise History of the Albanians*, London.

(1998), *Between Serb and Albanian: A History of Kosovo*, London.

(2020) *Albanian Nationalism after the Cold War*, Oxford.

and Pettifer, J. (1997), *Albania: From Anarchy to a Balkan Identity*, London.

Vranousis, E. (1970), *Hoi Horoi-Albanoi kai Arbanitae*, Athens.

Walbank, F. (1976), 'Southern Illyria in the third and second centuries BC', *Iliria*, 4, 265-72.

(1957-79), *A Historical Commentary on Polybius*, 3 vols, Oxford.

Ward-Perkins, B. (2005), *The Fall of Rome and the End of Civilization*, Oxford.

Wilkes, J. (1969), *Dalmatia*, London.

(1976), 'Arthur Evans in the Balkans, 1878-1881', *Bulletin of the Institute of Archaeology*, 13, 25-56.

(1992), *The Illyrians*, London.

Wilkinson, H. (1951), *Maps and Politics: A Review of the Ethnographic Cartography of Macedonia*, Liverpool.

Winnifrith, T. (1987), *The Vlachs: The History of a Balkan People*, London.

(1995), *Shattered Eagles: Balkan Fragments*, London.

(2002), *Badlands. Borderlands: A History of Southern Albania*, London.

West, R. (1941), *Black Lamb and Grey Falcon*, London.

Xhufi, P. 'La "debizantinizzazione" dell'Arbanon', in Gasparis, 59-77.

Young, A. (1997), *Albania. World Bibliographical Series*, vol. 94, Oxford and Santa Barbara.

Zamputi, I. (1966), 'Données sur la ville de Shkodër dans les trente premières années de la domination ottomane', *Studime Historike*, 3, 3, 47-60.

Zamputi, I. and S. Pulaha (1989-90), Dokumente të Shekuvje XVI-XVII për Historinë e Shqipërisë, 4 vols, Tirana.

INDEX

Adrianople, Battle of 12, 41, 43, 73-4, 78-80, 82, 198

Aetolians 58, 62-3

Agron, King 55, 58, 60, 64

Alaric, the Visigoth 12, 41, 79-82, 164

Alexander the Great 18, 35, 47, 53, 55, 64, 190

Ali Pasha of Ioannina 4-5, 113, 122-3

Alia, Ramiz 2, 148, 151, 188

Amery, Julian 145-6, 148, 188, 206

Anastasius, Emperor 79, 83, 85

Anjou, Charles of 60, 98-9, 101-4, 201

Apollonia 1, 14, 38, 40, 56, 58-60, 62, 190

Arianiti dynasty 6, 102-3, 111

Bajraktari, Muharrem 17, 143, 146-7

Bajram Curri (leader) see Curri, Bajram

Bajram Curri (town, formerly Kolgecaj) 1, 3, 28, 53, 71

Balaban Pasha 110

Balli Kombëtar party 145, 147-8

Balšić dynasty 10, 102-3, 105-7, 109, 122, 202, 204

Bar diocese 87-8, 115-16, 172

Bardylis, King 37, 55

Barlettius, Marinus 7, 108-9, 196, 202

Basil II, the Bulgar Slayer 42, 87, 90, 92-3, 98-9, 103

Bektashi Muslims 24-5, 33, 116, 124-5, 192

Berat 61, 87, 110

Berisha, Sali 2, 16-17, 28, 151-6, 209

Bizë 33, 147

Bllatë 182

Boris, Tsar of Bulgaria 87-8

Bushat 71

Bushati dynasty 113, 122-3, 203-4

Butrint 1, 6, 42, 85, 113, 116, 167

Byllis 11, 47, 53, 61, 71, 167-8

Byron, Lord 5-6, 122-3, 188

Caesar, Julius 12, 39-40, 67, 77, 197

Chryselioi dynasty 89-91, 99

Comnenus, Emperor Alexius 30, 88, 96-7

Comnenus, John (son) 96

Comnenus, Manuel (grandson) 96-7, 99, 102

Constantine, Emperor 41, 73-8, 87, 161, 168, 172, 198

Curri, Bajram 3, 140, 142-3

Dacia 41, 74, 76

Dalmatia 36, 39-40, 51, 59, 67-8, 76, 123, 135, 161, 163, 166, 172, 174, 197

Dardania 11, 37, 41-2, 68, 76, 83, 163, 167-8, 193, 197

Dardanians 36-8, 45, 47, 64-5

Davies, Brigadier 'Trotsky' 145, 147, 188, 206

Dečanski, Stephen 105

Delmatae 39, 65, 67-8

Dibër 6, 22, 25-6, 30, 32-3, 47, 110, 120, 125, 137, 140-1, 158-9, 164, 168-9, 180-2, 185, 209, 211

Dine, Fiqri 147-8

Dioclea 12, 87-8, 90, 95, 171-4

Dioclea, Priest of, see Priest of Dioclea

Diocletian, Emperor 12, 40-1, 73-8, 161, 198

Drin, River 20-1, 31-3, 47, 70, 150, 158, 191, 193, 197, 210

    Black Drin 11, 20, 32, 37, 47, 65, 71, 169

    White Drin 20, 161, 183

    Drin valley 44, 71, 74-7, 81, 83, 118, 159, 162-5, 169-70

    Drin as border 20-1, 27-8, 37, 41,

48, 59, 62-4, 69, 76, 86, 88, 137-8, 160, 180-2, 196

Drisht 87, 106

Ducas, Michael 103, 203

Dukagjin family 7, 28-9, 103, 106-7, 120, 122, 172; see also Kanun of Lek Dukagjin

Duklja 86, 95-7, 103

Durham, Edith 3-4, 26-8, 31-2, 87, 111, 116, 119-21, 128-9, 155-6, 162-4, 178, 188, 191, 193, 203, 205-6, 210

Durrës 1, 14, 23, 25, 30, 38, 54, 71, 88, 112, 116, 121, 134-8, 142, 144, 152, 154, 181, 197

Dušan, Stephen 98, 101, 104-6

Dyrrachium 12-14, 38, 40, 42, 45, 48, 54-5, 58-60, 64, 66-7, 71, 81, 83-91, 93-7, 99, 101, 103-4, 121, 166, 173-4, 190, 197

Elbasan (formerly Scampa) 9, 25, 29, 33, 40, 77, 91, 110, 136-7, 147, 166, 173

Epidamnus 54-6, 64, 86

Epirus 11-13, 15, 37, 41, 56-8, 60-1, 66, 68-9, 76-7, 80, 83, 86, 97, 103-4, 160, 165-7, 175, 196, 210

Esad Pasha 14, 128, 133-7, 141, 178

Evans, Sir Arthur 162-4, 169, 197, 200, 210

Fan, River 20, 27, 32, 209

Fier 143, 153

Fishta, Gjergj 10, 17-18, 34-6, 65, 127, 129, 208

Fourth Crusade 6-7, 93-4, 97-8, 101-2, 157, 201

Frashëri family 35, 126-7, 137, 159, 168-9, 179, 189, 199, 202, 205, 208-9

Gentius, King 35, 48, 51, 64-6, 71, 102, 158-9

Ghegs 2, 76

Giles, Colonel Frank 144, 179-85, 211-12

Gjakova 154, 161-3, 180, 182-3

Gjirokastër 5, 107

Gjoni, Marko 140, 142

Gollobordë 23, 33, 127, 182, 192

Grazdhan 71, 75, 158-60, 167-70, 209

Gruda 27, 34, 127, 184

Gurakuqi, Luigj 136-7, 140-2

Hasan Bey Prishtina 40, 142-3

Hasluck, Margaret Masson 3, 27, 111, 119, 121, 146-7, 188, 190, 193, 203, 206

Hibbert, Sir Reginald 145, 188, 206

Hoti 27, 34, 120, 127, 184

Hoxha, Enver 2-3, 7, 14, 16-17, 21, 26, 31, 33-5, 50, 64, 83, 109-10, 114, 121, 126, 129, 131-3, 144, 148-51, 188, 190-1, 205-8

Justinian, Emperor 11-12, 42, 79, 82-3, 85-6, 93, 160, 162, 165-70, 198, 210

Kadare, Ismail 151, 207

Kalojan 9, 98

Kanun of Lek Dukagjin 103, 106, 114, 120-1, 205

Kastrat 26, 120

Kastrioti 49, 102, 107, 110, 112, 202

Kelmendi tribe 113, 118-19, 144

Kemp, Peter 145-7, 188, 206

Kičevo 158-9

Komani-Kruja 11, 53, 85, 200

Korab, Mount 20-1, 159, 183

Kruja 6, 30, 86, 88, 102, 106, 108-10, 116, 118, 134-6, 148

Krum 86, 88

Kryeziu family 17, 141-2, 144, 146-7

Kukës 1, 11, 20, 26-7, 31-2, 48, 65, 71, 150, 153-5, 161, 164, 191, 210

Kupi, Abas 17, 118, 144-8

League of Nations 138-40, 181

Legalitet 132, 145, 148

Lezhë (ancient Lissus) 6, 26-7, 31, 53, 71, 88, 109, 162-3, 165, 194

Lissus 11, 13, 27, 31-2, 59, 62-3, 66,

68, 70-1, 75, 85, 161-7, 170, 197

Lurë 20, 22, 169

Mat, River 20, 27, 32-3, 43-4, 49, 118, 135, 138, 140-1

Mirditë 25-8, 34, 48-9, 118, 120, 126, 134-5, 140, 143, 147

Mjgeni 23

Monunius, King 38, 55-6, 58, 60

Mother Teresa 17-18, 127, 190, 208

Murphy, Dervla 3, 31

Musachi 102-3

Mytilus 55-6, 58, 60

Naissus 11, 31-2, 70-1, 75, 80, 161-5, 170

Nano, Fatos 2, 153-5

Napoleonic Wars 5, 113, 123, 205

Nemanjid dynasty 10, 98, 103-5, 200

Nicopolis 86, 88-9

Noli, Fan 138-42, 202, 206

Ohrid, Lake 11, 20-1, 30, 38, 55, 63-5, 88, 101-2, 164, 181, 191

Palaeologus, Michael 98-9, 102, 104

Parthini tribe 40, 48, 60-1, 63-4, 66, 68, 196-7

Peć 103, 105, 115

Penestae tribe 158

Peshkopi 1, 23, 26, 32, 75, 86, 159, 165, 169, 182

Peutinger Table 31-2, 48, 70-1, 75, 161-2, 164

Philip of Macedon 47, 53, 55-7, 61-4, 159, 209

Pindus Mountains 47-8, 118, 159, 209

Pleuratus, King 35, 48, 60, 62-5, 159

Praevalitana province 11, 41-2, 68, 76, 165, 167-8, 174, 198, 210

Prenk Bib Doda, chief 126, 128, 134-7, 140

Prespa, Lake 23, 63, 90, 175, 191-2

Priest of Dioclea 8, 82, 87, 89-91, 95-6, 171-4, 189, 198

Prizren 22, 32, 125-7, 154, 161, 180, 182-3, 185, 205, 211

League of Prizren 125-7, 205

Procopius 11-12, 26, 28, 42, 79, 82-3, 160, 162, 165-70, 173, 189, 193, 198, 210

Progon dynasty 101-2, 201

Protocol of Florence 22,175

Pukë 28, 31-2, 70, 162, 191

Pyrrhus 35, 37, 53, 56-8, 64, 109

Qemal Bey Vlora 128, 132-5, 206

Rilindjë 125, 127, 205

Rosunjë 53, 71, 164

Rubik 27

Samuel, Tsar 10, 84, 86-93, 95, 99, 173, 198

Sarda 159, 162, 164, 168

Scampa (now Elbasan) 77, 81, 166

Scanderbeg (Gjergj Kastrioti) 6-7, 15, 17, 29-30, 35, 49, 64, 85, 94, 98, 103, 107-13, 117, 120-2, 125, 130, 132, 157, 164, 187, 189, 196, 202-4

Scanderbeg Square 15, 17, 108, 130, 133, 152

Scerdilaidas 60-5

Scodra (now Shkodër) 13, 66, 68-71, 197

Shala 26-7, 156, 163-4

Shkodër 1, 4-5, 20, 25, 28, 30-2, 40-41, 54, 71, 82, 87, 101, 103, 106-8, 112, 115, 121-3, 125, 128-9, 134-5, 137-8, 148, 151, 153, 162, 164, 166, 180, 189, 194, 205

Lake Shkodër 39, 48, 58

Shkumbin, River 5, 15, 25, 31, 33, 37, 47-8, 69, 76, 83, 88, 98, 104, 116

Sirmium 74-5

Smiley, David 145, 206

Spaç 27, 150

Sveti Naum 181, 183, 211

Tanzimat 123, 157

Taulantini 48, 54-6, 60, 65, 196

Teuta, Queen 13, 35, 58-60, 102

Theodosius, Emperor 41, 78-9

Theth 150, 155-6, 164

Thopia family 102-3, 106-7, 112
  Thopia, Charles 8-9, 102, 106, 202
Tirana 15, 20-1, 25, 32-3, 102, 129-31, 134, 138, 140, 142-3, 148, 151-2, 185
Tosks 2, 76, 148
Tropojë 26, 28, 38, 47, 147, 149, 154-5
Turhan Pasha 137-8
Ulcinj 71, 82, 87-8, 127, 129, 180, 184
Uscana 14, 47, 62, 66, 71, 158-60, 168, 209
Valbona, River 54, 71, 143, 163
Vasa, Pashko 125-6, 205
Vermosh 155-6, 180, 183-4
Via Egnatia 13, 29-32, 40, 66, 68-9, 75, 81, 93, 95, 104, 161, 164
Vig 31, 70, 162, 164
Vlachs 9, 23, 30, 47, 51-3, 85, 88-9, 91, 97-8, 118-19, 122, 127, 163, 166, 174-5, 192, 199, 202
Vlorë 107, 134, 138, 142, 152
Vraka 23, 156, 192
Wilder, Rose Lane 3-4, 144, 188
William of Wied, King 133-7, 142, 206
Xoxe, Koçi 144, 148-9
Zeta 71, 96, 105, 122
Zgerdesh 53, 70, 194
Zog, King (Ahmet Zogu) 3-4, 14, 17, 25-6, 28, 34, 49, 64, 118, 131-147, 149, 151, 178, 181, 187-8, 190-1, 205-6